AN HISTORICAL ACCOUNT OF WINCHESTER, WITH DESCRIPTIVE WALKS

AN HISTORICAL ACCOUNT OF WINCHESTER, WITH DESCRIPTIVE WALKS

Charles Ball

First Published in Winchester in 1818

Published by the Winchester University Press 2009

Copyright © Winchester University Press
University of Winchester
Winchester SO22 4NR

This edition first published 1818
This digitally printed version 2009

By permission of the Warden and Scholars of Winchester College, this Winchester Series Edition has been created from Winchester College's copy of the first edition of Charles Ball's *An Historical Account of Winchester, With Descriptive Walks.*

British Library Cataloguing-in-Publication Data
A CIP catalogue record for this book is available
from the British Library.

ISBN: 978-1-906113-02-5

Printed and Bound in Great Britain

THE WINCHESTER SERIES PREFACE

Winchester University Press takes as a special interest the hinterland of Winchester, a city whose reach in time and space goes a great way. The scope of that hinterland provides the topics and titles for books in the Press's Winchester Series.

The beginnings of Winchester are suggested by the evolution of its name from suppositious Celtic through attested Latin to everyday English. Caergwinntguic becomes Cair-Guntin, Caergwintwg, Caer Gwent, Venta Belgarum, Venta Castra, Wintanceastre, Wincestre, Vincestre and finally Winchester. The names chart the city's passage over a thousand years from Britonic through Roman to Saxon possession, and they give a historical and linguistic starting point for the Winchester Series.

From the sixth to the eleventh century, Winchester was in the Westseaxna Rice, the kingdom of Wessex, the home of the West Saxons. They ruled land between the south coast and the River Thames. They contested their northern and eastern boundaries with the kingdom of Mercia; what are now the counties of Oxfordshire, Sussex and Kent were sometimes part of the one kingdom and sometimes part of the other. To the west, Wessex was bounded by the River Taw or by the River Tamar as today's Devon was contested with the British kingdom of Dumnonia. At highpoints, the West Saxon kings claimed rule over the whole of England, but the heart of their kingdom was Hampshire, the Isle of

Wight, Berkshire, Wiltshire, Dorset, and Somerset. This is the heartland of the Winchester Series.

Under the Normans, the hinterland of Winchester was given new boundaries. It remained a place where kings held court, but it no longer had its own kingdom; instead, it became the cathedral city of a diocese that extended northeast through Surrey to border the River Thames at Southwark and southwest to Dorset. It still includes the Channel Islands, but it lost Surrey and Portsmouth in 1927. Within the Anglican Church, the bishops of Winchester are second only to the archbishops of Canterbury and York, and Winchester Cathedral is one of the architectural glories of Europe. This diocese is a dimension of the Winchester Series.

In the nineteenth century, Thomas Hardy revived the name of the ancient kingdom of Wessex and created through his novels a new notion of the hinterland of Winchester. The heart of his imaginary land is Wiltshire, his Mid-Wessex, and the other counties in his Wessex are Berkshire, Devon, Dorset, Hampshire, and Somerset. Hardy brings attention to the literary riches of the Winchester hinterland within which have lived and written Jane Austen, William Blake, William Cobbett, Charles Dickens, Benjamin Franklin, Elizabeth Gaskell, Edward Gibbon, William Hazlitt, George Herbert, John Keats, John Keble, Alfred Tennyson, Izaak Walton, H.G. Wells, Gilbert White, Charlotte Mary Yonge. The territory of these writers provides another focus for the Winchester Series.

In the twentieth century, Winchester was placed in what was described in various official documents as the South East England Region. Originally designated as a Civil Defence Area, the Region has expanded and contracted but presently includes the counties of Buckinghamshire, Oxfordshire, Berkshire, Hampshire, the Isle of Wight, Surrey, East Sussex, West Sussex and Kent. Hampshire and Winchester now look east and associate with Sussex and Kent. The old associate counties, Wiltshire, Dorset and Somerset, have been designated part of the South West England Region. Hampshire was once the place where the West Country began but no longer. The expansion of London has made it more a Home than a Shire county, and European Route 5 - running from Greenock to Algeciras by way of Southampton and Le Havre – makes twenty-first-century Hampshire more immediately part of Europe than it has been since the end of the Hundred Years War. The South East England Region too shapes the Winchester Series.

The Winchester Series is a collection of titles that relate to Winchester in the broad outlines described, and it is a series in which newly-authored books will be commissioned, but its starting point is the wealth of books held in the libraries of Winchester Cathedral, Winchester City, Winchester College, and the University of Winchester. Many of these books deserve to be reprinted in a portable and affordable form, and Winchester University Press is proud to be doing so.

The Editors
Winchester University Press

7

WINCHESTER, WITH DESCRIPTIVE WALKS
AN INTRODUCTION

Charles Ball published *An Historical Account of Winchester, with Descriptive Walks* in 1818. The core of the book is six walks in and around the city. Ball introduces them with a history of Winchester from the earliest times to his own day. He follows the walks with two appendices, one giving the names of the bishops of Winchester and the other providing extracts from historical documents. Ball emphasizes in his 'Address' to his readers that he has written his book because the earlier histories of the city are dry catalogues and the later histories are contentious polemics.

His own historical account successfully avoids both dryness and contentiousness. He moves deftly through the nearly three thousand years of Winchester's history, and he scores few sectarian points on the way. He is at the same time both scholarly and pious. His scholarship is shown by his listing eleven major sources and by the numerous footnotes supporting his pages. His piety is shown by his frequent celebrations of the mildness and glory of Christianity and by his placing Winchester's cathedral and its bishops at the centre of his story.

His piety, however, is of an interesting kind. By his use of the term 'Christianity', he avoids sectarian specificity but he conveys a sense of a Church running uninterrupted over one thousand years from the time of St Birinus, the first bishop of Winchester consecrated in the reign of King Kinegils, to Brownlow North, the eighty-first bishop consecrated in the reign of King George III. In emphasizing the continuity between Birinus and North, Ball reveals his sympathy for pre-Reformation Christianity, and it is clear that he loves the medieval world. His Account of Winchester is a subtle predictor of a High Anglicanism that did not become more general in his church until later in the nineteenth century.

In 1818, Winchester remained the county town of an undiminished Hampshire; it was the cathedral centre of a major diocese; it was the location of a Crown court. It retained, as it still does, the aura of a city that had once been great in the kingdom. Nonetheless, nothing great had taken place in Winchester since the seventeenth century. Had Charles II completed the Winchester Palace that he started in 1683, things might have been different, but he died too soon to see it finished, and no subsequent monarch made it a home.

For Ball, things went wrong for Winchester many hundreds of years before the death of Charles II, and, indeed, he dates the decline of the city from the death of Henry I in 1135. It was at that point that the crown of England was usurped by Stephen of Blois and the country fell into decades of disarray. Ball sees those years, in which Winchester suffered so much, as the period in which London confirmed its ascendancy over the ancient capital city. Winchester's high point, in Ball's telling, was but a few years before, in 1110, when a great new abbey at Hyde, to the north of the city, was consecrated with a procession of monks moving from their habitation close by the Cathedral and carrying with them the bones of King Alfred. At the moment when the new Hyde foundation was completed, Winchester, he believes, 'stood unrivalled amongst the cities of England'. There were in the city two great palaces, a powerful castle, a magnificent cathedral, three royal monasteries, and very many churches, chapels and houses of noblemen. But within twenty-five years and through the ambition of Stephen, the decline set in: 'it affords,' says Ball, 'a melancholy illustration of the instability of human grandeur.'[1]

Ball associates grandeur above all with royal favour and presence, and at times his story is reduced to identifying years in which royal visits were made to Winchester, the saddest that of Charles I when a prisoner in 1647 on his way to execution. The turn out of the Mayor and Aldermen to pay their respects to their distressed monarch was in Ball's view worth all the ceremonial greetings of better times and enough in itself to immortalize Winchester.[2] Melancholy and decline are the themes of Ball's history. 'Winchester,' he says at one point, 'appears to have remained undisturbed in its advance towards obscurity.'[3]

When Charles Ball was describing Winchester in 1818, he was doing so at a moment when its preservation as a model of the English county town was about to be assured by the Industrial Revolution. The transformation that made Manchester a cathedral city composed of great streets, great factories and workers' homes had no effect on Winchester. If there had been any coal in Hampshire, Winchester might have grown, but there was none, and Winchester came to represent the restful South as Manchester to represent the active North. In North and South, Elizabeth Gaskell makes Hampshire stand for all that the North is not. Her heroine, who describes herself as coming from Hampshire but living in the North, lives 'with an unspoken lament in her heart for the sweet profusion of the South'.[4] She has to learn, of course, that there is as much virtue, and certainly more love, in the North as in the South, but the contrast is complete. Gaskell for her part moved south at the end of her life to live in Hampshire at Holybourne where she began the writing of Wives and Daughters, left incomplete by her death.[5]

Charles Ball has no sense of the lucky escape that was to be Winchester's from the ravages of industrialization, and he feels instead the loss of the city's ancient grandeur. However, Ball seems rather to enjoy his melancholy, and it does not prevent him from being an instructive and entertaining guide, the role he adopts on page 83 when he begins the description of his first Winchester walk. What we know about him must largely be inferred from his book. He has no entry in the Dictionary of National Biography. However, the Hampshire County Archives hold a burial record for a Charles Ball, aged 57, who died on 6 July 1823 in Micheldever, and this may be the author of An Historical Record. The book itself tells us that he was a scholarly man, a gentleman and a proto-Anglo-Catholic. His book also tells us that he had a great admiration for William of Wykeham, a figure frequently mentioned and always in terms of extravagant praise: 'his memory will be immortal'; 'that truly great man'.[6] These might be words spoken by a son of Wykeham, but Winchester College does not believe that Charles Ball was at the school.

On the other hand, his Winchester has been long famous as a guide to the city, and the six descriptive walks that Ball made in 1818 can still be followed much as he took them. Where we find that sometimes something that Ball described no longer exists, we are brought to a lively realization of the nearly two hundred years that have passed since his day, and a reading of his three-thousand year history of the city is the best preparation for taking his walks. What he sees are monuments, evidences of kings and princes, ravages of time, proofs of long-gone glory. In that respect, Ball is not ahead of his time as he is in religious sentiment but actually rather behind it. His love of the Gothic is of an eighteenth-century kind, and that is evident in what he chooses to point out as he guides his reader round Winchester.

The first walk begins at the Westgate and leads by way of the Great Hall, which he calls the Chapel of the old Castle, through the barracks, now a luxury housing estate, to the Cathedral. Guide and reader return by way of the Priory Gate from the Inner Close along St Swithun Street and Symonds Street to the High Street where the walk ends. This is not the longest of the walks, but it is longest in description, and Ball spends most of the time in the

Cathedral. Here we can feel that we are in a space that has not changed with time, and all the details that he asks us to note we can still find there. This walk is to be found on pages 83 to 144.

The second walk again begins at the Westgate and focuses its attention on the great Castle of Winchester. Ball spends a considerable time lamenting the 'consummate hypocrisy and cunning'[7] of Oliver Cromwell whose batteries first broke the castle down and whose sappers then demolished it completely. For Ball, the Castle's most conspicuous traits 'are those of violence and suffering',[8] and he provides a lengthy list of distinguished people done to death within its wall. After that Ball makes his way to Canon Street to lead the reader to view Winchester College and the ruins of Wolvesey Palace. This walk is to be found on pages 145 to 176.

The third walk starts in the High Street at what he calls the Cross and what is now known as the Butter Cross. Ball describes the High Street in some details and then cross the bridge to climb St Giles's Hill and take the great view of the City and Cathedral looking west. This is another occasion to lament the decline of Winchester because the hill used to be the site of the annual great Fair of St Giles, instituted by William the Conqueror and at its height, famed through Europe. The emphasis of this walk is the changes within Winchester and all the churches and chapels that it has lost. In 1282, there were forty-seven of them, of which the majority had been pulled down by 1818.[9] More have been pulled down since 1818. This walk is to be found on pages 177 to 190.

The fourth walk starts at what Ball calls the Soke Bridge, the bridge over the River Itchen at east end of the High Street. It takes a route along Water Lane, 'a dirty avenue',[10] to visit St John on the Hill. He provides a beautiful and evocative description of this the oldest parish church in Winchester. Ball returns by way of a sleepy road following the remnants of the old north wall. That track has become the roaring one-way route called North Walls. The fourth walk goes to places often left unexplored by today's visitors and is to be found on pages 191 to 200.

The fifth walk starts in what Ball calls Gaol Street (what used to be called Jewry Street and is now again called Jewry Street). The focus of this walk is to be Hyde Abbey, but it starts with a fascinating account of the great architectural development of Jewry/Gaol Street in 1805, the effects of which can still be seen. Ball's description of Hyde Abbey is among his saddest. That once magnificent repository of the bones of King Alfred has not only been knocked down but, as recently as 1788, has been made the site of a prison. Here is Winchester's most lamentable demonstration of the mutability of the human condition: 'the stately abode of mitred Abbots levelled with the dust and mingled with the filth and rubbish of the cow yard!'[11] This walk is to be found on pages 201 to 214.

The sixth walk describes a route out of Winchester along Kingsgate Street to the Hospital of St Cross and then back along the St Cross Road to the city centre. More needs to be said about this walk to be found on pages 215 to 238.

Ball's aesthetic, historical sensibility is an Augustan one; his prose is that of a writer schooled in the style of Addison and Steele, and his sentiments, especially in relation to landscape and to Nature have nothing of the Romantic about them. He does not appear to be a man who would be reading William Wordsworth or Samuel Taylor Coleridge who had startled the literary and wider world in 1798 with the publication of The Lyrical Ballads. Twenty years on, those first Romantic poets had changed the tenor of English verse, and younger poets were making new impressions on the critics and receiving even more scandalized reviews.

It is difficult to know then what Charles Ball would have made of the Romantic poet into whom he might have bumped in the summer of 1819. That was when John Keats was visiting Winchester with his friend Charles Brown. They arrived in the middle of August and stayed until the end of September, and their business was to take advantage of Winchester's lack of business in order to find the peace and quiet that they needed to write. They were collaborating on a drama called Otho the Great, and in addition Keats was completing, or trying to complete, The Fall of Hyperion.[12]

Introduction

In a letter to his friend Benjamin Bailey, dated Saturday, 14
August 1819, Keats wrote to say that he and Brown had left
the Isle of Wight, and:

> We removed to Winchester for the convenience of a
> library, and find it an exceedingly pleasant town,
> enriched with a beautiful cathedral, and surrounded
> by a fresh-looking country. We are in tolerably good
> and cheap lodgings.[13]

What delighted Keats about Winchester was what Ball so
much regretted. The city had declined into a place where
the activity of the world had ceased. On 22 September 1819,
he wrote to John Hamilton Reynolds, a fellow poet and
London friend:

> The side streets here are excessively maiden-lady
> like; the door-steps always fresh from the flannel.
> The knockers have a staid, serious, nay, almost awful
> quietness about them. I never saw so quiet a
> collection of lions' and rams' heads. The doors [are]
> most part black, with a little brass handle just above
> the keyhole, so that in Winchester a man may very
> quietly shut himself out of his own house.[14]

One of the things that Keats loved to do in this sleepy place
was to go for walks, and it is the firm belief in Winchester
that Keats had a copy of An Historical Account of
Winchester, With Descriptive Walks that he used it as a
guide to the city. Of the walks that Ball lays out, the sixth

and last one, describing the route to the Hospital of St
Cross, became Keats's favourite. It was one that he liked to
take in the evening before dinner,[15] and it brought him to
create a poem that that was not part of his writing plan for
Winchester. His letter to Reynolds shifts from talking about
the streets of Winchester to talking about the beauty of its
countryside in late September:

> How beautiful the season is now. How fine the air—
> a temperate sharpness about it. Really, without
> joking, chaste weather—Dian skies. I never liked
> stubble-fields so much as now—aye, better than the
> chilly green of the Spring. Somehow, a stubble field
> looks warm, in the same way that some pictures look
> warm. This struck me so much in my Sunday's walk
> that I composed upon it.[16]

He then writes out his ode 'To Autumn':

> Season of mists and mellow fruitfulness!
>   Close bosom-friend of the maturing sun;
> Conspiring with him how to load and bless
>   With fruit the vines that round the thatch-eaves run;
> To bend with apples the moss'd cottage-trees,
>   And fill all fruit with ripeness to the core;
>   To swell the gourd, and plump the hazel shells
>   With a sweet kernel; to set budding more,
> And still more, later flowers for the bees,
> Until they think warm days will never cease,
>   For Summer has o'er-brimm'd their clammy cells.

Who hath not seen thee oft amid thy store?
    Sometimes whoever seeks abroad may find
Thee sitting careless on a granary floor,
    Thy hair soft-lifted by the winnowing wind;
Or on a half-reap'd furrow sound asleep,
    Drowsed with the fume of poppies, while thy hook
      Spares the next swath and all its twined flowers;
And sometime like a gleaner thou dost keep
Steady thy laden head across a brook;
Or by a cider-press, with patient look,
    Thou watchest the last oozings, hours by hours.

Where are the songs of Spring? Ay, where are they?
    Think not of them, thou hast thy music too,
While barred clouds bloom the soft-dying day,
    And touch the stubble-plains with rosy hue;
Then in a wailful choir the small gnats mourn
    Among the river sallows, borne aloft
      Or sinking as the light wind lives or dies;
    And full-grown lambs loud bleat from hilly bourn;
Hedge-crickets sing; and now with treble soft
The redbreast whistles from a garden-croft,
    And gathering swallows twitter in the skies.[17]

The ode moves from appeals to taste and smell in the first stanza through appeals to the ear in the second and to appeals to the eye in the third. And, from first stanza to last stanza, there is a shift from late summer to late autumn, from morning to evening. It is a majestic response to the Winchester water meadows, and its intrinsic beauty contrasts with the reaction of Charles Ball to the same scene.

'Continuing our walk southwards,' says Ball, 'we shortly pass, in a meadow at the end of King'sgate Street, the scite of the parish church of St Faith, which, with others, was destroyed to its foundations in the early part of the sixteenth century.'[18] Charles Ball is going where John Keats is going but seeing such different things and seeing so differently. Ball's meadow at the end of Kingsgate Street shows how open the countryside remained in 1818. Winchester College has much extended on the left side of Kingsgate going out of town, and houses now line the full length on the right side. The west-bank meadows of the Itchen have become playing fields, and Keats' 'stubble-fields' have been much built upon, but the landscape remains superlative.

'Continuing our progress by the path through the meadow,' says Ball, 'we approach at a short distance the principal object of our Walk.'[19] That object was the Hospital of St Cross, and the path would have taken the walker close to the River Itchen, the river among whose sallows, Keats's 'small gnats mourn'. The fact they are doing so 'in a wailful choir' might well be because Keats also was walking to St Cross, the church Ball calls 'a cathedral in miniature'.[20]

Keats describes the walk and the church in a letter given the dates 17 September to 27 September; it is one of the very long pieces that he used to send to his brother George who by then lived in Kentucky. Keats speaks not only of Winchester's 'beautifully clear river' running by St Cross but also of the scandals associated that ancient foundation. It had been established to help the aged poor; now, it was exploited by 'a relation of the Bishop' who lived in splendour.[21] Ball, who has a great deal to say about the depredations and excesses of earlier times, is always discrete in his reference to what may or may not have being going on in his own times, and he makes no reference to the behaviour of the Master of St Cross.

To read An Historical Account of Winchester, With Descriptive Walks of 1818 and to use it as a guide in the twenty-first century makes the reader-walker move through time as well as space. It brings together a mix of sensibilities, and it draws attention not only to what is there but also to what is not there. Ball describes buildings which are no longer standing, and he talks about customs that are no longer practised. The absences are as instructive as the presences. Ball's Winchester speaks richly of history, religion, and monument, but it says little of landscape. That we are able to see what Ball does not see is thanks to writers like Keats.

Ball and Keats lived at the same time and, for a very short while, they lived in the same place, but their sensibilities were years apart. It is unlikely that either would have liked her novels, but another Winchester writer, Jane Austen, shared some of Ball's Augustan virtues and some of Keats's Romantic values. She had died in College Street, a year before An Historical Account of Winchester, With Descriptive Walks was published. Ball takes us past her house but, of course, he makes no mention of her name.

While we are at Jane Austen's house, we might take the opportunity to note Wells, the booksellers to the right of it. In 1818, the shop was owned by James Robbins, the publisher of The Hampshire Chronicle. The newspaper was printed in the building at the back of the shop, and in that same shop An Historical Account of Winchester, with Descriptive Walks was printed. As its title page notes, John Robbins was its publisher. In 1844, Robbins went bankrupt, and, when he did, Winchester College intervened to persuade a London dealer, David Nutt, to take over. In addition to the business, Nutt took on Robbins's apprentice, Joseph Wells. He was the son of the College beer butler. In 1862, after a successful spell as manager, Joseph Wells became a partner in the business.[22] The shop still bears his name. That is just one of the many continuities between the Winchester of Charles Ball and the Winchester of today.

Christopher Mulvey
Winchester
September 2009

NOTES

1. Charles Ball, *An Historical Account of Winchester* (Winchester: Winchester University Press, 2009), 24-25.

2. Ball, 69.

3. Ball, 52.

4. Elizabeth Gaskell, *North and South* (Leipzig: Tauchnitz, 1855), 68.

5. Dorothy Eagle and Hilary Carnell, *Oxford Literary Guide* (Oxford: Clarendon Press, 1980), 135.

6. Ball, 49, 189.

7. Ball, 149.

8. Ball, 147.

9. Ball, 203.

10. Ball, 191.

11. Ball, 207-208.

12. Walter Jackson Bate, *John Keats* (Cambridge: Harvard University Press, 1963), 563.

13. Richard Monckton Milnes, first Baron Houghton, *The Life and Letters of John Keats* (London: Dent, 1969), 176.

14. Milnes, 183-84.

15. Bate, 580.

16. Milnes, 184.

17. John Keats, *The Poetical Works of John Keats* (London: Moxon, 1847), 219.

18. Ball, 218.

19. Ball, 219.

20. Ball, 228.

21. Bate, 580.

22. Geoffrey Day, the Fellows' Librarian of Winchester College, supplied the history of Wells bookshop. He also drew the attention of Winchester University Press to Charles Ball's *An Historical Account of Winchester, With Descriptive Walks* and its links to John Keats, for which the Press thanks him.

WINCHESTER.

AN

HISTORICAL ACCOUNT

OF

𝔚𝔦𝔫𝔠𝔥𝔢𝔰𝔱𝔢𝔯,

WITH

DESCRIPTIVE WALKS.

BY CHARLES BALL.

WINCHESTER:

PRINTED AND SOLD BY JAMES ROBBINS, COLLEGE-STREET.

SOLD ALSO BY MESSRS. LAW AND WHITTAKER, AVE-MARIA-LANE, LONDON.

1818.

ADDRESS.

OF the various Publications issued from the Press, under the title of " The History of Winchester," which the Author of the following pages has perused, he has had invariably to remark, that while the earlier accounts were little better than dry unconnected catalogues of historical fact, intermingled with a series of doubtful occurrences, or filled with tedious details of obsolete charters, equally uninstructive and uninteresting, even the more scientific and elaborate Work of a later period was found liable to objection, from the general tone of controversy that seemed to pervade, and in some instances almost obscure, the professed object of the Writer.

The Author has also had frequent opportunities of observing, that the inhabitants of Winchester in particular, as well as strangers who visited it generally, were often compelled to remain ignorant, or with at best but a partial knowledge, of many of the important traits of its History, and the more interesting and venerable Memorials of Antiquity yet preserved within it, for want of some commodious channel of authentic information; inasmuch as, besides the voluminousness of the only work extant, which with many persons operated as an insuperable bar to the perusal of it, there was another objection, that the generality of Readers found perhaps equally insurmountable, namely, the price. *Thus he considered that there were many who could afford to purchase, did not read, because they wanted inclination for the perusal of* two quarto volumes; *while at the same time others, who might have the necessary inclination, could not prudently indulge themselves with the gratification of it.*

In the summer of 1815, *the Author, acting under this impression, was encouraged in his design of preparing some brief notice of the History and Antiquities of Winchester, by the approbation of a short article upon the subject, which he had then an opportunity of laying before* JOHN BRITTON, *Esq. Author of " The Cathedral Antiquities of England," who not only approved the idea, but suggested the immediate attention of the Author to some concise account, in the nature of a Guide, which might supply the vacancy in the Literary Annals of Winchester.*

Encouraged by the approbation of this Gentleman, the design was pursued; and after a considerable time, during which the Author had had recourse to a number of curious and important works illustrative of the subject, he felt that he should, by adhering to the usual narrow limits of a mere Guide, of necessity omit much valuable, and, as he thought, original information ; he therefore at once decided upon the extension of his plan, which he subsequently arranged in the manner it is now offered to the Public.

Thus actuated, he submits to the Public a Work, compiled as well from the various sources of information afforded by the labours of Trussell, Gale, Warton, Wavel, and Milner, as from the more general and important researches of Verstegan, Stowe, Godwin, Heylin, Dugdale, Hume, and other writers of equal authority and eminence, which, together with an extensive and unwearied personal survey and inquiry, he trusts will be found to pourtray the History and Antiquities of our City; without, on the one hand, being liable to the objection of prolixity and excessive price; or, on the other, of withholding any information useful to the Reader.

Perfection not being within the reach of mortality, the Author is confident that some allowance will be made for the errors of his Work; and although he naturally hopes those are not many, he cannot but regret that the want of a Literary Friend, to whom he might have submitted his MS, and by whom it might have been corrected and improved, may have left a greater share of imper-fections in his first essay than under more favour-able circumstances would have appeared.

The Author feels, that in concluding this Ad-dress, it would be ungrateful not to offer his most sincere acknowledgements to those Gentlemen by whom he has been favoured with the inspection of many curious and valuable documents, necessary to the production of an authenticated Work of this nature, and to express his regret that he is not at liberty to particularize the individual kindness with which, on various occasions, his inquiries have been honoured.

To the Publisher also he considers his thanks are due for the handsome and liberal manner in which the Work has been presented to the notice of the Public, both so far as regards Typographical beauty, and the number and nature of the Embel-lishments, the latter of which have been executed, at a considerable expence, from original drawings, made by Mr. C. F. PORDEN, expressly for the Work.

CHARLES BALL.

WINCHESTER,
1st *January*, 1818.

TABLE OF REFERENCE.

	Page.
HISTORICAL Account of the City and Environs of Winchester	1

First Walk, comprising the West Gate—Guildhall—the Cross—St. Lawrence's Church—the Square—Bishop Morley's College—scite of the Newan Minstre, or Abbey of St. Grimbald—the Cathedral, and its Environs—St. Swithun's Church, over King's-gate—Christ's Hospital—St. Thomas's Church   - - - - -   83

Second Walk, comprising the County Hall—Scite of the Castle of Winchester—the Barracks—the Female Asylum—the College of St. Mary—Wolvesey Ruins—Bishop Morley's Palace—Scite of St. Elizabeth's College—St. Catherine's Hill   - - - - - -   145

Third Walk, comprising the County Hospital—the Market House—St. Maurice's Church—Scite of the Charnel House for the City—the City Bridewell—Scite of St. Mary's Abbey—the Central Schools—the Silk Mills—St. John's House and Chapel—Eastgate House—the Bridge—St. Giles's Hill—Magdalen Hill—Church of St. Peter Cheesehill—the Wires   - - - - - - - -   177

Fourth Walk, comprising the Old Barrack—St. John's Church—Winnall—the Church of St. Martin—the Bourne Gate—the City Wall—Denemarck Mead—St. Peter's Chapel—the Benedictine Convent   - - - - - - - - - - - - - - -   191

Fifth Walk, comprising the County Gaol—the Theatre—Scite of the Palace of Henry the Second—Staple Gardens—Scite of the North Gate of the City—Ruins of Hyde Abbey—Scite of the Church—the County Bridewell—Hyde Abbey School—North-west Wall of the City—the Hermit's Tower—the Obelisk—Oram's Arbour   201

Sixth Walk, comprising St. Michael's Church—Scite of the Carmelite Convent—Scite of St. Faith's Church—the Hospital and Church of St. Cross—the Priory—South Gate of the City   - - - - -   215

APPENDIX,

No. I. List of the Bishops of Winchester   - - - - - - - -   239

No. II. Extracts from the Report of the Committee on the Public Records of the Kingdom, so far as it relates to Winchester   - -   257

LIST OF EMBELLISHMENTS.

GENERAL View of Winchester, from the brow of St. Giles's Hill, - - - - - - - - - - - - To face the Title Page.

Interior View of the Ruins of Wolvesey Castle, - - On the Title Page.

Arms of the City and Diocese—Ancient Measures, Maces, &c.   page 1

View of the West Gate and the City Cross - - - - - - - - 83

North-west View of the Cathedral - - - - - - - - - - 89

View of the Barracks - - - - - - - - - - - - - - 145

View of the Chapel and Dormitories of the College - - - - - - 154

View of the Library and Cloisters of the College - - - - - - 163

Interior of the Chapel of St. Mary Magdalen - - - - - - - 177

View of the County Gaol, and the Theatre - - - - - - - - 191

View of the North Entrance to Hyde Abbey - - - - - - - 201

View of the Tower, Refectory. and Cloister of the Hospital of St. Cross 215

AN
HISTORICAL ACCOUNT
OF
THE CITY AND ENVIRONS
OF
𝔚𝔦𝔫𝔠𝔥𝔢𝔰𝔱𝔢𝔯.

WHEN offering to the world a Descriptive Account of the Antiquities of a City whose origin may, perhaps, be dated from a period almost ten centuries earlier than the Christian æra,[1] and is, at all events, enveloped by the mist of uncertainty and romance which characterises the early History of our Island; the Historian has too often been induced to extend his labours beyond the bounds of legitimate inquiry, and to wander amongst the fascinating but dangerous labyrinths of tradition and conjecture;

---

[1] Wavel's History of Winchester, v. i. p. 2. See also City Tables, Warton's Hist. Win. p. 1. &c. &c.

we, however, with a view of avoiding so pleasing, yet eventually so fatal an indulgence, shall studiously confine ourselves to a relation of such facts as have not only the external recommendation of probability, but have also the sanction of a well-grounded and unimpeachable authenticity as a claim to historic notice.

The first event in the History of Winchester of which we have any authentic relation, appears to be that of its occupation by the Belgæ, about two centuries and a half before the birth of Christ;[1] a part of the warlike nation, of which they formed a tribe or clan, having, about that period, landed from the opposite coast of Gaul, and reduced a considerable extent of the maritime line of Britain to their authority, seated themselves in the fertile province of Hampshire, and extirpating or expelling the former inhabitants of *Cær Gwent,*[2] which then seems to have been the appellation of our City, established themselves within it.

From this early period Cær Gwent may be said to have commenced its progress towards a state of civilization and improvement, inasmuch as its new occupiers were, to a considerable degree, less rude and barbarous than their predecessors the Celtic Britons.[3]   It is, however, from the circumstance of

---

[1] Whitaker's Hist. Manchester, b. xii.

[2] Milner's Hist. Winchester, i, 5, &c.   See also Trussell, Warton, and others.

[3] Cæs. Com. l. ii.   Whitaker's Hist. Manch. b. xii.   Miln. i. 12.

their intercourse and traffic with foreigners, of which, from their convenient situation with regard to harbours, they very soon began to enjoy an important share,[1] that we chiefly draw our conclusion of their superiority in the scale of civilization to the savage and uncultivated natives whom they succeeded.

Still it must not be supposed that the City, under the dominion of its Belgic masters, could have attained any very considerable height of improvement. It was found by them a mere collection of cabins or huts, built of the branches of trees or of mud covered with reeds, sheltered and protected by the overspreading boughs and almost impenetrable depths of the neighbouring forests.[2] However superior to the former, its present occupiers were still barbarians; and although the circumstance of their applying themselves more particularly to agriculture than its original owners, must no doubt have contributed in some degree to the improvement of their dwellings; yet Cær Gwent, as well as their cities in general, was so little improved in appearance or comfort, as scarcely to be distinguished, by the Roman invaders, from the intrenched woods and miserable huts of the Aborigines in the interior of the island.[3]

When, about fifty-five years before Christ, the Romans, who, under the guidance of Cæsar, had recently subdued all Gaul, from the Alps to the British Channel, had crossed the latter in order to bring this

---

[1] Cæs. Com. l. iv.   [2] Cæs. l. v.   [3] Cæs. l. v. vi.

country under the tributary yoke, it appears that our Belgic inhabitants were, in common with others, very shortly compelled to submit themselves to the authority of the invaders, who, after exacting a proportion of tribute from Cær Gwent, the name of which they changed to *Venta Belgarum*,[1] returned to the Continent; and from this period, during the space of nearly a century, the Britons, being free from any foreign attack, it is not unnatural to suppose that Venta was greatly improved and aggrandized in consequence of the successes both in arms and commerce of the Belgæ, whose acknowledged capital it had then become; and, among the various causes that operated to the increase of its welfare and importance, may be reckoned the establishment of the chief foreign mart for tin in the neighbouring Isle of Wight,[2] and the consequent enlarged intercourse with the manners and improvements of more civilized nations which was thereby opened to our City.

The period was now fast approaching which was to accelerate the already rapid progress of improvement in the manners and appearance of Venta; but it was preceded by the severe discipline of defeat and subjection. Some of the native Princes of Britain having neglected or refused to pay the accustomed tribute to the Romans, as also to give up some criminals who had taken refuge within their territo-

---

[1] Heylin, 373. Wavel, ii. 3. Warton, &c.
[2] Whitaker, b. xi. Milner, i. 16.

ries,[1] the Emperor Claudius at length determined upon the complete subjugation of the whole Island; and landing, in A. D. 44,[2] with his unconquerable legions upon the British coast, after a short but severe struggle received the submission of great part of the Island, and with it that of Venta Belgarum.

A considerable number of the natives, who upon this event had retired into Wales, having greatly harrassed the various Roman stations by their continual inroads, once more drew the serious attention of Claudius towards our shores. Accordingly, in A. D. 50,[3] the General, who had held the command from the time of the Emperor's departure from the Island, was replaced by a more active successor, who, upon his arrival, found the Roman authority almost destroyed, and the country of their allies the Belgæ, invaded and laid waste.[4] Having repulsed the Britons with much slaughter, his next care was to secure the Roman province, as it was called, from similar calamities in future; and with this view he disarmed such of the neighbouring provinces as were suspected favourable to revolt, and fortified in a regular manner all the cities of consequence within the limits of his authority.[5] It is therefore to this period we may probably ascribe the first construction of our City in a regular form,[6] and the erection of the massy walls with which it has been surrounded.

---

[1] Trussell's MSS. l. ii. 32. Stowe, 15   [2] Ibid.   Milner, i. 18, 20.
[3] Milner, i. 21.   [4] Ibid.   [5] Ibid.   [6] Ibid. i. 23.

Next to the abolition of the Druidical sacrifices and funerals, the greatest benefit conferred by the Romans upon the inhabitants of Venta, in exchange for their independence, was the revival of their commerce, which had been fatally interrupted by the ambition of some of the native Princes. Manufactories adapted to its local situation and natural products were established,[1] and appear to have been considered under the special protection of the Emperor, as we find that at this early period it was celebrated for its magnificent embroideries wrought chiefly for the Imperial Court, and as the place where the tackling and sails of the Roman fleets on the coast of Britain were almost exclusively prepared.[2]

Venta now for a considerable time continued to enjoy the fruits of peace and civilization without interruption; and, after a succession of Princes uniformly distinguished for their submission to the Roman authority, we arrive at the period, when under the sanction of its sovereign and benefactor Lucius, the pure rays of Christianity began to disperse the intellectual darkness that enveloped the inhabitants of our island.

Accordingly, we find that, A. D. 165, Lucius, King of the Belgæ,[3] after receiving baptism with his Queen and a great number of his subjects in this his capital, proceeded to convert the idol temples of

---

[1] Wavel, ii. 5.   [2] Trussell's MSS. I. ii. 33.   Wavel, ii. 5.

[3] Wavel, i. 7. See also Verstegan's Restitution of Decayed Intelligence, p. vi.

his ancestors into places for Christian worship, and began the erection of a Cathedral, which was finished and consecrated A. D. 169, in the name of the Holy Saviour.[1] This, however, with every other sacred edifice, was totally destroyed during the religious persecution, set on foot by the Emperor Maximilian at the latter end of the third century, an interruption which does not seem to have been of very long continuance; and Christianity having been re-established by Constantius in 312,[2] the inhabitants of Venta exerted themselves in rebuilding their Cathedral, which they completed in the course of five years and dedicated with great pomp to St. Amphibalus the Martyr.[3]

We again find our City continuing to flourish in tranquility until some time after the arrival of the Saxons under Hengist and Horsa, who, in 447, had landed in the Isle of Thanet, by the invitation of Vortigern, King of Britain;[4] and, after remaining a considerable period as the allies of the unsuspicious and confiding natives, during which time they were strengthened by repeated accessions of their armed countrymen, at length found a pretext for hostilities, and in the course of their ravages, entering this City,[5] put the inhabitants without distinction to the sword, immolating the Clergy upon their altars, and destroying almost every edifice devoted to Christian

---

[1] Stevens's Monasticon, ii. 217.   [5] Stowe, 17.
[2] Trussell's MSS. l. ii .34.   [4] Verstegan, 117.   [3] Wavel, ii. 6.   Stowe, 19.

worship.[1] In the midst of this work of destruction, they were, however, arrested by Ambrosius, the successor of Vortigern, who came to the relief of our City, and driving out the Saxons with much slaughter, restored it to its liberty and its religion.[2] This triumph unhappily was but of short duration, for Ambrosius marching against Cerdic, who had landed at Southampton with a great body of Saxons, a battle ensued near Chardford, A. D. 516, in which Ambrosius was defeated and killed, with 5000 of his men,[3] and the conquerors immediately advanced upon this City, where they gave loose to all the horrors of Pagan vengeance.[4]

After this frightful visitation but little remained of Venta except a part of the walls and a few houses, merely adequate to the number of the conquerors that could be spared to replace its former inhabitants.[5] The Cathedral indeed remained; but the altars of the God of Mercy had become subservient to the gloomy and impure rites of the Saxon deities. The arts, the commerce, and the splendour of our City were destroyed; and amongst the other important changes it experienced at this period was that of its name, being no longer called Venta Belgarum, but *Wintanceaster*, since contracted to *Winchester*,[6] and which latter appellation it has since borne to the present time.

Still, however, under all its disadvantages, Win-

---

[1] Milner, i. 60.   [2] Ibid. i. 61.   [3] Rapin, i. 37.
[4] Wavel, ii. 7.   Milner, i. 71.   [5] Trussell's MSS. ii. 36.   Milner, i. 71.
[6] Milner, i. 71.   Wavel, i. 1. ii. 9.

chester shortly became the chief city of the most powerful monarch in the island, as we find that Cerdic, after reducing the surrounding districts to his authority, resolved to declare himself King of the West Saxons, and, assembling the chief of his people in this city, which he had rebuilt, caused himself to be solemnly crowned, A. D. 519, in the Temple of Thor, formerly the cathedral church, with the usual ceremonies of his nation.[1]

After a succession of warlike and successful mo‐ narchs, whose seat of government was chiefly at Winchester for upwards of a century, it cannot be doubted that its population and condition must have greatly increased and improved, since the time when Cerdic had new founded it as a Saxon city. It seems, however, during this period, to have regained but little of its former state of civilization, which had been so fatally interrupted by that event: its rude and warlike inhabitants were strangers to the use of let‐ ters or the advantages of commerce; and its religion seems to have been of the same gloomy complexion with its manners. In this state of ignorance and barbarism it continued until the reign of Kinegils, who succeeded to the throne of the West Saxons, A. D. 612, and was converted to Christianity[2], with many of his people, about 635, by St. Birinus,[3] an Ita‐ lian monk, who had obtained permission from Pope Honorius to carry the mild and persuasive tenets of

---

[1] Milner, i. 72.   [2] Verstegan, 146.   [3] Godwin's Lives of the Bishops, 158. Milner, i. 90.

the Christian religion into those parts of our island, from whence it had been so long and so frightfully expelled.

St. Birinus remained in this city and its neighbourhood until Christianity had once more taken a deep root, and its monarch, with great part of the inhabitants, had been baptized.[1]   Kinegils, whose early passion for war was now absorbed in excess of zeal for the religion he had adopted, immediately began the foundation of a cathedral,[2] which should, by its magnificence, be worthy of himself and of his capital. His death, however, happened shortly after the commencement of his pious work, and he was buried in the centre of the pile which he had began to erect, and which his successor, Kenewalch, was enjoined to complete.[3]

This Prince, however, being young, and not having the same predilection for a religion whose precepts, breathing only peace and moderation, could not but be considered irksome by those whose headstrong passions were excited, and barbarous propensities encouraged, by the gloomy and warlike rites of their Pagan deities, soon forgot or neglected his father's dying injunctions; and, although he did not actually re-establish the sanguinary worship of his ancestors, yet, by his total indifference to the cause, the building of the church was for many years at a

---

[1] Godwin's Lives of the Bishops, 158.   [2] Trussell's MSS. lib. ii. 34. Dugdale's Monasticon, i. 11.   Warton, 69.   Wavel, i. 9. ii. 22.   Milner, i. 92.   [3] Ibid.

stand.[1] It appears, however, that, after some considerable vicissitudes in his affairs, he at last set about finishing the cathedral in the most magnificent and splendid manner that the age was acquainted with; and the whole being complete, was dedicated to the Holy Trinity and St. Peter and St. Paul, by St. Birinus, A.D. 648.[2] He also, with a view of inducing Bishop Agilbert, the successor of St. Birinus, to fix his residence at this his capital city, gave him a superb edifice, erected for a royal palace by Kinegils, on the south east side of the cathedral,[3] and appointed it thenceforward the principal episcopal seat of the Bishops of the West Saxons.

Henceforward, until the dissolution of the Heptarchy under Egbert, in 827, when Winchester became the metropolis of England, there appears but little to remark in the history of this city, other than its continued advances towards civilization and improvement, the benefits of which had already began to mark their influence upon the manners and condition of the inhabitants; so that, in the year 856, its trade and commerce continuing to flourish exceedingly, the principal citizens formed themselves, under the protection of Ethelwolph, King of England and father of the illustrious Alfred, into a society of merchants, under the denomination of a Guild, being the first association of the kind recorded in history.[4]

---

[1] Milner, i. 93.   [2] Trussell's MSS. l. ii. 34, 40.   Monasticon, i. 11. Stowe, 24.   Milner, i. 95.   [3] Trussell's MSS. l. ii. 30, 40.   [4] Trussell's MSS. l. ii. 44.   Milner, i. 121.

But Winchester was again fated to experience the sanguinary and unbridled rage of an invading enemy. The Danes having, in 860,[1] landed in great numbers at Southampton, shortly made themselves masters of this city, wherein they committed the most horrid and lamentable excesses. The barbarians, however, paid dear for the calamities they had occasioned; for, having incumbered themselves with an immense booty, they were attacked as they were conveying it to their ships, and routed with great slaughter, while the spoil they had taken was returned in triumph to the places from whence it had been torn.[2]

In this attack our cathedral seems to have owed its safety to the fortifications raised round it some few years before, at the request of St. Swithin, by Ethelbald, King of England,[3] the probable remains of which, at the south-west corner of the church-yard, are still visible. But its fate was not entirely averted by this precaution; for these barbarians, having been reinforced by fresh numbers of their countrymen, after fighting several battles with the West Saxons, again entered our city, A. D. 871, and, after plundering and nearly demolishing the cathedral, massacred every individual belonging to it or found within its precincts, while at the same time the city was undergoing all the horrors of fire and pillage.[4]

Alfred having established himself upon the throne

----

[1] Stowe, 27.   [2] Milner, i. 123.   [3] Ibid.   [4] Milner, 125.

of England, about 880,[1] rebuilt and considerably enlarged the city,[2] which had been reduced almost to a heap of solitary ruins by the merciless Danes; those of its inhabitants who were fortunate enough to escape their fury having mostly fled into Wales.[3] By his care, however, it soon recovered its ancient state and dignity, and once more became the seat of government, and the depository of the records of the kingdom; and, in furtherance of his design to render it a truly royal city, he began the erection of a monastery, intended as a place of burial for his family and a retreat for St. Grimbald, a pious monk, whom he honoured with his regard, and from whom it was afterwards named. The foundations were accordingly laid on the north-east side of, parallel with, and at a very short distance from, the cathedral church,[4] and a magnificent monastery, completed and dedicated to the Holy Trinity, A. D. 903. He also assisted his Queen, Alswytha, in building another monastery in this city, for persons of her own sex, and which was, some time after her death, completed by King Edward, and called the Nunna Mynstre, or Abbey of St. Mary.[5]

About 923, Athelstan, the second monarch from Alfred, being considerably harrassed by the incursions of the Danes, who landed in almost every part of his kingdom, was, after various battles, overpowered by numbers, and obliged to seek refuge within

---

[1] Hume, i. 89. [2] Rapin, vol. i. 96. [3] Milner, i. 131,
[4] Dugdale, i. 208. [5] Dugdale, i. 212.

the walls of his capital, whither he was quickly followed by the conquerors, who, after a long siege, proposed to decide the question of mastership by the swords of their respective champions.[1]   A combat is accordingly said to have taken place, immediately without the north gate of the city, between Sir Guy of Warwick and Colbrande the Danish giant,[2] which terminated in the death of the latter; and thereupon the Danes fled with precipitation from the neighbourhood.   Perhaps the more reasonable cause of their flight might be found in the great strength of our fortifications, and the number and desperation of the forces shut up within them, which left the besiegers scarcely any possibility of taking the place by storm, while, from its great resources, they were rendered equally hopeless of starving it to a surrender.   These were the most probable reasons for the retreat of the Danes; and although the accounts which have been handed down respecting this famous combat, are not to be rejected as entirely fabulous; yet the relation has too much an air of romance,[3] for many of the circumstances attending, it to be considered otherwise than as agreeable inventions of the monkish writers.

Some idea of the prosperity of Winchester during the present reign, may be collected from the fact of there having been no less than six Mints,[4] for as

---

[1] Milner, i. 146.   See also Trussell's MSS. lib. iii. 51, &c.   [2] Ibid. id. Stowe, 29.   [3] Drayton's Narrative, see Trussell's MSS. l. ii. 52, &c. [4] Trussell's MSS. l. ii. 49.

many different kinds of money, established in it by Athelstan, which appear to have been situated in the centre of the city, and near the present Piazza, in the High Street, which then formed the scite of the Royal Palace.[1]

In the year 944 Winchester was severely afflicted with the plague, which, about that time, raged with great fury throughout the whole island; and, during the continuance of this calamity, aggravated by the horrors of famine, it was, unfortunately for the wretched inhabitants, set on fire, and the greatest part of it reduced to ashes.[2]

During the splendid reign of Edgar, who seems to have been one of the most illustrious of our West Saxon Monarchs, great confusion and fraud having existed throughout the kingdom, from the diversity of the measures then in use, a standard was made of the various divisions of weight and measure, which was deposited here; and at the same time a law was ordained, that the Winchester measure should be observed as that of the whole kingdom.[3] Of these measures, the original bushel is still preserved in the Guildhall of the city. It was also this Monarch, who, with a regard to the comfort and safety of some parts of his kingdom, which had long been greatly infested with wolves, imposed upon one of his vassal princes an annual tribute of three hundred wolves' heads, which were to be deposited by him at the palace of the Bishop of Winchester near

---

[1] Trussell's MSS. l. ii. 49.　[2] Trussell's MSS. l. iii. 52.　[3] Milner, i. 157. &c.

this city, the erection, as we have before mentioned, of Kinegils, and which, from this circumstance, seems to have derived the appellation of Wolvesey,[1] by which it is still called.

During this reign also, St. Ethelwold, Bishop of Winchester, entirely rebuilt the cathedral church, which he lived to finish and dedicate to St. Swithun and other saints, A. D. 980;[2] and, amongst the other great works undertaken by this prelate for the benefit of our city, that of a supply of water, which he effected by making several canals at a great expence, seems to have been productive of the most lasting benefit to Winchester of any of the works undertaken for its advantage.

In 981 we find the Danes once more landing at Southampton,[3] which, with the neighbouring country, they pillaged; but at this period we may conclude that Winchester was more strongly fortified than usual, from the circumstance of the invaders, who, in 994, 998, and 1001, held their head quarters at Southampton and in the Isle of Wight, not attempting to molest it;[4] and it would be well for the character of our city had this been the real and only motive for their forbearance; but, in fact, the inhabitants are charged[5] with having purchased an exemption from attack, by supplying the enemy with whatever provisions they required. This infamous privilege from their share of the common dan-

---

[1] Trussell's MSS. lib. iii. 58.   [2] Milner, i. 159.   [3] Milner, i. 170.
[4] Milner, i. 171.   [5] Ibid. id.

ger, was, however, but of short duration, and it was lost by an event truly worthy of those who had enjoyed it: for the invaders had no sooner withdrawn their main strength from the country, than Etheldred secretly directed the immediate massacre of all the unarmed Danes in the kingdom.[1] Here, in 1002, it accordingly appears,[2] the work of blood commenced, and here also, as soon as it was completed, certain revels, known by the name of Hock-tide Sports, were instituted, in memory of the event.

The horrible cruelties which the exasperated Danes inflicted upon every native who fell into their hands when they again landed upon our shores, a short time after this transaction, appear too frightfully disgusting for repetition.[3] As to this city, which was summoned by Sueyne, in 1013, it instantly opened its gates to the conquerors, submitting itself to whatever terms they might think proper to impose. Their vengeance, however, seems by this time to have been nearly exhausted, inasmuch as we do not find a recurrence of those destructive ravages, with which, on former occasions, they had visited our city; on the contrary, we now find them strengthening the fortifications, and honouring it with the ceremony of a coronation.[4]

Winchester, under the mild and impartial sway of Cnute, shortly recovered its original splendour; and it appears that in 1016, and again in 1020,[5] a

---

[1] Stowe, 31.   [2] Trussell's MSS. l. iii. 62, 66.   [3] Stowe, 31. See Milner, i. 172, note.   [4] Wavel's History of Winchester, vol. ii. p. 35.   [5] Ibid.

general assembly of the nobility was held in it, during which a number of wise and equitable laws were framed, tending to the welfare and security of the whole kingdom.

In 1044[1] our city was remarkable for the trial of Emma, mother of Edward the Confessor, who, being charged with criminal familiarity with Bishop Alwyn, insisted upon undergoing the proof, so usual in those days, of the fiery ordeal; and accordingly is said to have accomplished her purgation by walking, unhurt, over red-hot ploughshares, in the cathedral,[2] and thereby succeeded in establishing her innocence. Nor was the benefit of her triumph confined to the Queen herself: as we find that considerable gifts[3] were made by the King, and others, to our cathedral, upon the occasion of her deliverance.

Upon the invasion of England by the Normans, in 1066, Winchester found but little reason to rejoice in the change which it immediately experienced; although, perhaps, much of the rigour with which it was treated by the Conqueror, might have arisen from the unusual circumstance of the Abbot and part of the Monks of St. Grimbald's Abbey having been so imprudent as to follow Harold, to whom the Abbot was related, to the battle of Hastings, where they all paid with their lives for their temerity.[3] This punishment, although severe, did not appease the anger of William, who, immediately upon his

---

[1] Trussell's MSS. 1. iii. 60.   [2] Ibid. Monasticon, i. 34. Godwin, 168.   [3] Monasticon, i. 34.   [4] Monasticon, i. 210.

arrival at Winchester, gave orders for the seizure of the abbey and all its possessions, which he forthwith divided amongst his followers.[1] The abbey, which he had retained to himself, was, however, after a few years, restored to the monks, who at the same time were permitted to elect a new Abbot; and, in furtherance of his avowed design of restitution, certain possessions were given to the fraternity, of equal value to those of which it had been despoiled.

From this city it was that so many of the severe and oppressive ordinances, which affected the nation at large, were issued by the Conqueror; amongst which the regulation,[2] obliging his subjects to extinguish their fires and lights at the ringing of the Curfeu, or evening bell, was not one of the least annoying; and which regulation, so far as sound is concerned, is continued in our city to the present time.

According to the acknowledged policy of William, who relied chiefly for the stability of his conquest on the fortresses which he himself built, or obliged his followers to build, throughout the country, he very early began the erection of a Castle,[3] for the security of this his capital, and the depository of his treasures and records. This structure, of which we shall hereafter have particular occasion to speak, was situated at the western extremity of the city, and appears, from its great strength and command-

---

[1] Dugdale, i. 501.   [2] Trussell's MSS. l. iii. 68.   [3] Milner, i. 189

ing situation,[1] admirably adapted to the designs of the founder.

Winchester has the merit of giving, at this early period, the great and important example of the first trial *per pares*, that is extant upon record.[2] Waltheof, Earl of Huntingdon and Northampton,[3] having been accused of entertaining some rash projects for throwing off the Norman yoke, was brought to trial in the newly-erected castle, and, being found guilty by a jury of his peers, was condemned to the axe; which sentence it appears was accordingly carried into execution on the 29th of April, 1075,[4] upon the brow of the cliff at the east end of the city.

A parliament was held here in 1079, during which William demanded, and obtained, the extensive tract in this county since called the New Forest, as a place wherein he might give loose to the indulgence of his favourite amusement of the chace; and, he in consequence, devastated and laid waste the country for an extent of more than thirty miles.[5] This measure was, however, most probably effected from a far different motive than the ostensible one of amusement; as the consideration that, in the event of a general insurrection of the natives, he might find, amidst the recesses of the forest, a safe retreat for his Normans, upon the coast directly opposite

---

[1] Heylin, 373.   [2] Trussell's MSS. l. iii. 67.   [3] Hume, v. i. c. iv. 282. Stowe, 39.   [4] Hume, i. c. iv. 285.   [5] Stowe. 40.   Hume, i. 297.

to that of their own country,[1] must have had considerable weight with a leader of such acknowledged policy as William.

About the like period, viz. 1079, Walkelyn, a relation of the Conqueror, having been appointed to the see of Winchester, commenced rebuilding a part of the cathedral, and the whole of the adjoining monastery, from the ground, at his own expence.[2] This work, however, with regard to the cathedral, seems to have been confined merely to the tower, and a very small portion of the transepts and body of the church;[3] and this, with the new monastery, being complete in 1093, almost all the Bishops and Abbots in England assembled in Winchester,

---

[1] Trussell's MSS. l. iii. p. 70.   [2] Dugdale, i. 218.   Heylin,149.   Warton, 63.   Trussell's MSS. l. iii. 72.

[3] Survey—It has been generally considered that Walkelyn rebuilt the whole church from the ground; but in opposition to this we would observe, that it had been completely erected by Ethelwold, little more than a century previous to his time, in which short period it can hardly be supposed to have become so dilapidated as to require building anew. Walkelyn most undoubtedly built the present tower, and probably new roofed the body of the church and transepts, which he heightened; but it must be sufficiently obvious to the most cursory observer, upon a very slight examination of the masonry of the transepts, and such parts of the nave as were not re-fashioned by Wickham, that they were the workmanship of a very distinct period from that of the tower; as, independent of the difference of the stone, there is a manifest variation in the style of workmanship; nor do we consider ourselves as presuming too far, when we offer our opinion that the greatest part of the transepts, as well as the body of the present church, was erected at least a century earlier than has been commonly supposed; and this idea is considerably strengthened by a comparison of the masonry of the transepts with that of the eastern crypt, the acknowledged work of Ethelwold, who finished his church A. D. 980.

to honour the ceremony of its consecration, which took place on the festival of St. Swithun, to whom it was again dedicated.[1]

The rich citizens, being thus incited to liberality by the example of their Bishop, greatly exerted themselves in founding various religious establishments and splendid edifices, which, shortly after this period, ornamented every quarter of the city; and Winchester appears now to have flourished and increased to a surprising degree, in consequence of the enlargement of its commerce by the communication opened to it with William's Norman territories, assisted by the wealth and splendour of the Government, of which it continued the principal seat.

William Rufus followed the example of his father in keeping his court here, and especially so during the great festival of Easter;[2] on one of which occasions, being on a hunting party in the neighbouring forest, famous for the devastations of his father, and the premature deaths of his brother and his nephew,[3] he met with his own untimely end by the glancing of an arrow. The next day, viz. 2d August, 1100, his corpse was brought to this city, and buried in the centre of the choir of the cathedral, under a plain tomb of grey marble. That this

---

[1] Dugdale, i. 218.   Milner, i. 195.   [2] Trussell's MSS. l. iii. 72.

[3] Hume, i. 329.   Richard, second son of the Conqueror, was gored to death by a stag; and Richard, youngest son of Duke Robert, the eldest son of the Conqueror, had his neck broken by a fall from his horse, while hunting, in 1087.   Trussell's MSS. l. iii. 69, 71.

Prince was not too highly rated in the opinions of his subjects in this city, may be collected from the circumstance of their attributing the fall of one of the old Saxon towers of the cathedral, which happened the following year, and covered his tomb with its ruins, to the marked displeasure of Heaven that he had been permitted to receive Christian burial.[1]

Henry, the younger son of the Conqueror, being, at the time of his brother's death, in this city, was immediately saluted by the chief nobility upon the spot, King of England; and, repairing to Westminster for the ceremony of his coronation, afterwards returned hither to celebrate his nuptials, under a dispensation from the Pope, with Matilda, daughter of Malcolm, King of Scotland, who had taken the veil in the royal abbey of St. Mary, in this city;[2] and in consequence of the birth of a son, which happened in 1101, he granted a charter of privileges to Winchester,[3] as a mark of regard to the city to which he was indebted both for his Queen and his son.

The exultation of the citizens, and, in some degree, of the King himself, upon the joyful occasion of the birth of an heir to the throne, was soon after repressed by a terrible and unforeseen calamity. In 1102,[4] a fire burst out in the centre of the city, which totally destroyed the Royal Palace, the Mint, Guild-

---

[1] Milner, i. 198. [2] Trussell's MSS. l. iii. 72. [3] Milner, i. 200.
[4] Ibid. N. B. Trussell's MSS. l. iii. p. 72, states this calamity to have happened in 1112.

hall, and many of the houses of the inhabitants; and, upon this occasion, the ancient charters and most of the records of the city, became a prey to the devouring element.[1]

About 1110, the important circumstance of the removal of the religious fraternity of the Nunna Mynstre, or St. Grimbald's Abbey, founded, as we have before observed, by Alfred, in 890, took place.[2] This transaction seems to have become necessary, from the encroachments which had been made upon its boundaries by the Conqueror, for the scite of his palace,[3] and the increasing unhealthiness of the situation, arising from the waters, which, running from the castle ditches down the city, settled round the abbey in a stagnant condition; added to this, was the inconvenience arising from its contiguity to the cathedral, with which it was parallel, and in consequence of which the voices and organs of the respective choirs, while at the celebration of divine service, mutually interrupted and confounded each other.[4] These grievances, connected with others, induced the Bishop (Giffard) to undertake their removal; and a magnificent church and monastery having been erected in Hyde Meadows, the monks of St. Grimbald abandoned the situation their fraternity had occupied for more than two centuries, and went in solemn procession to their new Abbey of Hyde, carrying with them not only

---

[1] Trussell's MSS. l. iii. p. 72.   [2] Monasticon, i. 208, 510.
[3] Trussell's MSS. l. iii. 73.   [4] Trussell's MSS. l. iii. 74.

the relics of their saints, but also the remains of the illustrious founder, and other eminent persons who had rested within their precinct; and the situation, thus abandoned, was again restored to the monks of the cathedral,[1] to whom it had in the first instance belonged.

Winchester, invariably distinguished by the kind and liberal protection and regard of its Monarch, at this period seems to have stood unrivalled amongst the cities of England.[2] It was, as we have before remarked, the chief seat of Government, and the residence of the Sovereign, wherein he assembled the nobility of his kingdom at the principal festivals of the year. Defended by a royal and stately castle, surrounded with high and strong walls, and ornamented with two palaces of great extent and grandeur, and with a great number of noble edifices for public use, and the residence of the illustrious personages who were accustomed to inhabit it;[3] it was also enriched with a magnificent cathedral, besides three royal monasteries and other religious houses of less note, and a multitude of churches and chapels.[4] It was the principal key and thoroughfare of the eastern and western parts of the

---

[1] Milner, ii. 231.   [2] Trussell's MSS. l. iii. 75.   [3] Trussell's MSS. l. iii. 75, 76, &c.   [4] Milner, i. 208, refers to Trussell for the limits of the city and suburbs, which he states to have extended westward almost as far as the village of Week; northward, to Hyde Barton; eastward, to St. Magdalen Hill; and southward, to St. Cross. But it does not appear that any passage in Trussell can be found to warrant the reference.

kingdom; and was resorted to from every part of the country, on account of its celebrated fairs. It also enjoyed a considerable woollen manufactory, and an extensive traffic with the Continent, from which it annually imported great quantities of wine, in return for its manufactured woollens and other commodities.[1] But Winchester had now arrived at the climax of its prosperity, and henceforward it affords a melancholy illustration of the instability of human grandeur; since the almost uninterrupted task of the historian, from this period, will be to relate the gradations by which this city, although for a long time one of the most considerable places in the kingdom, has sunk to its present state of comparative unimportance.

Upon the death of Henry, in 1135, and the usurpation of the crown by his nephew Stephen, Winchester received its first impulse towards the retrograde path in which it was thenceforward destined to move.

Stephen having seized the palaces, or rather castles, of the Bishops,[2] shortly after his accession to the throne, under the pretext that it was not lawful for the clergy to hold castles, but in reality with a view to curtail their power, and to get possession of the immense treasures deposited in some of them, a synod was held in this city,[3] to protest against the injustice that had been done, and, if possible, to obtain redress. By this assembly, sum-

---

[1] Trussell'. MSS. l. iii. 76, 77, &c.   [2] Hume, i. 383.   [3] Trussell's MSS. l. iii. 78.

moned by Henry de Blois, the King's brother, as Cardinal Legate and Bishop of Winchester, and attended by Theobald, Archbishop of Canterbury, and most of the other Prelates, Stephen was peremptorily summoned to appear, and give plenary satisfaction for what he had done, or suffered to be done, against the privileges of the Clergy or the rights of the Church. Accordingly, in apparent show of obedience, the King speedily repaired to his palace in this city, from whence he sent certain of his nobles to know the cause of so imperious a mandate. After some negociation between the Prelates and the messengers of the King, the farce seems to have ended with the complete humiliation of the former, who forthwith broke up the synod without coming to any decisive measure on the subject of their discontents; and the Legate, with the Archbishop of Canterbury, being afterwards admitted to the royal presence, fell upon their knees, and in the most submissive manner besought the King to do that justice to their cause voluntarily, which the recent exercise of their assumed power had been unable forcibly to extort from him. To this latter measure, he, it seems, paid still less attention than he had done to the first; and withdrawing angrily from his suitors, departed for London, leaving the assembled prelates, as well as the inhabitants of our city in general, highly dissatisfied with his conduct.[1]

---

[1] Trussell's MSS. l. iii. 78, 79, 80.

In this untoward situation of affairs, the Empress Maud, daughter of Henry the First, landed with her adherents on the coast of Sussex,[1] in order to dispute the right to the crown, in favour of her son. Winchester seems, in the first instance, to have been favourably inclined towards the cause of the Empress, in opposition to the wishes of its Bishop, Henry de Blois, who, in order to put a speedy end to the miseries he foresaw would result to his country from a cruel intestine war, invited a great number of the nobility and chief men, whom he suspected were in her interest, to an entertainment in his castle of Wolvesey,[2] which he had then lately completed in a style of great magnificence, upon the scite of the original Saxon palace of Kinegils;[3] and after the entertainment, causing the gates to be closed, endeavoured, by various means, to induce them to give up, to his brother, the fortresses of which they were in possession. The scheme, so far as related to the castle of Winchester, totally failed, by the absence of its Governor from the feast,[4] and that fortress was firmly secured in the interests of Matilda, although, by the influence of De Blois, the city preserved its allegiance to the King.

In the course of the civil war that immediately ensued, Stephen was taken prisoner; and great part of the kingdom, having declared in favour of the

---

[1] Milner, i. 211. Stowe, 52.   [2] Milner, i. 211.   [3] Trussell's MSS. l. iii. 78. Gale, 33. Warton, &c.   [4] Trussell's MSS. l. iii. 79.

Empress,[1] our Bishop found it necessary to glide with the current he had vainly endeavoured to stem; and, after a short negociation, the scene of which appears to have been Magdalen Hill,[2] admitted her with her partizans into the city, which was accordingly entered by them in great pomp, on the 2d of March, 1141.[3]

The haughtiness of Matilda having occasioned much dissatisfaction, and the public opinion in her favour being on the decline, the Bishop, ever attentive to the interests of the prevailing party, very soon neglected to treat the Empress with the deference and respect attached to her high rank and pretensions; and upon being summoned to attend her, thought it necesssary to throw off the mask of obedience, by retiring to Wolvesey, and putting it in a proper condition to weather the impending storm.[4] The fortress was very soon afterwards invested[5] by the troops of the Empress, commanded by her uncle the King of Scotland, and her natural brother Robert, Earl of Gloucester. This event was the signal for a general movement on the part of Stephen's friends, who, hastening in considerable force to Winchester, relieved the Prelate, and attacked, in turn, those who had besieged him.[6] The armies, on both sides, appear to have been numerous and brave; and, unhappily for Winchester, carried on

---

[1] Hume, i. 386.   [2] Trussell's MSS. l. iii. 79.   [3] Stowe, 53. Hume, 387.   [4] Hume, i. 389. Trussell's MSS. l. iii. 30.   [5] Milner, i. 213.   [6] Hume, i. 390.

their destructive operations in the very heart of it, for the space of seven weeks,[1] during which the royal army, by degrees, obtained possession of the city, and in the end confined the partizans of Matilda to the castle. These advantages, however, were not obtained until after many sanguinary conflicts in the streets, nor, indeed, until the whole northern division of the city, including the royal palace and the new monastery of St. Grimbald, with the large suburb of Hyde, and forty churches, were totally destroyed.[2] At length the imperialists, straightened for provisions, and particularly so for a supply of water, were driven to extremity; but, careless of their own fate, their anxiety seems to have had the safety of Matilda for its principal object; in consequence, by one of those extraordinary expedients which could originate only in desperation, a stratagem was conceived and executed, which, aided by the romantic and almost supernatural fortitude of the Empress, fully answered the most sanguine hopes of her adherents. A report was industriously circulated, that Matilda had died in the castle; and, after a suitable time had elapsed, during which a truce had been obtained from the enemy, she was enclosed like a corpse, in a sheet of lead, and in that state, accompanied by some of her most distinguished friends properly disguised, carried upon a horse litter, through the besieging army.[3] At a

----

[1] Trussell's MSS. l. iii. 81. [2] Ibid. [3] Hume, i. 390. Trussell's MSS. l. iii. 82.

proper distance she was freed from her dismal envelope, and ultimately succeeded in effecting her escape to a place of safety.

One of the first concerns of Stephen, on regaining possession of the castle, was to strengthen it with new fortifications. This he effected to a considerable extent;[1] but whilst busied in the undertaking, a large army collected against him from the neighbouring counties, and forced him to abandon the completion of his design.

The war continued for about ten years after this transaction, with little intermission and various success; and at length Stephen, after losing his Queen, his only son, and his brother, was induced to open a negociation[2] with the adverse party, and a final conclusion was thus put to its ravages, by a treaty with Henry Fitz-Empress, in 1153, which was subsequently ratified at Winchester, with the consent of the whole nation.[3]

Henry de Blois, Bishop of Winchester, who appears to have borne so conspicuous a part in the transactions of this eventful period, was, upon the whole, a prelate of great abilities and some virtues, united with an ardent attachment to his see, the revenues of which he considerably improved; he also seems to have greatly strengthened and repaired the fabric of his cathedral,[4] and to have col-

---

[1] Milner, i. 216.

[2] Trussell's MSS. l. iii. 83.   Hume, i. 394.   [3] Ibid.   Stowe, 55.

[4] Godwin, 171.   Milner, i. 223.

lected together the remains of many illustrious and royal personages, who had been interred in different parts of it, and which he deposited in chests or coffins of lead, placed round the sanctuary. But among the various acts of munificence and princely liberality which distinguished him, one of the most conspicuous, and that which has chiefly contributed to perpetuate his memory, was his foundation, about 1136, of the Hospital and Church of St. Cross.[1] This institution he endowed with ample revenues, for the maintenance of thirteen resident persons, and the daily support of one hundred more of the most indigent that could be found in the city. There was also a provision made for the necessary officers of such an establishment; and the religious Brotherhood of St. John of Jerusalem were appointed comptrollers and governors of the whole.

The Brotherhood of St. John do not, however, appear to have conducted themselves, in their administration, to the satisfaction of the succeeding Bishop of this see, Richard Toclyve, to whom, and his successors, they shortly resigned their charge;[2] and Toclyve, being anxious for the improvement of the charity, among other alterations, extended its beneficial operation to the daily support of one hundred poor persons, besides those appointed by the founder, the revenues being at that time fully

---

[1] Trussell's MSS. l. iii. 72. Gale, 97. Wavel, ii. 212. Lowth's Wickham, 65. Godwin, 171. See 𝕾𝖎𝖗𝖙𝖍 𝖂𝖆𝖑𝖐. [2] Wavel, ii. 217. Milner, ii. 154. Lowth, 70.

equal to so great a charge. This prelate also, it is conjectured,[1] afterwards founded an Hospital upon the hill, on the eastern side of the city, which he dedicated to St. Mary Magdalen,[2] and endowed for the support of aged and infirm persons, upon a similar principle to the hospital of St. Cross; but, unhappily, every record, which might have thrown a light upon the original foundation and early history of this charity, has perished, with almost every vestige of its existence, by the conjoint efforts of time and violence.

Winchester appears to have been a favourite residence of Henry the Second, who spent much of his time in it, and rebuilt the royal palace at the north-west extremity,[3] which had been laid in ruins during the late war; and, in short, under the patronage of this Prince, the city was almost entirely rebuilt, and once more in a flourishing condition, although not to the extent of its prosperity during the reign of the Conqueror and his two sons. Among the many valuable privileges granted to it by Henry the Second, he conferred upon it, in 1184, a charter, by which it was ordained that Winchester should be governed by a Mayor and Bailiffs, &c.[4] a privilege which was not obtained by London until twenty-five years afterwards, viz. in 1209; and the first of our citizens invested with the important charge, appears to have been Florence de Lunn, who, it

---

[1] Milner, ii. 214.　　[2] See **Third Walk**.　　[3] Trussell's MSS. l. iii. 86.
[4] Trussell's MSS. l. iii. 87.

seems, remained in his office during the years 1184 and 1185.[1]

Upon the death of Henry the Second, in 1189, Richard Cœur de Lion hastened to this place, where he possessed himself of the royal treasury, and received the homage of the nobility on his accession to the throne. During the considerable period which followed this event without any serious interruption to the welfare of the city, our Bishop, Godfrey de Lucy, the successor of Toclyve,[2] was devoting his vast revenues in aid of its splendour and prosperity. Among the various benefits conferred upon it by this prelate, the most important and useful appears to have been the restoration of the navigation of the river Itchen, which he effected from Alresford to Southampton.[3] Nor did he neglect those duties more immediately attached to his situation; inasmuch as the repairs and works undertaken by him in his cathedral, justly entitle him to rank among its principal benefactors; the whole eastern end, from the back of the choir to the then extremity of the Lady Chapel, having been rebuilt by him.[4]

Winchester does not (especially so far as its ecclesiastical welfare is considered) appear to have been a favourite with Richard, who, immediately upon his arrival here, in March, 1194, from his long and rigorous captivity in Germany, began to reward the unshaken attachment of his subjects, by

---

[1] City Tables, St. John's House.   [2] Godwin, 172.   [3] Trussell's MSS. l. iii. 93.   [4] Milner, i. 230, note.

a general resumption of the grants which had been made by him previous to his departure on the Crusades.[1] The church was therefore hastily dispossessed of several manors, and the Bishop obliged to resign the castle and honours which had been purchased by him at an exhorbitant price.[2] By these, and many other, acts of unexpected rigour, he appears to have materially weakened the affections of his subjects in this city, from whence, in the same year, he departed for Normandy, and was destined never to return.

In 1207, King John held an assembly of the Barons and chief men of the kingdom in this city,[3] by which a tax was imposed upon the people of a thirteenth part of all moveable property; a measure which caused great and almost universal disstisfaction. Here also, in October of the same year, his Queen, Isabella, was delivered of a son,[4] who was surnamed, from his birth-place, Henry of Winchester; and his joy at this event, added to his design of raising money by every possible method, shortly afterwards induced him, for two hundred marks paid down, and an agreement for the annual payment of one hundred more, to confer upon Winchester a charter of incorporation, together with several valuable privileges, and to confirm those it had anciently possessed.[5] Here too, in the chapter house of our cathedral,[6] was this miserable tyrant absolved, by the as-

---

[1] Trussell's MSS. l. iii. 88.   Stowe, 66.   [2] Trussell's MSS. l. iii. 89.
[3] Ibid.   [4] Ibid.   [5] Trussell's MSS. l. iii. 91, 92.   [6] Trussell's MSS.
l. iii. 90.   Echard's History of England, l. ii. 104.

sembled prelates, from the sentence of excommuni-
cation issued against him by the Pope, to whom,
in the person of his Legate, he had previously made
the most abject and disgraceful submissions at Dover
for that purpose.

These concessions on the part of John, seem,
unfortunately, to have been the mere effect of cow-
ardice, united with the most consummate duplicity;
as his conduct towards his subjects, in a very
short time became more tyrannical and oppressive
than at any former period. Hence arose that
powerful confederacy of the Barons, the result of
which is, to this day, the main support and ornament of our constitution. In the transactions which
immediately followed the decisive conduct of the
Barons, our city appears to have early fallen into
their hands;[1] and was retained in their possession
until, by the signature of the Great Charter, on
the 19th June, 1215, it was, with other parts of
the kingdom, restored to its allegiance.[2] The field
of Runnimede, however, like the chapter house of
our cathedral, was merely the scene of John's
momentary submission, and of oaths intended to be
broken, as opportunity and renovated power should
offer; and having rashly attempted to invalidate
the only act which casts a gleam of light over the
deep hue of hypocrisy and tyrannical injustice that
pervades the whole of his reign, the Barons, indig-
nant at his perfidy, had again recourse to arms;

---

[1] Milner, i. 238.   [2] Hume, ii. 86.

and, in the excess of their resentment, invited
Lewis, the Dauphin of France, to the throne of
England.[1] John appears to have fixed his head
quarters at Winchester, where he hoisted the royal
standard;[2] but upon the approach of the Dauphin,
he appointed a governor of the city, and hastily retired to Gloucester. Savarac de Maulon, his new
governor, following the example of his master,
shortly afterwards also withdrew from the city, first
setting fire to it in various places,[3] in which condition it was abandoned to Lewis, and, with the surrounding country, given up to pillage.

Upon the death of John, in 1216, the Barons,
jealous of the growing effects of a measure, which,
originating in the fury of resentment, tended eventually to reduce this country to a province of France,
assembled a parliament at Bristol, and there confirmed the title of Henry, son of the late King, who
a short time before had been crowned at Gloucester, by the Bishops of Winchester and Bath.[4] This
Prince, during his long minority, seems to have held
his court frequently at Winchester, under the guardianship of Peter de la Roche, or de Rupibus, then
Bishop of this see,[5] to whom, upon the death of the
Earl of Pembroke, the regency of the kingdom de-
volved, in conjunction with Hubert de Burgh, then
Chief Justice.[6] This circumstance, in some mea-

---

[1] Hume, ii. 96.   [2] Trussell's MSS. l. iii. 93.   [3] Ibid. l. iii. 92.   Milner,
i. 239.   [4] Hume, ii. 147.   Echard, l. ii. 109.   [5] Godwin, 173.
Hume, ii. 163.   [6] Ibid.   Echard, l. ii. 111.

sure, restored the consequence of the city, which
had greatly suffered in the late contentions; but the
advantages arising from the King's residence were
in a considerable degree counteracted by the asso-
ciations formed within it, for the purposes of rapine
and plunder, in which many of the principal inhabitants of the city, as likewise several of the King's
household and body guard, were concerned.[1] These
alarming combinations were at length broken, in
1249, through the perseverance and spirit of Henry,[2]
and many of the guilty executed, notwithstanding
the excuse offered by those of the royal household,
" that they received no wages from the King, and
were obliged to rob for a maintenance."[3]

During the contentions which arose in 1261,
between Henry and his Barons, our city suffered
greatly; both parties alternately getting possession,
and alternately committing ravages. Still, when
peace had obtained the ascendancy, Henry was not
unmindful of the natural tie that connected him
with his birth-place, and although he did not actually extend its privileges, he was particularly tena-
cious of infringing those it already possessed. He
also was the first of our Monarchs who granted to
the Corporation a common seal,[4] and appears, on
all solemn occasions, to have worn his crown in
state, within the city. We may conjecture that
the behaviour of our citizens had been such as to

---

[1] Trussell's MSS. l. iii. 98.   Echard, l. ii. 120.   [2] Hume, ii. 232.
[3] Ibid. 233.   Echard, ii. 120.   [4] Wavel, ii. 70.

deserve the honour thus conferred upon them, as, independent of these marks of the royal favour, we find that, in 1266, a parliament was assembled in Winchester by Henry, under the authority of which the charters and privileges of the city of London, and many other places that had taken active measures in the late rebellion, were declared forfeited.[1]

Among other causes which operated to the advantage of Winchester, one of the most important seems to have arisen from the canal, which, as we have before mentioned, had been recently made from Alresford to Southampton, and by which the commerce of this city with the continental territories of Henry, had been greatly facilitated; its domestic trade had been also much increased and supported by the privileged marts held here, and particularly by the fair on St. Giles's Hill, which was then the greatest in the kingdom.[2] The increasing importance of London, however, on the other hand, operated much in its disfavour; and although Edward the First held several parliaments here, in one of which the celebrated Statutes of Winchester were passed, yet the royal domicile was in a great degree removed, and with it, of course, the attendants of the court, and others engaged in public affairs, whose affluence and expenditure had hitherto greatly contributed to prop the decaying prosperity of the city.

During the visit of Edward to this place, in 1276, he renewed the charters, and restored to it the pri-

---

Echard, l. ii. 125.　　　[2] Milner, i. 264.　See 𝕿𝖍𝖎𝖗𝖉 𝖂𝖆𝖑𝖐.

vilege of choosing its own officers. This power it appears to have lost in the course of the civil dissentions, which, originating in the turbulent and unsettled state of the kingdom, had prevailed within it for a considerable time, and it was probably during this visit that he bestowed a new seal upon the Corporation, which is still made use of by them in affairs of particular importance.[1]

In 1282, John de Pointes, or Pontissara, a person of extensive learning and great talents, united with considerable experience, was appointed to the bishopric of Winchester.[2] The most important act of his episcopal government seems to have been the establishment of a College for the propagation of literature and piety, which was erected by him at a short distance from his castle of Wolvesey, and dedicated to St. Elizabeth, of Hungary,[3] The foundation, which was completed in 1301, appears to have been for a warden, six priests, three deacons and sub-deacons, besides clerks and students, who were required by their statutes to be " obedient to their chief in all things lawful, grave in their habit and behaviour, modest, sober, good livers, and of good conversation remote from laymen. No female was to be admitted into any part of the college, and the members were to be rigidly examined previously to their admission, and to swear to the observance of the statutes." This foundation, which was liberally endowed, was not, however, fated to extend

---

[1] Milner, i. 268. [2] Godwin, 178 [3] Dugdale, i. 349.

its beneficial influence, like that of its subsequent neighbour, to modern times, as we shall hereafter have to notice it amongst the list of those establishments, which, in the reign of the Eighth Henry, were engulphed in the vortex of avarice and impiety.

In the course of 1303, a dispute occurred between our citizens and those of London, respecting the exorbitant duties required by the latter from the merchants of Winchester, upon the sale of their merchandizes within the limits of the city of London, from which our citizens insisted on their exemption; and after a considerable period, during which the matter was contested with great obstinacy on either side, the dispute was terminated, without having recourse to the usual excesses of the age, by the production of the charter of privileges granted to our city by Henry the First, upon the sight of which the Londoners resigned their pretensions.[1]

During the year 1304, the Hospital of St. John the Baptist, near the east gate of this city, which had been erected upon the scite of an institution founded by St. Brinstan, Bishop of Winchester, about 933, and subsequently destroyed by the Danes, was re-established and endowed by John le Devenish, a magistrate of Winchester, for the " sole relief of sick and lame soldiers, poor pilgrims, and wayfaring men, to have their lodging and diet gratis there for one night, or longer, as their inability to travel might require;[2] but this establishment, origi-

---

[1] Trussell's MSS. l. iii. 105.   [2] Trussell's MSS. l. iii. 102.

nating in, and acting upon, the most singularly benevolent principles, was, with many others of a far
less useful nature, totally suppressed in the latter
part of the reign of Henry the Eighth.

The royal favour which Winchester had hitherto
enjoyed, was unfortunately lost in 1305, by the escape
from the castle of a foreign hostage of great importance and high rank.[1]   Such an event, in the reign
of so warlike and impetuous a Prince as Edward,
could not but be attended with the most severe consequences.   Accordingly, all its liberties were declared void by the King, its magistrates imprisoned
in the Tower of London, and an excessive pecuni-
ary fine levied upon them for their negligence. The
good offices of the Queen, who seems to have been
struck with the severity of the punishment, soon,
however, procured the restoration of the privileges
of the city, as well as the liberty of its magistrates,
and the remainder of the sentence was also finally
remitted by her interposition.[2]

Edward the Second succeeded his father in 1307,
upon the throne of this kingdom, and is said to
have been a benefactor to our cathedral, although
there are no traces of his bounty to the city, in
which it does not appear that he ever resided, except during the festival of Christmas, in 1319.

Our city, in consequence of the unhappy circumstances of this reign, which present to history the
unnatural picture of a King and Queen of Eng-

---

[1] Trussell's MSS. l. iii. 105.   [2] Ibid.

land at open war with each other, was obliged, among other indignities, to submit to a direct violation of its charters, by the savage execution of Hugh de Spencer, Earl of Winchester, who had been taken by the Queen, in 1326, while gallantly defending Bristol for his royal master. The venerable nobleman, who had nearly reached the 90th year of his age at the time he fell into the hands of this merciless woman, was, without either trial or accusation, condemned to suffer death,[1] and he was instantly hung upon a gibbet, his body afterwards cut in pieces and thrown to the dogs, and his head, by the orders of the Queen, affixed upon the walls of this city, for the avowed purpose of terrifying the citizens, who were known to be equally attached, with the venerable Earl, to the cause of their unhappy Monarch.[2]

Shortly after the dethronement and murder of Edward the Second, on the 21st of September, 1327,[3] a parliament was held in Winchester, by the Queen and her creature Mortimer; in the course of which, finding that many of the Barons, who had hitherto supported them, began to grow impatient under their disgraceful yoke, as, indeed, this city had shewn itself from the beginning of their rule,[4] they resolved to make a terrible display of their vengeance, in order to intimidate such as might attempt to shake off their authority. To do this effectually, they thought

---

[1] Hume, ii. 367.   [2] Trussell's MSS. 1. iii. 108.
[3] Hume, ii. 371.   [4] Milner, i. 282.

G 2

it necessary to sacrifice one, who, united with illustrious rank a great share of the popular affection : and their victim was the King's uncle, Edmund of Woodstock, Earl of Kent, a nobleman of the most exemplary character and universally beloved,[1] but, unhappily, too credulous to withstand the arts which were used to ensnare him. The consequence was that he was attainted of high treason and condemned, in the parliament then assembled at this place, to suffer death. On the morning appointed for his execution he was led to a scaffold, erected before the castle gate ; but such appears to have been the general detestation of the act, that no person[2] could be induced by rewards or threats to perform the office of headsman, until, in the evening, it was undertaken by a criminal from one of the prisons, who, to prolong his own wretched existence, consented to terminate that of the Earl, whose body was afterwards interred by stealth in the chapel of the castle.[3]

The reign of Edward the Third seemed at one time to promise much benefit to Winchester, in consequence of the attention he paid to the staple commodity of the realm, which was also the article of trade that particularly concerned this city ; and it being found requisite that there should be fixed markets or staples for wool in convenient places throughout the kingdom, our city, in 1353, was

---

[1] Hume, ii. 389. Trussell's MSS. l. iii. 110. Stowe, 114.
[2] Trussell's MSS. l. iii. 130, 131. Hume, ii. 390. [3] Trussell's MSS. l. iii. 111.

appointed one of them ;[1] and the merchants, upon the faith of the King's promise not to revoke the appointment, began eagerly to avail themselves of the circumstance by purchasing land and erecting large warehouses and buildings for the convenience of the trade.[2] By this measure Winchester once more seemed destined to resume its former station as a great commercial city. But the sudden and unexpected removal of the wool staple to Calais, in 1363, in direct violation of the royal pledge,[3] gave a severe check to its commercial welfare, from which it never after fully recovered. The dissolution of the various clothing manufactories and other great establishments, being naturally accompanied by continual migrations, whole streets were at length deserted ; the navigation became neglected and choaked up;[4] and, by degrees, the appearance of trade and activity, once so conspicuous in this city, gave place to desertion and decay.

Still, however fallen as a city, Winchester continued to be the second bishopric in point of dignity, and the first in point of opulence, in the kingdom; and its prelate, William de Edyngton, in high favour with the Sovereign. With respect to the Bishop, it appears, that, in addition to the prelacy of the newly instituted Order of the Garter, which had been conferred upon him by Edward, he was, in 1366, elected to the metropolitical see of Canterbury, which he positively refused to accept.[5] Bishop Edyngton seems

---

[1] Trussell's MSS. l. iii. 110.   Hume, i. 513.
[2] Trussell's MSS. l. iii. 110.   [3] Ibid.   [4] Ibid.   [5] Godwin, 181.

to have been a considerable benefactor to the poor and to his cathedral, in which he had actually began the great work of rebuilding the nave,[1] when his progress was arrested by the hand of death in 1366, a very few months after the refusal we have before noticed.

Upon the death of Edyngton, the see of Winchester came into the hands of the celebrated William de Wykeham, the stately monuments of whose active benevolence and unrivalled talents being daily in our view, surrounded with all the splendour of living usefulness, have rendered him by far the most admired and renowned of any of our Bishops. Of the origin of this truly great man, there is considerable difference of opinion;[2] but it is evident that he was naturally endowed with the most brilliant talents, and that he began from his early youth to cultivate them with unexampled diligence. It appears that under the patronage of Nicholas de Uvedale, Governor of Winchester castle,[3] he received his education at a school near this city, which stood on the very spot that he afterwards chose for the scite of his college, and that, in his character as a student, he was distinguished no less for his piety than his literary attainments. Accustomed every morning to frequent the cathedral church, and to dedicate the day by hearing mass in a certain chapel of the Virgin, the pious sentiments which he imbibed upon this spot in his youth seem

---

[1] Godwin, 187.   [2] Godwin, 182. Lowth's Life of Wickham, p. 9.
[3] Godwin, 183.   Lowth, 12.

to have determined him in the choice which he afterwards made of it for his sepulchre.[1] To his superior skill in mathematics, it appears that he chiefly owed his rise to dignity and fame; and his first office at court, which was that of Surveyor of the King's Works, seems to mark the talents for which he was then most celebrated, while the buildings or repairs which he executed at Dover, Windsor, and other castles,[2] gave ample scope for the exercise of them. His abilities were afterwards found to be equally calculated for the management of more important duties, and he became progressively Secretary of State, Keeper of the Privy Seal, Chancellor of the kingdom, and the King's chief confidential adviser in the management of all matters of importance;[3] insomuch that a cotemporary historian, who, from his situation about the court, had every facility in ascertaining the truth of what he advanced upon the subject, says, " At this time reigned a priest called William de Wican. This William de Wican was so much in favour with the King of England, that every thing was done by him, and nothing was done without him."[4] Upon the death of Edyngton in 1366, he was, at the recommendation of Edward, unanimously elected, by the prior and monks of our cathedral, to the bishopric of Winchester; but about nine years after this event, viz. in the beginning of 1376, upon the

---

[1] Lowth, 255.　　[2] Godwin, 183. Lowth, 18.　　[3] Godwin, 182, 184, &c. Lowth, 28, 43, 53.　　[4] See an extract from Froissart's Chronicle, in Lowth, 33. Godwin, 184.

representations of the Duke of Lancaster, who laid numerous misdemeanors to his charge, and among others that of embezzling the public money,[1] the revenues of his see were sequestered, and himself ordered to retire from the court.[2] This unmerited disgrace was, however, but of short duration; and in July, 1377, he received an ample pardon from the King,[3] which concludes with the following honourable testimony of his innocence and integrity: " Although we have granted to our said cousin the Bishop of Winchester, the said pardons and graces, nevertheless we do not think the said bishop to be in any wise chargeable in the sight of God with any matters thus by us pardoned or released unto him, but do hold him to be, as to all and every of them, wholly innocent and guiltless."[4]

Having now recovered his temporalities, Wickham forthwith set about executing those great designs which he had planned in his retirement for the advantage of his diocese and of posterity in general. To this end he founded the magnificent structure of the New College in Oxford, which was completed in 1386;[5] as also another, which he began in the ensuing year at Winchester,[6] designed as a nursery for the former, in order that his diocese might have a constant and uninterrupted supply of learned and pious clergy. He also built, or rather entirely new modelled, nearly the whole of the west

---

[1] Godwin, 185. Lowth, 103. [2] Godwin, 185. Lowth, 116.
[3] Godwin, 186. [4] Lowth, 134, 135. [5] Lowth, 167. Godwin. 186.
[6] Godwin, 187.

end of his cathedral in the manner it now appears;[1] and among the rest of his useful acts, by a vigorous perseverance, he recovered the Hospital of St. Cross from the deplorable effects of the rapacity of its successive masters, and restored it to the original purposes of its founder.[2]

After a long and honourable life, unstained by a single blot, William de Wykeham, the nineteenth bishop of Winchester from the Conquest, whose memory will be immortal as his benevolence was active, died on the 27th of September, 1404, in the 80th year of his age,[3] and was buried in a superb chantry, which had been prepared by his direction, in the south aisle of his cathedral.

To return more particularly to the general subject of our History, we find that in 1388, Richard the Second and his Queen visited this city, in the course of their progress through the western part of the kingdom; and that, in 1392, a parliament was here assembled, in consequence of the city of London having been deprived of its charters.[4] These occurrences, and the marriage of Henry the Fourth with the Duchess of Brittany, which was celebrated in our cathedral in 1401,[5] appears to have been the only events of any importance recorded of Winchester during a considerable period.

Previous to the departure of our Fifth Henry to atchieve those conquests, the brilliancy of which

---

[1] Lowth, 195. Godwin, 187.   [2] Lowth, 82. See Sixth Walk.
[3] Godwin, 187. Lowth, 259.   [4] Stowe, 136.   [5] Wavel, ii. 90.

have illumined the brightest pages of English history, he honoured our city with his presence ; where, surrounded by the Princes of the Blood and the chief nobility of the kingdom, he received, in 1415, the ambassadors of the French King,[1] who came with proposals of peace, but upon terms incompatible with the high spirit of Henry and the honour of his kingdom ; they were accordingly rejected, and the King shortly afterwards proceeded with his army to Southampton, from whence they embarked for France.[2]

During the prelacy of Cardinal Beaufort, who succeeded Wykeham, in 1405, the hospitable foundation of De Blois, at St. Cross, was in a considerable degree improved, and the greater part of the present buildings erected;[3] additional funds were also added to the endowment, for the support of thirty-five more brethren and two chaplains, as also for three women who were to attend and minister to the brethren when sick. Besides the revenues appropriated to these purposes, the Cardinal employed large sums of money in relieving poor prisoners, and in completing some parts of his cathedral which had been left unfinished at the death of his predecessor;[4] and upon his decease, on the 11th of April, 1447, he was interred within a most stately monument, erected by him at the east end of his cathedral.[5]

---

[1] Echard, l. ii. 183.　　[2] Stowe, 146.　　[3] Godwin, 189. Monasticon, ii. 481.　Wavel, ii. 226.　Vide **Sixth Walk.**　　[4] Milner, i. 301.　[5] Godwin, 189.　**See First Walk.**

Henry the Sixth appears to have been a benefactor to our city, and greatly attached to its different religious and literary establishments, and especially to those of Wykeham; inasmuch as his collegiate foundations at Eton and Cambridge were modelled upon the exact plan of those of our venerable prelate.[1] As a proof, however, of the encreasing decay of the city during the present reign, Henry granted, at his first visit here in 1440, the sum of forty marks annually to the Mayor and Aldermen for its benefit,[2] which they continued regularly to enjoy for about ten years, when, being deprived of it by an Act of Parliament, particularly relating to grants made to corporate bodies, they found it necessary to petition the King for a renewal of his bounty; stating, among other reasons for the necessity of the application, that the trade and population of the city had so greatly decreased that no less than seventeen parish churches and 992 houses had actually fallen to ruin within the last fourscore years for want of inhabitants and the means of keeping them in repair. The petition concludes thus: " The desolacōn of yᵉ said poure cittie yˢ soe grete, and yerely fallynge farther intoe syche decaye and ruwyne, yᵗ, withᵒᵗ yᵉ gratious comforte of yᵉ Kynge oure Soueraigne Lord, yᵉ Maire and yᵉ Balyffs must of necessitie cesse and deliuer uppe yᵉ cittie and yᵉ keyes intoe yᵉ Kynges handes."[3] The King, however, granted

---

[1] Lowth, 180.   Wavel, ii. 92.   [2] Milner, i. 305.
[3] Wavel's History of Winchester, Appendix, ii. 243.

the request of the petitioners, and the proposed surrender was averted.

During the period of anarchy which followed the
dethronement of this imbecile Monarch, in 1461,
the succession of Edward the Fourth in the same
year, and the usurpation of the crown in 1483, by
that remorseless tyrant Richard the Third, Winchester appears to have remained undisturbed in its
advance towards obscurity: equally unnoticed by
every party, it was free from the dangerous consequences of their jealousy; and we therefore find no
event of any importance in its history until that of
the pregnancy of Elizabeth, Queen to Henry the
Seventh, who, from motives of state policy,[1] was
conducted to this city for her acouchement, and in
the castle of which she was, on the 20th of September, 1486, delivered of a son.[2]

In the year 1502 Richard Fox, Bishop of Durham, a prelate of the most exemplary character,
and who appears to have been in high favour with
the Sovereign, was appointed to this see, then vacant
by the death of Thomas Langton.[3] Bishop Fox, a
worthy successor to the episcopal throne of the illustrious Wykeham, was also, like him, indefatigable
in the discharge of his duties, unbounded in his charities to the poor, and a munificent benefactor to the
cause of learning and piety; and there is little doubt
but that the condition of Winchester must have been
greatly ameliorated during his prelacy, although the

---

[1] Milner, i. 344.   [2] Hume, iii. 338.   [3] Godwin, 192.

monuments which have more particularly tended to the preservation of his memory here are the great repairs and improvements which he effected in his cathedral,[1] and which, on the whole, have perhaps never been equalled for their beauty, elegance of design, and execution. Of these works, the magnificent stone screen at the back of the altar,[2] would have ensured him the gratitude of his church and the admiration of posterity; but he also erected the partition walls of the choir, whereon he placed a series of mortuary chests containing the relics of several monarchs and prelates which had been removed from their sepulchres in the early part of the twelfth century, by Bishop de Blois;[3] he also finished the roof of the presbytery, from the eastern extremity of Walkelyn's tower to the end, and embellished it and the parallel aisles with superb windows of stained glass; and in addition to this, he fronted the eastern boundary of the choir, on the outside, with a rich display of ornamental Gothic architecture, among which, under a beautiful canopy, supported by his favourite device the pelican, his statue, clothed in the episcopal habit, is placed.

During the prelacy of this Bishop, the depopulation and consequent decay of the city having so greatly increased that many of its parishes were unable to repair their churches or maintain their ministers,[4] a number of the churches were ordered

---

[1] Godwin, 193.   [2] See First Walk.
[3] Gale, 26.   Dugdale, i. 219.   Godwin, 193.   [4] Wavel, ii. 95.

to be demolished and the respective parishes united, that there might be some chance left of supporting the remainder.

In the latter part of June 1522, Henry the Eighth, and his imperial guest Charles the Fifth, spent some days together in this city,[1] and appear to have been particularly attracted by the Round Table then kept in the castle, and traditionally asserted to have been placed there by the British King, Arthur, about ten centuries before that period, for the purpose of celebrating the banquets of knighthood and chivalry.[2] Whatever may have been the reasons in 1522 for believing such a tradition, they have certainly not reached the present times unimpaired, or we must give our ancestors credit for a greater share of credulity than some might be willing to allow, since it seems to have been very clearly demonstrated by a learned historian and antiquary of our city,[3] that the scene of the romantic magnificence and festive banquets of the renowned Arthur was the Cær Gwent of Monmouthshire, and that the history of this table, so far as relates to its erection by that personage, is a dream of fiction, which has become, as it were, embodied into the substance and appearance of reality, from the singular coincidence in name of our city with that of his actual residence. That this table is of some antiquity there is no reason to doubt; it being admitted that at the period of Henry's visit to Winchester, when it was

---

[1] Wavel, i. 5. ii. 94,　　[2] Ibid. i. 5.　　[3] Milner, i. 73.

defaced or decorated, as it now appears,[1] many incontrovertible proofs of its great age were destroyed; and, perhaps, if it is allowed to be of a date coeval with the repairs of the castle by Stephen, in 1142, about which time the institution of the Round Table was formed by that Sovereign,[2] we shall have given it credit for a sufficient degree of antiquity to authorise all the curiosity excited by its present elevated situation in the original chapel of the castle, to which it was removed upon the demolition of the other parts of that structure in 1645.

Upon the death of Bishop Fox, in 1528, the celebrated Cardinal Wolsey was translated to the bishopric of Winchester, which he held but for a short period, as it became vacant by his death in November, 1530. Winchester does not appear to have been much benefited by the Cardinal, or even honoured with his presence, as he took possession of his cathedral by proxy;[3] and the only use which he seems to have made of his power was to dissolve certain monasteries and churches in his diocese, in order to confer their revenues and possessions upon the magnificent colleges which he was building at Oxford and Ipswich.[4]

This see, upon the death of Wolsey, remained vacant nearly four years, when Henry bestowed it upon the famous Stephen Gardiner,[5] during whose prelacy the final dissolution of the monastic institu-

---

[1] Trussell's MSS. 1. ii. 37. [2] Milner, and authorities, v. ii. 183, and notes. [3] Milner, i. 323, 324. [4] Stowe, 201. Godwin, 193, 489. [5] Godwin, 194. Hume, iv. 140.

tions, and consequent destruction of religious houses, took from Winchester all that had been hitherto left of its lingering grandeur and importance.

The dissolution of our venerable priory of St. Swithun,[1] which had flourished in magnificence and splendour for upwards of nine centuries, was among the earliest consequences of the Reformation. Its yearly revenue, which at this period was valued at 1507*l.* 17*s.* 2*d.* seems, for the most part, to have been appropriated to the use of the new foundation established by Henry in 1538,[2] which consisted of a dean, twelve prebends, six minor canons, ten singing men, and eight choristers, with clerks and other officers, and was dedicated to the Holy and Undivided Trinity; William Basyng, or Kingesmill, the last prior, being at the same time, in consequence of his voluntary resignation, appointed the first dean upon the new establishment.

The dissolution of the royal Abbey of Hyde, the foundation of the illustrious Alfred; of St. Mary's Abbey, endowed by his Queen; and in short of all the other monastic establishments of Winchester, immediately followed the suppression of the priory of St. Swithun; nor did the catalogue of destruction end with them, as the hospitable foundations of St. Cross,[3] St. Mary Magdalen, and other charitable institutions, were either materially despoiled of their possessions, or, like the College of St. Eli-

---

[1] Warton, 74.   Wavel, i. 23. ii. 97.   [2] Dugdale, i. 35.   Wavel, ii. 31.
[3] Wavel, i. 35, 36.

zabeth, founded by Bishop Pontissara, and the Hospital of St. John the Baptist, endowed by John le Devenish, were entirely suppressed.

Whatever might have been the objections to the existence of monastic institutions, as connected with the spiritual welfare of the kingdom in general, it is certain that in no part of it were the temporal effects, produced by their suppression, more sensibly felt than at Winchester. It had fallen from its station as a royal and as a commercial city, and it was chiefly to the number and splendour of its religious establishments that it had for a considerable time owed the little remains of consequence and exterior appearance it possessed. These, however, being dissolved, and the edifices themselves pulled down or falling in ruins, it became literally the mere skeleton of its former self, and, with the decline of monasticism, seems to have lost its last and oldest claim to distinction and importance.

We have little to notice during the short reign of the Sixth Edward, except the natural consequences of the foregoing measures, a further depopulation of the city, and the excessive dissentions of the clergy and others, with respect to the policy of the important revolution that had taken place in the spiritual concerns of the kingdom, in the course of which our Prelate Gardiner was sent to the Tower, and afterwards, in 1550, deprived of his bishopric.[1]

Upon the accession of the Princess Mary, in

---

[1] Godwin, 194. Hume, iv. 370.

1553, one of the first acts of her power was the reinstatement of Gardiner in the possession of his see; and within a few weeks afterwards we find him appointed Chancellor of the kingdom, and performing at the ceremony of her coronation.[1]

In 1554, Winchester became the scene of the meeting and subsequent nuptials of Queen Mary with Philip of Spain, which were solemnized with great magnificence in the chapel of the Blessed Virgin, at the east end of our cathedral.[2] Upon this occasion the charters were renewed, and various marks of royal favour manifested to the citizens and clergy, which were immediately followed by the restitution of many large estates that had been alienated from the bishopric during the preceding reign.[3] It does not, however, appear that any of the ancient establishments of Winchester were actually restored to existence, if we except the hospital of St. John, near East Gate, which about this time was refounded by one Richard Lambe,[4] for the support of six poor widows of citizens, who were placed under the controul and superintendance of the Corporation for the time being. The city itself does not appear to have been materially benefited; and, in truth, its progress towards decay seems to have been much too far advanced for an expectation of its reverting to its original prosperity, although the general measures which were adopted during this

---

[1] Hume, iv. 403.   [2] Stowe, 258.   Wavel, ii. 98.   Echard, I. iii. 321.
[3] Heylin, 101.   [4] Warton, 12.

reign in favour of the church might probably contribute in some degree to a momentary revival of its hopes.

Amongst the list of sufferers in the cause of Protestantism, which have cast a hue of blood over the records of this bigoted reign, Winchester appears to have furnished but few victims, and those not of importance [1], except from the examples which, amongst others, they afforded of the unconquerable spirit of the religion they had embraced, whose influence supported its votaries through all the tortures that cruelty could devise or malice execute, and soothed the agonies of death with the well-earned hope of a blissful immortality.

Shortly after the coronation of Queen Elizabeth, in 1558, she honoured our city with a visit; and although she expressed her great concern at its declining state,[2] we do not find that she bestowed any particular marks of royal beneficence in aid of its deplorable condition for several years after her visit.

The next bishop at all distinguished in this diocese was Robert Horne, who, we find, was consecrated to Winchester in 1560.[3] The appointment of this person, so far as his temporal character is considered, appears to have been a calamity both to his church and the city at large, inasmuch as to him is ascribed the destruction of almost every ornament with which his cathedral was then adorned;[4]

---

[1] Milner, i. 360.   [2] Wavel, ii. 98.
[3] Godwin, 195.   [4] Gale, 104. Milner, i. 370.

the statues of saints and remarkable persons were indiscriminately destroyed, the numerous paintings throughout the church defaced or obliterated, and the various chapels demolished or despoiled of their beauty; the venerable chapter house and the cloisters on the south-west side of the cathedral were also razed to their foundations by his order, and the whole fabric of the church, by his mistaken notions of improvement, irretrievably injured and despoiled.[1]

During the latter part of the reign of Elizabeth, viz. in 1587, a charter was obtained for our city through the mediation of Sir Francis Walsingham its recorder, which, as being the last of the kind ever granted to our citizens, is that by which, at the present day, they hold their privileges.

By the tenor of this charter,[2] Winchester is declared to be a corporation of itself, and a free city, under the government of a mayor, recorder, six aldermen, one deputy recorder or town clerk, two bailiffs, two coroners, and two constables, with a council of twenty-four honest and discreet citizens, to be called " The Four-and-Twenty Men." The mayor, recorder, and aldermen, are appointed justices of the peace for the city, with usual powers, and exempted from the jurisdiction or interference of the county magistrates. They are also empowered to assess and receive fines, &c. without accounting for the same to the Queen. The mayor is appointed

---

[1] Collier, ii. 471. Milner, i. 370. Wavell, ii. 99. Warton, 22.

[2] See Charter, 30th Elizabeth.

escheator for the Queen and her successors, within the city, and empowered to hold courts of record, and borough-mote courts. Two markets are appointed to be held in each week, on Wednesday and Saturday, and three fairs to be held annually, at the times therein limited. The mayor and commonalty to have return of writs within the city. The citizens are exempted from all suits of hundred and county courts, and their former exemptions from tolls, duties, and customs, confirmed. The mayor appointed clerk of the markets, with power to make assize of bread, wine, &c. The mayor and commonalty authorized to erect companies of different trades or occupations in the city or suburbs; all former rights and privileges granted to the city are confirmed; and finally, all questions respecting the guardianship of the Hospital of St. John established by John Lambe, Esq. in the preceding reign, are settled, and the difficulties concerning the title to the same removed.

The principal aim of this charter was evidently to save the city from the extreme consequences of further depopulation; and by tolerating foreigners to exercise their arts or occupations within it, free from the restraints usual in such cases in other privileged cities, to counteract, in some degree, the effect of the perpetual migrations it had so long experienced. But the salutary ends it was hoped it would have produced, being unfortunately anticipated by the confusion of the times, before there had been sufficient opportunity to mature and disseminate its natural consequences, the effect was, that although many advantages were derived from it, Winchester never enjoyed the full extent of the benefits which their charter of Elizabeth was intended to convey.

Amongst the other ancient privileges confirmed by this charter was that of keeping the standard weights and measures of the kingdom; and accordingly, in the course of the next year, 1588, a new set of them, bearing the arms and name of the Queen, were presented by her to the city, and in 1589 she further honoured it with the gift of a new seal.[1]

The commencement of 1603 was distinguished at Winchester by the remarkable event of James the Sixth of Scotland being proclaimed King of England, by the sole authority of Sir Benjamin Tichborne, sheriff of Hants, who, having received intelligence of the Queen's death while at his family seat in the neighbourhood of this city, hastened hither, and issued the proclamation of accession without waiting for orders from the Privy Council in London, who, for several hours after the transaction, were still deliberating upon the subject.[2] This spirited and decisive conduct of the sheriff was deservedly rewarded by James, who granted to him and his heirs, in perpetuity, the royal castle of this city, together with an annual pension during the

---

[1] Milner, i. 375. Warton, 33. Wavel, 99, 117, with variations.
[2] Milner, i. 389.

life of himself and his eldest son, whom he also knighted; and it was probably owing to the King's partiality for the city from the foregoing circumstance, that, upon the plague breaking out in London in 1604, the courts of justice were removed to Winchester,[1] which was also shortly afterwards crowded with the great officers of state and the nobility, who were summoned to the trial of the conspirators in Sir Walter Raleigh's plot, some of whom were afterwards executed before the gate of the castle.[2]

While these transactions were going forward, our city, from the conflux of great personages and the expenditure naturally occasioned by them, must have exhibited some faint image of its former importance and activity. It seems also that James occasionally honoured it with his presence, although it does not appear that he conferred any permanent advantage upon it; and indeed there is quite sufficiency of evidence to convince us that its tendency to decay was in no wise interrupted by the beneficence of the Monarch.

About the commencement of the reign of Charles the First, in 1625, a severe pestilence broke out amongst the inhabitants of Winchester, which carried them off in great numbers,[3] but without extending to other parts of the kingdom, or even to the towns in the immediate neighbourhood; and the effects of it had scarcely subsided, when, as if in

---

[1] Stowe, 451. Milner, i. 394.   [2] Stowe, 452.   [3] Warton, 34.

aggravation of the calamity, a large body of soldiers were marched into the city and quartered upon the private inhabitants, in whose houses and families they appear to have committed such violent and disgraceful excesses[1] that many of the better sort, who had providentially escaped the plague, were absolutely forced to quit their homes that they might avoid so unjust and unreasonable an imposition, which in some instances promised to be of more fatal consequence to their happiness than even the plague itself. This extraordinary instance of oppression, added to that of levying ship-money, which followed in 1634, gave birth to an universal discontent and apprehension among the citizens, insomuch that the mayor and his brethren presented a remonstrance and petition to the King, in which they depicted the grievous calamities of their ancient city, as well the kingdom at large, arising from the unconstitutional measures that had been adopted, and earnestly prayed for their discontinuance.[2] The only visible effect, however, which this remonstrance seems to have had was that of a most marked neglect and indifference on the part of Charles towards those by whom it was presented. Nor can we upon this occasion justly attach any peculiar blame to the conduct of this unhappy yet amiable Monarch, since, from the very commencement of his reign, he seems to have been absolutely forced to act with a degree of harshness and indifference to the opinions

---

[1] Wavel. ii. 118.　　　　[2] Wavel, 119.

of his subjects, equally foreign to his inclination and his interest; and this through the studied opposition and overbearing insolence of those on whom he most naturally depended for assistance and advice.

The next prelate whom we shall notice, as bearing any distinguished rank in the annals of our church, was Dr. Walter Curle, Bishop of Rochester, who was translated to this see in 1631,[1] and appears to have considerably improved the cathedral and its environs, by removing various nuisances and encroachments with which it was then incumbered and disgraced. The avenue at the south-west end of the cathedral, had, since the demolition of the cloisters by Bishop Horne in 1560,[2] been blocked up by a cluster of mean houses, in consequence of which there was no immediate way from the close into the city without passing through the church. This inconvenience was now removed, and a passage opened upon the scite of the buildings. The inside of the cathedral was also considerably altered and embellished, the ancient rood-loft taken away, and a screen of the Composite order, after a design of Inigo Jones, erected in its place. The ceiling of the choir under the tower was also made and decorated in the manner it now appears; new ornaments of plate and tapestry were provided for the service of the altar, and various other improvements effected.[3] Whilst these mat-

---

[1] Gale, 106. Monasticon, i. 13.   [2] Ante, p. 59.
[3] Warton, 89. Milner, i. 401.

K

ters were in progress, Charles with his Queen honoured our city with a visit, on which occasion their arms, richly emblazoned on glass, were put up in the hall of the deanry, where they still remain in high preservation.[1]

During the troubles which characterise the eventful reign of this ill-fated Monarch, Winchester, with its castle, were early secured for the Parliament by Sir William Waller,[2] the possession of which gave him the command of a considerable extent of country to the west; and although he seems to have been fully sensible of the advantage, yet, towards the conclusion of 1643, the castle was seized and garrisoned by the royalists under Sir William Ogle, and our city appointed the general rendezvous of the royal army, then forming in the western part of the kingdom.[3] Fortifications were accordingly thrown up round the city, particularly on the east and west sides, on the latter of which the deep entrenchments still remain.[4] The activity of Waller, and the defeat of Lord Hopton on Cheriton Down, in 1644, rendered these precautions unfortunately of little avail, and the Parliamentary General again obtained possession of the city.[5] The castle, however, into which the Mayor and principal citizens had retired, still continued, under the command of Lord Ogle, to hold out for the King; and Waller, finding all his endeavours ineffectual for its reduc-

---

[1] See First Walk.
the Rebellion, l. viii.   [4] See Fifth Walk.

[2] Echard, ii. 555.

[3] Clarendon's History of

[5] Echard, ii. 595.

tion, turned his revenge upon the defenceless city. Under these circumstances, the ungovernable violence of the soldiery, encouraged by recent victory and inflamed by unexpected opposition, fell chiefly upon our venerable cathedral, which was defaced and plundered in a most wanton and shameless manner.[1] Fortunately for posterity, the exquisite altar-screen of Fox was protected from their violence by a parallel wall erected immediately before it, of a height sufficient to entirely conceal it from observation;[2] but the surrounding parts of the church did not escape their fury, which was vented by breaking to pieces the carved work of the choir, destroying the organ, and throwing down the communion table, the rails and furniture of which they used for firing. They also defaced the monuments; and, tearing down the mortuary chests from the walls of the choir, threw the bones contained in them against the painted windows,[3] which they destroyed throughout the church, with the exception of the window at the east end, and this being less exposed to their violence than the rest, fortunately escaped entire. Happily, in this merciless epoch, the tomb and chantry of William de Wykeham was exempted from the general havoc, by means of an officer in Waller's army, who had received his education in the college of that illustrious prelate,[4] and who, notwithstanding the cause in which he was engaged,

---

[1] Wavel, i. 43.   Gale, 25.   Milner, i. 408.   [2] Warton, 93.   Wavel, i. 42.
[3] Dugdale, i. 220.   [4] Wavel, i. 44.

retained a sufficient sense of honour and gratitude to protect, at the hazard of his personal safety, the monument and remains of his munificent benefactor. It is also attributed to the same influenee that the college itself was preserved from despoliation.

The wanton ravages of these ungovernable zealots would probably have extended to yet farther excesses, had not Waller withdrawn his troops for the purpose of besieging Oxford, on which occasion our city was again for a short time in the possession of the royalists. The fatal issue of the battle of Naseby, in 1645, rendering the King's affairs desperate, and most of the places in the west having submitted to the parliamentary forces, an army was dispatched under Oliver Cromwell for the reduction of Winchester.[1] On the 28th of September, 1645, he accordingly appeared before the city, which he immediately summoned; and upon receiving an answer from the Mayor that the Governor of the castle had alone the authority of surrendering the city,[2] an attack was commenced upon it from an eminence on the south-west side, which still preserves the memory of the event by the designation it bears of " Oliver's Battery." His chief efforts were, however, directed towards the castle,[3] which, after resisting the impression of his cannon for about a week, was surrendered to him, though not without strong suspicion of treachery on the part of Lord Ogle the governor.[4] No sooner was Crom-

---

[1] Wavel, ii. 126. [2] Ibid. 128. [3] Life of Cromwell, p. 31. [4] Milner, i. 409.

well master of the castle, than, in conformity with his usual practice, he began to demolish it by mining and blowing it up with gunpowder. The same policy was exercised upon the fortifications of the city; and in like manner the Bishop's castle of Wolvesey was reduced to a heap of ruins. The town hall and several churches and other edifices, both of a public and private description, were also demolished,[1] and, for a considerable time after the period in question, Winchester presented little more than a scene of desolation and distress.

On the 21st of December, 1647, Winchester again welcomed its Sovereign, but under far different circumstances from those in which it had received many of his predecessors—the unfortunate Charles, conducted as a prisoner, slept in this city, on the first night of his journey from Hurst Castle to Windsor,[2] but little more than a month previous to the horrible catastrophe which has left an indelible stain upon the annals of our country.

On the arrival of the King, the Mayor and Aldermen, notwithstanding the danger to which they were exposing the city in general and themselves personally, by their loyal and affectionate behaviour, received him with the most undisguised marks of duty and respect;[3] and during the few hours he was suffered to remain, the neighbouring gentry flocked hither in great numbers to express their devotion and attachment. It has been well expressed by the

---

[1] Wavel, ii. 129. [2] Echard, l. ii. 652. Milner, i. 410. [3] Echard, l. ii. 652.

Historian of Winchester,[1] that " such a reception of a captive King does more honour to this city than all its holiday addresses to successful Monarchs put together;" and he might have added, that loyalty so purely disinterested ought to immortalize Winchester when every other vestige of its existence shall have vanished from the surface of the island.

The murder of this unhappy Prince, on the 30th of January, 1648,[2] gave a fresh stimulus to the ebullitions of puritanical vengeance against every thing connected with the established religion and its ministers; accordingly a second Reformation, as it was called, was here set on foot and speedily effected; the Presbyterian church government was established by an ordinance of Parliament in all its forms and bearings; and the tyranny and insolence of the Puritans shortly arrived to such a height, that the regular clergy were not only forbidden, under severe penalties, from officiating at the altars of their Creator, but, after a little time, were actually expelled the city.[3]

Enthusiastic was the joy of the whole nation upon the restoration of Charles the Second, on the 29th of May, 1660; but in no part of it does that satisfaction appear to have been more sincerely expressed than at Winchester, which again recovered its episcopal dignity, of which it had been deprived ever since the death of Bishop Curle, in 1650. A new bishop, Dr. Brian Duppa, was now appointed

---

[1] Milner, i. 416. [2] England's Black Tribunal, p. 51.
[3] Wavel, ii. 130. Warton, 78.

to the see, and confirmed in the October follow-ing, about which time the cathedral chapter was re-stored;[1] and the established clergy, having regained possession of their churches, our cathedral naturally became an object of the first importance and atten-tion. The repairs, however, were chiefly effected during the prelacy of Bishop Morley, the successor of Duppa, in 1662, and the whole edifice was by degrees restored to a state of considerable beauty. Amongst the benefactions and charities of this pre-late to his see, it appears that he enriched it, and ornamented this city in particular with an Episcopal Palace, near the ruins of the once powerful Castle of Wolvesey, and endowed a College or Hospital for the support of Clergymen's Widows, on the north side of the cathedral burial ground.[2] About the same time that Winchester recovered its ecclesiastical importance, its civil and commercial interests began to experience a change for the better, by the revival of its navigation, which had been long in a state of decay, and was now restored under the sanction of an Act of Parliament.[3]

The next important event in the history of Win-chester was of the most awful description, viz. a severe visitation of the Plague, which broke out in the metropolis, in May, 1665, and extended to this city early in the following year, where it continued its ravages for nearly a twelvemonth.[4] On this

---

[1] Gale, 106. Milner, i. 423. [2] Wavel, i. 86. [3] Wavell, ii. 131,
[4] Wavel, ii. 132 Milner, i. 428. Warton, 34.

dreadful occasion all manner of trade or correspond-
ence with any other part of the kingdom was necessarily at an end; cart-loads of dead bodies were
daily carried out, and promiscuously deposited in
large pits dug for their reception on the neighbouring downs; nor was it without great difficulty that
the necessaries of life were procured for the wretched survivors. The markets were removed to a rising ground just without the west gate of the city,
where they were held once a week, and were regu-
lated by all the measures a prudent jealousy of life
could suggest, to prevent the spreading of the contagion. The method of bartering was thus: the
articles required for the markets were laid, by the
country people, upon a large stone, and fetched from
thence, upon their retiring to a certain distance, by
the townsmen, who, in return, deposited the money
agreed for, into a vessel of water provided for that
purpose.[1] By the deplorable effects of this malady,
Winchester was so greatly depopulated that, before
the disorder had materially abated, many of the
public streets were grown over with grass; nor
were its calamitous effects merely confined to external appearance: many of the wretched beings who
had escaped its fury, surviving but to lament the
dissolution of their nearest connections, and themselves reduced to a state of extreme poverty and in-
digence. And upon this melancholy occasion, the
humanity and benevolence of the more affluent citi-

---

[1] Wavel, ii. 132. Warton, 34, 35.

zens seem to have been exercised with peculiar effect.[1] Disregarding their private sorrows and personal dangers, they zealously applied themselves to the relief of their indigent fellow sufferers, and, by their timely assistance, preserved many from a cruel death who were actually languishing for want of nourishment and the common necessaries of life. They also formed themselves into a perpetual society for the relief and assistance of their fellow towns-men, under the designation of " The Natives' Society;" and the epoch of this truly benevolent transaction, as well as of the unfortunate occa-sion from whence it arose, has since been signalised by the erection of an Obelisk, with suitable inscrip-tions, upon the spot on which the markets were held, and the base of which is formed by the actual stone on which the traffic was conducted.[2]

During the latter part of the reign of Charles the Second, Winchester appeared in a fair way of re-trieving some considerable portion of its former greatness. Charles having made frequent visits to our city, at length determined upon erecting a Pa-lace upon the scite of the ancient castle.[3] Sir Chris-topher Wren was forthwith employed upon a design for the building, which appears to have been formed upon a scale of truly royal magnificence;[4] and, be-ing approved of, the King himself laid the founda-tion stone of the edifice on the 23d of March, 1683,

---

[1] Wavel, ii. 133.   [2] Ibid. 134.   Warton, 35.
[3] Wavel, i. 5.   Milner, i. 432.   [4] Milner, i. 433.

and the work commenced with the greatest ardour. The royal example was quickly followed by many of the nobility and gentry, and a number of handsome mansions were erected, and others designed, as well as various improvements in the general appearance of the city; and in the mean time Winchester began once more to assume a character of activity and importance, to which it had long been a stranger.[1]

Had the plan of Sir Christopher Wren, in all its parts, been carried into complete effect, Winchester would doubtless have become the most magnificent, if not the first, of the royal residences in the king- dom; but unhappily for it, in the very midst of these great designs and brilliant prospects, the sudden death of Charles, in 1685, burst like the explosion of a mine beneath it, and, with its well-founded hopes, its expectations of future greatness and pros- perity were scattered to the winds.

The short and turbulent reign of James the Second, was not of a description to allow him leisure for building palaces, and we accordingly find that the magnificent works of his royal predecessor were suspended immediately upon his accession to the throne;[2] nor was the universal depression of our citizens occasioned by the sudden change at all mi- tigated by the demand of their charters, accompa- nied with a writ of *quo warranto*, to enforce the production of them. The consequence of this pro- ceeding was, after a very spirited conduct on the

---

[1] Wavel, i. 6.　　　　[2] Wavel, ii. 137.　Milner, i. 434.

part of the Mayor and Corporation,[1] that the original charters were produced, and surrendered into the King's hands in 1686; but his arbitrary disposition having undergone some change, they were, with the charters of other cities, restored in 1688, with a confirmation of the privileges conveyed by them.

Among the very few occurrences of historical importance relative to Winchester during the present reign, that of the trial and execution of Mrs. Alicia Lisle, the widow of John Lisle, a regicide, and, to the disgrace of our city, a representative of it during the interregnum, deserves to be recorded.[2] This unfortunate woman, who seems to have outlived her husband merely to suffer the merited reward of his infamy, appears to have been, at the time of her execution, upwards of seventy years of age, and was tried for harbouring certain rebels after the battle of Sedgmore, in 1685. The jury, who repeatedly declared themselves dissatisfied with the evidence produced to establish her guilt, three times returned a verdict of acquittal; but were at last intimidated by the menaces and reproaches of Jefferies, who presided as judge, and ultimately pronounced her guilty of high treason. Sentence was immediately passed, and, notwithstanding all applications for pardon, she was executed in the market-place of our city, on the 2d of September,

---

[1] Wavel, ii. 140, 141.   [2] Warton, 35. Wavell, ii. 139. Hume, viii. 227. England's Black Tribunal, p. 24.

1685; and the stigma attached to the cruelty of the transaction was in no wise lessened by the answer of the King to the various applications for a pardon, " that he had promised Jefferies, before he set out with the commission, not to forgive her, and he should keep his word."[1]

At the time the navy of France was hovering upon the adjoining coast, in the subsequent reign of William the Third, Winchester was honoured with a visit from its Sovereign, who, at his departure, publicly thanked the Mayor and citizens for the attentions they had paid him,[2] as also for the loyalty and activity they had shewn in preparing to defend their city against the expected descent of the enemy.

About 1707 it was also visited by Queen Anne, accompanied by her royal consort Prince George of Denmark, the latter of whom seems to have been so delighted with the situation and noble appearance of the palace, that he procured it to be settled upon him, and an estimate was made of the expence of completing it according to the original design;[3] and the calculation being approved of, the completion was determined upon; but here again death interposed before any considerable progress had been made, and the unfinished building was left for years a disgrace to the city it had been originally intended to adorn.

Shortly after the visit of the Queen, in 1711, the present Guildhall was erected, and various other im-

---

[1] Hume, viii. 228.   [2] Wavel, ii. 143.   [3] Ibid.

provements made;[1] nor was the city alone attended to, as large sums were expended during the prelacy of Sir Jonathan Trelawney, in improving and decorating the cathedral.

In 1736 an Infirmary was established here, by a fund raised from voluntary subscriptions,[2] being the first institution of the kind out of the metropolis. This establishment seems chiefly to have owed its existence to the disinterested zeal and indefatigable exertions of Dr. Alured Clark, a prebendary of the cathedral and afterwards dean of Exeter, by whom its orders and constitutions were for the most part drawn up; and in 1752, the revenues of the institution having greatly increased by legacies and other benefactions, the mansion-house of Sir John Clobery, in Parchment-street, was purchased by the governors, and the present noble edifice erected upon its scite.[3]   This, under the designation of " The County Hospital," was opened for the reception of patients in 1759; and if we may judge from the rules by which it is governed, and the high professional character of the gentlemen who regularly attend it, it is impossible for the afflicted poor to be better attended to than in this hospital.

About the time that Winchester signalised itself by this splendid monument of humanity and benevolence, the unfinished but magnificent pile erected by Charles the Second for a royal palace, was, to

---

[1] Wavel, ii. 144.   Milner. i. 444.   [2] Wavel, ii. 146.   Milner, i. 445.
[3] Wavel, ii. 149.

the indescribable regret of our citizens, converted
into a depôt for the reception of prisoners of war,
of whom there were more than 5000 confined within
it at one period.[1]

Winchester upon the whole began at this time to
assume a military character, from the great number of that profession who were continually encamp-
ed upon the neighbouring downs or quartered within
the city, both as a precautionary measure with regard to any sudden attempt of the enemy upon the
adjacent coast, as for the more effectual security of
the unfortunate men who were, as we have before
mentioned, confined here. And these circumstances,
although at first they appear to have been greatly
disliked by our citizens, yet in the end have been
productive of considerable benefit to the city; as,
by the continual influx and departure of large bodies
of men, and the attendant increase of trade necessary to supply their occasions, a spirit of emulation
seems to have been diffused amongst the inhabitants
which has tended materially to their interests and
the improvement of the city.

In 1767 the navigation of the canal, which since
its re-establishment in 1676 had fallen into the
hands of a single proprietor, whereby a complete
monopoly of its advantages had existed for a considerable time, was, by the spirited interference of
some wealthy citizens, thrown open to the public;[2]

---

[1] Milner, i. 443. Wavel, ii. 151.   [2] Milner, i. 446. Wavel, ii. 152.

a measure which has been productive of incalculable benefit to the city and neighbouring country.

The spirit of improvement thus excited among the
citizens was considerably promoted in 1770, by an
Act of Parliament for paving and lighting the city;[1]
and in a short time after this event, a number
of respectable buildings were erected in different
parts of it, amongst which were the Theatre, the
County Bridewell, and other edifices of a public description; while the remaining city gates, which
from their contracted height and size had become
extremely inconvenient as entrances to the city, and
were mostly incumbered with a group of mean buildings, were, with a considerable part of the old wall
and other remains of our fortifications, taken down,
and the materials of them applied to the improvement and benefit of the city, which in their late condition they had become too ruinous to ornament,
and were happily unnecessary to defend. The different avenues to the city were thus materially improved, and the convenience of those resorting to,
or travelling through it, greatly increased, especially
at the east end, where the entrance for a considerable space was contracted by a number of old buildings which were now removed, and the scite of them
laid open to the High Street.

At the time our shores were inundated by the unfortunate clergy of France, who sought and obtained in this country a protection from the wild anar-

---

[1] Wavel, ii. 152.   Milner, i. 447.

chy and bloody proscriptions of their own, the King's House, as it is still frequently called, and which we have before mentioned as having formed a depôt for prisoners of war, was fitted up by Government for their reception, wherein at one time upwards of 1000 were comfortably sheltered and maintained; but the circumstances of the country rendering it necessary in 1796 to form a regular military depôt at Winchester, the unfortunate exiles were accordingly removed to various parts of the kingdom, and this noble edifice, the intended residence of Monarchs and hospitable asylum of distressed worth, was at last converted into a Barrack, to which purpose it has been ever since applied, and during the last war formed a regular station generally of about 2000 men.[1]

During the·present reign Winchester has been several times honoured with the visit *en passant* of its Sovereign, and at different times formed the residence of one or more branches of the Royal Family, who have generally on such occasions inhabited one of the prebendal houses in the Close. But the age of regal munificence to our ancient and honoured city, has, like the day-beam of its splendour, vanished probably for ever, as we do not find upon any occasion, during the last century, that it has received a single memorial of the beneficence or peculiar attention of its Sovereign.

In conclusion, although Winchester has fallen

---

[1] Milner, i. 450.

from its eminent rank as a royal and commercial city, although it has become a stranger to the consequence and activity for which it was once so renowned, it is nevertheless far from being without attraction or importance. The venerable memorials of its ancient greatness, with which it is still profusely enriched; the fine and open country with which it is surrounded; the various Schools and Charities of a public and private description established within it; and the number of highly respectable characters by which it is constantly inhabited, unite in rendering it an enviable example to other and more fortunate cities, and in giving it a well-grounded claim to the attention of the antiquary and the traveller; while, independent of these circumstances, an importance naturally attaches to it as the capital of the county, in which of course all business of a public nature is transacted, and wherein the Assizes and Sessions are invariably held. For amusement, it has its Theatre, its Assemblies, its Races; each of which may be ranked far above mediocrity, and in themselves possess no inconsiderable share of attraction; but on the other hand, it is to be regretted that much of the interest which might attach to our city is lost for want of a Public Library or some Literary Institution of a general character, which, if once established and judiciously managed, would probably have the effect of inducing a more social and general intercourse with the neighbouring gentry as well as strangers; and from

M

its nature, as a measure of undoubted public utility, it could not fail of being properly and effectually supported.

~~~~~~~~~~

Having thus completed a general Historic Sketch of Winchester, from the earliest recorded event connected with its existence to the present time, we shall conduct the reader through a series of Descriptive Walks, in the course of which we shall endeavour to point out every object within the limits of the city or its environs, at all distinguished by its importance or remarkable for its antiquity.
~~~~~~~~~~

1 West Gate.—2. The Guildhall.—3. The Cross.—4. St. Lawrence Church.—5. The Square.—6. The Matrons' College.—7. The Cathedral.—S. The Deanry.—9. King's Gate.—10. Symonds's College.—11. St. Thomas Church.

The First Walk.

AMONG the more prominent objects which may be supposed to engage the attention of a stranger on his arrival in Winchester, the ancient Gate of the city, which terminates the western extremity of the High Street, will necessarily, from its antiquity, become a subject of curiosity; and from its situation, as forming a principal entrance, will be a proper station from which to commence our First Walk.

This venerable structure consists of a massy square tower over a spacious gateway, crowned on the west side with machicoliations, and ornamented

with shields in quatrefoils, bearing the arms of the
city and kingdom; the grooves for the portcullis are
still remaining at the west side of the arch, as are
the massy hooks for supporting the gates. Near the
east end, on the south side, we observe the entrance
to the keep of the tower, which is now used as a
billiard-room; on the east side, the fabric is supported by three large buttresses, two of which terminate in plain niches with canopies. The substance of this gate appears to have been built by
the Normans at the time the walls were strengthened and repaired and the castle erected in 1072.[1]

Proceeding from hence along the south side of
the High-street, we pass Trafalgar-street, which
formerly, under the denomination of Gar-street,
extended nearly to the southern extremity of the
city, having in its limits the churches of St. Mary,
St. Andrew, St. Margaret, and St. Paul.[2]   The next
object on this side is Southgate-street, originally
Gould-street, at the end of which stood the South
Gate of the city.   The whole of this street, except
near the north end, is now chiefly occupied with the
blank walls of gardens and the inclosure of the barrack ground; although, like Gar-street, it originally
contained no less than four churches, viz. those of St.
Boniface, St. Nicholas, Allhallows, and St. Mary
Odes.[3]   Of these sacred edifices, or of the numerous habitations that surrounded them, not a ves-

---

[1] Historical Account, p. 19.
[2] Ancient Ichnography of Winchester.   [3] Ibid.

tige is now to be seen. Proceeding, therefore, along the High-street, we arrive at St. Thomas, or Calpe-street, on the east side of which, near its junction with the High-street, is the entrance to the Hall of the Guild of Merchants of Winchester, or, as more commonly expressed, " The Town Hall." Of this guild or society we have before spoken as being the most ancient in the kingdom.[1] The present hall was erected at the commencement of the last century, and is neatly and commodiously fitted up for holding the sessions and transacting the other public business of the city.

Besides the archives of the city, there are several articles curious for their antiquity kept in this hall, as the various measures of length and quantity, given by different Monarchs to the city, the ancient seals, &c. From a low square tower over the west end, the heavy tones of the curfeu announce regularly their now unheeded summons, as in mockery of the feudal ordinance from which the custom originated, established by the Conqueror nearly eight centuries back.[1] Descending from the hall, we observe in the High-street the noble columns which support the edifice, nearly buried amongst the projecting shop-widows, which most fatally for the appearance of the chief public building of the Corporation, have been suffered to rise between them. From the front of the structure a large clock, the gift of W. Powlett Powlett, Esq. in 1816, projects

---

[1] Historical Account, 11.　　　[2] Ibid. 19.

considerably into the street; and in a central niche below, is a statue of Queen Anne, in her regalia, presented to the Corporation about 1713 by one of the members for the city; upon a tablet beneath the figure we read the following inscription :

" ANNO PACIFICO ANNA REGINA."

Continuing our walk eastward, we arrive at the City Cross. This structure, from its stile of architecture, is supposed to have been erected about the beginning of the 15th century,[1] and does not appear to have suffered materially, except from the injuries of time. It is of a square form, standing upon an octagonal base of five steps, and consists of three distinct tiers of Gothic arch-work with ornamented niches and canopies, under each of which, in the middle division, it is not improbable there was originally a statue. The extreme height of this piece of antiquity, from the bottom of the lower step to the cross at the top, is rather more than 43 feet, and the greatest circumference of the whole is 49 feet. A statue of the natural size, which remains on the west side, appears to be that of a man in the Roman costume, bearing in his right hand a palm-branch, the emblem of martyrdom, and in his left a small square mass of stone, the design of which it is now impossible to trace. It is conjectured by an old historian[2] that this figure was intended to represent St. John, and that the corresponding niches

---

[1] Wavel, i. 227. Milner, ii. 194.   [2] Wavel, i. 227.

were occupied by the statues of the three other
Evangelists. This interpretation, has, however,
been disputed,[1] and perhaps correctly; but from the
total absence of any peculiar inditia, it is probable
that the real design will never be correctly ascertained; and in the mean time, that explanation
which at least carries with it an air of probability,
may, it is presumed, continue to be offered.

We now turn to the little passage on the south-
west side of the cross, and at its extremity on the
left perceive the only entrance to the parish church
of St. Lawrence, which, like the other parish
churches of this city, is of considerable antiquity,
being mentioned in the Register of Bishop Pontissara, in 1282,[2] at which time it had been apparently
erected a considerable number of years. Into this,
as being the mother church of the city, the Bishop
of Winchester makes a solemn entry on taking possession of his see.

This edifice consists of one large aisle, without
the least attempt at beauty or decoration. The altar
is very plain, and stands immediately under the east
window, which is large and of a date considerably
earlier than the rest of the present church, which
appears to have been entirely rebuilt in 1674. The
font bears some traces of antiquity; but the monuments are not particularly worth noticing, if we except the marble tablet which records the death of
John Wilkes, Esq. of Milland House, near Liphook,

---

[1] Milner, ii. 194.   [2] Bishop's Registers, No. 1, fo. 156.

who commenced in this city the printing, and with the most indefatigable perseverance edited and conducted, " The Encyclopedia Londinensis," and various other works of respectability, and is interred in this church.

Leaving St. Lawrence Church, we proceed southward along Great Minster-street into the Square, the scite of a Palace of William the Conqueror,[1] destroyed by Bishop de Blois, who used the materials in building his magnificent castle of Wolvesey in 1138.[2]   At the south-west corner of the Square are the Meat Shambles, and over them stands the original Theatre, now used as a store-loft.   Passing the west end of this, we enter the Burial-ground of the Cathedral, and looking down the avenue on the left, observe, against the houses, the low remains of the stone wall which formed the boundary of the cathedral inclosure towards the north.   A short distance beyond this, on the same side, is the Matrons' College, erected by Bishop Morley, in 1672, and endowed for the support of ten clergymen's widows.   The scite of this building, and the adjoining ground to the east, was formerly that of the church and monastery of St. Grimbald, founded by Alfred the Great,[3] in 898, as a royal chantry or burial-place, and a retreat for the abbot, after whom it was named. This foundation was richly endowed by Alfred, and also found benefactors in most of the succeeding Princes; of

---

[1] Milner, i. 188.   [2] Historical Account, 28.   [3] Ibid. 13.

one of whom, viz. Cnute, it is recorded that he bestowed upon it a large cross for the high altar, of silver gilt, enriched with precious stones, which had not its fellow in the kingdom, and was considered equal in value to a whole year's revenue of it. As there are not any traces left of this edifice, which was abandoned in 1110 by its inmates for a new and more commodious establishment in Hyde Meadows, we shall not here enlarge upon its history, but proceed up the avenue towards the Cathedral.

Of the original foundation of an edifice devoted to the rites of Christianity by Lucius, King of Britain, in 169, we have before spoken.[1] The church erected by him appears to have stood about 120 years,

---

[1] Historical Account, 9.

when it was levelled with the ground, and the clergy belonging to it put to death, in the persecution under Dioclesian, towards the end of the third century. It was however soon after restored, and dedicated to St. Amphibalus the Martyr, by Bishop Constans, early in the fourth century. From this period until the city fell into the hands of the Saxons under the ferocious Cerdic, in 516, our church appears to have flourished with little interruption; but upon that occasion, the barbarians having obtained possession of the cathedral, all its clergy were swept away in one promiscuous slaughter, and the cathedral itself devoted to the worship of the Saxon deities.[1] Upon the conversion of Kinegils, in 635, the edifice, which had been so profaned by the gloomy and unhallowed rites of Thor, was destroyed, and the foundations of a new cathedral began. The progress of the new building, after a short interruption by the death of Kinegils, and the neglect of his son Kenewalch, was at length brought to a completion; and the cathedral thus raised remained unimpaired, until the ravages of the Danes in 871, when its clergy were again destroyed, and the fabric itself considerably injured, by their violence.[2]

The principal part of the present structure appears to have been erected about the middle of the tenth century by St. Ethelwold, Bishop of Winchester, who entirely rebuilt his cathedral from the ground, which he lived to finish, and dedicate to St.

---

[1] Historical Account, 11, 12.   [2] Ibid. 17.

Swithun, A. D. 980; and this cathedral, after suffering considerable injury from the violence of the Danes, was, about 1079, repaired by Bishop Walkelyn, who erected the present tower, with a part of the nave and transepts.[1] He also built, on the south-west side of the cathedral, new cloisters for the monks, with other suitable offices for their accommodation; and the church thus repaired was solemnly dedicated to St. Swithun and St. Peter and St. Paul, A. D. 1093.

About a century after this event, the eastern end of the church, from the great east window, was rebuilt by Godfrey de Lucy, Bishop of Winchester.[2]

The whole western extremity of the church was considerably improved in the course of the fourteenth century by its successive Bishops, Edyngton and Wykeham; the latter of whom may be almost said to have rebuilt that part of his cathedral, having altered it from its original rudeness to the finished state in which it now appears.[3] But in order to appreciate the full value of the improvements effected by the illustrious Wykeham, it will be necessary to survey for a moment the plain naked walls, huge unadorned pillars, and uncovered timbers, of the interior of the transepts, the stile of which, previous to this change, was that of the whole church; and comparing these with the high-finished and elegant Gothic architecture of the nave and side aisles, we shall readily be sensible of the advantage produced by the alteration.

---

[1] Historical Account, 29.   [2] Ibid. 44.   [3] Ibid. 63.

The west end of the structure was now complete;
but the intermediate space of the eastern part, from
the Norman tower of Walkelyn to the works of
De Lucy, still retained its original Saxon features,
and corresponded but ill with the more finished
works of Wykeham, which it joined on the west
side.   But this incongruity was removed by Bishop
Fox,[1] who, in the early part of the sixteenth century, rebuilt this part of the church in a superior
stile of Gothic elegance, and whose statue, under a
superb canopy, terminates the eastern boundary of
his improvements.

After these general observations, we shall approach the Great Entrance of the Cathedral, at the
west end, the appearance of which, with its open
galleries and majestic window, supported by massive side-towers and pinnacles, and terminating
in a superb canopy over a statue of Wykeham,
is admirably adapted to the air of solemn grandeur
which pervades the interior of the edifice; and it
would perhaps be a difficult task to express the sen-
sations that are excited on entering it for the first
time—the prospect, which at once opens before us
from the grand western door, through the whole
extent of the lofty aisle, terminated by the magnificent window at the back of the choir, is calculated
to affect even the most indifferent spectator with
mingled emotions of admiration and religious awe.

Having indulged for a few moments the delight-

---

[1] Historical Account, 69.

ful feelings which a view like this is so peculiarly adapted to call forth and expand, we shall commence our walk round the interior of the cathedral, from the west end of the south aisle.

Opposite the second arch from the entrance, we observe, against the south wall, the monument erected by the present Bishop of Winchester to the memory of his deceased Lady, executed by Flaxman in a stile of elegant simplicity. The design consists of two figures, one of which, representing a young female, in the attitude of Grief, is bending over a funereal urn. On the opposite side, a matron-like figure, bearing the attributes of Faith, points to Heaven as the source of comfort and hope to the mourner. Near the summit of a pyramid, which forms the back-ground, is inscribed, in letters of gold,

THE JUST SHALL LIVE BY FAITH.

And, upon a tablet forming the base of the whole design, is the following epitaph:

To the memory of
HENRIETTA MARIA NORTH,
Second daughter of John Bannister, Esq. and Elizabeth his wife,
Married to
The Honble and R^{t} Revd Brownlow North, Bishop of Winchester,
Who in the 46th year of her age, and on the 16th day of Novr. 1796,
Virtuous, amiable, and accomplished,
Dignified by every moral,
Graced by every social excellence,
Firm in reliance upon her God,
Stedfast in the faith of her Redeemer, Christ,
Terminated her exemplary and valuable life.
This testimony of his perfect admiration, undiminished gratitude,

And never-ceasing regret,
Is placed by her affectionate and ever-mindful
Widower.

Advancing a few paces, we reach the monument of Thomas Cheyney, Dean of Winchester. This memorial is composed of the finest jaspar and statuary marbles, the beauty of which is only equalled by the execution of the design sculptured upon them. On an oval tablet, in front of a quadrangular urn, which forms the centre of the monument, a figure, denoting Religion, is beheld opening a sarcophagus, from which the deceased appears rising ; while above the whole, an angel is represented, sounding the last trumpet. On the one side of the urn, Wisdom is seated; on the other, Hope; and above them, a Phœnix, the emblem of Immortality, rises from the midst of her characteristic flames. Upon a tablet, surmounting the family arms of the Dean, is the following inscription :

HIC JUXTA SEPULTUS EST

THOMAS CHEYNEY, S. T. P.

Hujusce Ecclesiæ Decanus,

Et Collegii Wintoniensis Socius.

Qui,
Cum in omni negotiorum genere,
Sagaci admodum judicio & rerum usu,
Prudens, habilis, & fidelis, semper haberetur;
Nemo enim, ingenia moresq; hominum
Aut interiùs vidit, aut penitiùs intellixit ;
Cum principibus viris diù placuisset,
Et ad altiora feliciter aspirare potuerit ;
Hic, tamen in otio & umbratili vitâ

Sed ingenuo, sed literato homine verè dignâ,

Hic, amicorum commercio frui,

Et sibi, suisq; placere maluit,

Donec luctuosâ & diuturnâ valetudine fractus,

Et ingravescente demum ætate,

Deo bonorum remuneratori,

Et supremo omnium judici,

Animam immortalem piè reddidit.

Obiit 27° die Januarii,

Anno { Domini, 1760,
        Ætatis,   66.

We now observe, on our left hand, the chantry and tomb of William de Wykeham, which occupies the fifth arch from the west end of the church. The chantry is richly ornamented with Gothic tracery, and is divided in its length into three arches, the lower parts of, which are again divided into seven compartments, and secured with ornamented bars of iron. At the four octangular ends of the chantry are rich canopies and pedestals, formerly occupied by statues, the staples by which they were fastened being yet remaining. Within the chantry, which also presents a series of highly-finished canopies, with pedestals, &c. the marble figure of Wykeham, richly dressed in complete episcopal costume, lies upon a superb altar-tomb of veined marble, surrounded with escutcheons bearing his arms and devices. The head, resting upon a cushion, is supported on each side by an angel, and at the feet sit three friars, as offering up their prayers for the repose of his soul. The epitaph, which is engraved on brass, surrounds the upper part of the tomb, and is as follows:

Wilhelmus dictus Wykeham jacet hic nece victus,
Istius ecclesiæ præsul, reparabit eamq3
Largus erat dapifer, probat hoc cum divite pauper,
Consilijs pariter regni fuerat bene dexter.
Hunc docet esse pium fundatio Collegiorum
Oxoniæ primum stat, Wintoniæq3 secundum
Jugiter oretis tumulum quicunq3 videtis
Pro tantis meritis ut sit sibi vita perennis.

Against the south-east side of the chantry, is a monumental tablet, with an inscription, to the memory of Dr. William Harris, who died in 1700, and bequeathed a considerable sum of money for the improvement and decoration of the choir, the particulars of which we shall shortly have occasion to notice.

The next object to which our attention is directed, is the noble monument of Bishop Willis, who died in 1734, and is interred near this part of the church. The principal design of this memorial is a sarcophagus, upon which a figure, of the natural size, representing the Bishop, reclines, supporting himself by the left arm upon a pile of books, and having the right extended towards Heaven. The side-columns supporting the pediment, under which the figure is placed, are of a beautiful veined marble, and the architecture of the whole presents a finished specimen of the Composite order.

The inscription upon this monument is as follows:

In Memoriam

Reverendi admodum in Christo Patris

RICHARDI WILLIS,

Episcopi Wintoniensis ;

Viri

Eâ morum simplicitate,

Eâ animi integritate, et verborum fide,

Ut qui illum optimè noverint,

Ij maxime æstimaverint,

Propensissime dilexerint,

Patriam, principem, et libertatem publicam

Unicè amavit ;

Religionem interea verè Christiq;

Sanctissime coluit

Acerrime vindicavit.

Nullâ temporum varietate

Debilitari, aut frangi potuit.

In republicâ, in ecclesiâ,

Fidelis, constans, et sui similis

Egregiis hisce virtutibus instructus,

In mediis quos abunde meruit honoribus,

Felicissime consenuit,

Donec annorum plenus.

Obiit, 10 die Augusti, anno { Domini, 1734, ÆEtatis, 71.

JOHANNES WILLIS, armiger,

Filius ejus et hæres,

Piè memor

Posuit.

Opposite the next arch, is a tablet erected to the memory of Dean Naylor, who died in 1739, the inscription upon which is as follows:

M. S.

CAROLI NAYLOR, LL. D.

Parochiâ de Oddington,

Apud Dobunos Rectoris,

Necnon Cancellarii Sarisburiensis,

Et Ecclesiæ hujus Decani.

Quâ, illi

Et grandes virtutes fuerint,

Tostentur posteris et quæ obijt muniæ

Et propensus præsuli egregii favor.
Illius nempe,
Cujus lateri quam proximè,
Ex voto defunctus, apponitur,
Ut cui per varios honorum gradus
Adhæserat, vivo comes individuus
Etiam mortuus adjungeretur.
Animam,
Wakefieldiæ, in agro Ebor; acceptam,
Wintoniæ, paralysi correptus, reddidit.

Junii 23° anno { Salutis, 1739,
{ Ætatis,   47.

ELIZ^{A.} NAYLOR et FANIA EATON,
Sorores et ex asse hæredes L. M. P.

Beneath this inscription is an oval of white marble, upon which are sculptured, in bas relief, the emblems of Death, Judgment, Time, and Eternity; and the whole is pointed by the awful and emphatic word:

MEMENTO!

Under the ninth window is the elegant mural monument of Thomas Knollys, Earl of Banbury, who died in 1793, with an epitaph commemorating his domestic and public virtues; and in an oval beneath, is a memorial of his Countess, who died in 1798.

In the adjoining arch stands the chantry and tomb of William de Edynton, Bishop of Winchester,[1] somewhat similar in design to that of Wykeham, but executed in a far less ornamental stile of architecture. The chantry consists of a series of

---

[1] Historical Account, 45.

arches surmounted with a cornice, without canopies or vaulting, leaving the area of the tomb entirely open. The figure of the Bishop, which is of alabaster, and has been somewhat mutilated, lies, as in the preceding chantry, upon a tomb in the centre, and the following epitaph is inscribed, in brass letters, round the edge of the slab which supports it:

Edyndon natus: Wills hic est tumulatus:
Presul prægratus: in Wintonia Cathedratus:
Qui pertransitis: ejus memorare velitis:
Providus et mitis: ausit cum mille peritis:
Pervigil Anglorz fuit adjutor populorum:
Dulcis egenor: pater et protectorz eorz
M. C. tribz junctum: post L. X. A, sit I punctum:
Octavo functum: notat hunc Octobris juuctuz

On the pavement, adjoining the south side of this chantry, a flat stone covers the grave of Bishop Thomas, the tutor of his present Majesty, who died in 1781. The epitaph inscribed upon this stone is as follows:

H. S. E.
JOHANNES THOMAS, S.T.P.
Natus est, XVII° die Augusti, anno
M.DC.XCVI.
Collegii omnium animarum, in Oxon, Socius, 1720.
Ecclesiæ S^{ti.} Benedicti juxta ædem S^{ti.} Pauli Rector, 1731.
Dein, Ecclesiæ Paulinæ Canonicus Residentiarius, 1742.
Episcopus Petriburgensis, 1747.
Augustissimi Principis, Georgii III^{ti.} Præceptor, 1753.
Episcobus Sarisburiensis, 1757.
Wintoniensis denique, 1761.
Obijt 1mo. die Maij,
M.DCC.LXXXI.
Uxorem habuit, hìc etiam sepultam,
Susannam, Thomæ Mulso de Twywell,

In agro Northamptoniæ armigeri, filiam,
Quæ, annos nata LXXV. decessit.
XIX die Novembris,
M.DCC.LXX.VIII.

Against the south wall, in front of Edynton's chantry, is the monument of the late Dr. Balguy, Archdeacon of Winchester. This memorial consists of an urn of Parian marble, in front of a large pyramid, which is charged with arms, and supported by a tablet bearing the following inscription :

Near this place lies interred
The Revd. THOMAS BALGUY, D. D.
Archdeacon of Winchester, Prebendary of this Church,
And Vicar of Alton.
Born 27th Septr. 1716, died 19th Jany. 1795.
A sincere and exemplary Christian,
A sound and accurate scholar,
A strenuous and able defender of the Christian religion,
And of the Church of England.
His preferments had been accepted with gratitude,
Not sought by him.
In 1781 George III. named to the Bishopric of
Gloucester,
Which, on account of his infirmities, he desired
Leave to decline.

Passing the choir steps, we presently enter the south transept; the stile of which, as we have before mentioned, was that of the whole body of the church previous to its alteration by Wykeham.[1] The west aisle of this transept, which is portioned off from the rest, appears to have been originally the sacristy, and now forms the chapter-room and treasury

---

[1] Ante, 91.

of the cathedral. Towards the end on the west side is the modern entrance to the chapter room, &c. ornamented with a rich wainscoting of oak, carved in various devices to correspond with the ancient presses which are ranged along the south wall of the transept. These presses are carved in scrolls and terminate in canopies, bearing on the cornice the initial and device of Prior Silkstede, by whom they were probably erected for the purpose of containing the rich vestments worn on all solemn occasions by the monks of the cathedral. Near the centre of the south side, a door way conducts us to a passage originally communicating with the ancient offices of the monastery; on our left hand was the calefactory; and on the right, a staircase lead to the dormitories and offices of the monks, now used as the library of the cathedral and the apartment appropriated as a music room for the choristers.

The east aisle of the transept is divided into two chapels, the southernmost of which is called Silkstede'schapel, from the letters of his christian name (𝕿 𝖍 𝕺 𝔪 𝖆 𝖘𝖘) being carved with various devices on the cornice of the screen which encloses it. Near the window at the south-east end of the chapel is a monument erected to the memory of Dr. John Nicholas, a Prebendary of the cathedral, consisting of a large urn standing under a Doric arch, bearing the family arms and crest, and ornamented with sepulchral lamps; a scroll beneath is supported at the ends by winged sculls, and bears upon it the following inscription :—

H. S. E.
JOHANNES NICHOLAS S. T. P.
Hujus Ecclesiæ Præbendarius, Εὐεργέτης ;
Utrumq; Collegii Wiccamici scholaris, et socius, et custos ;
In utroq; reliquit perennia munificentiæ suæ monumenta :
Collegia disciplinâ excoluit, ædificiis auxit, et exornavit,
Scholam suis penè sumptibus extruxit, Wiccamo suo sanè dignissimam,
Inter hæc omnia, pauperibus, largus bonorum
Erogator, et præsentissimum levamen.
Hæc opera verè magna magnum loquuntur auctorem,
Et seræ posteritate enarrabunt.
Diem suum obiit Feb. 27°.
Anno { Dom. } 1711.
{ Ætat. } 74.

On the ground, immediately in front of the above, a flat stone with an inscription to the memory of his Lady, seems to convey a modest censure upon this pompous display of virtue and goodness, by the following lines after the record of her name :

Adeò a laudibus abhorruit posthumis,
Ut ipsius morituræ votis dandum est,
Quod virtutes alias atq; alias
Religio sit silere.

Opposite the entrance of the chapel, a flat stone bears the following memorial of the venerable Isaac Walton, author of a celebrated and ingenious Treatise upon Angling :

Here resteth the body of
Mr. ISAAC WALTON,
Who died the 15th of December,
1683.
Alas ! hee's gone before,
Gone, to returne noe more.
Our panting breasts aspire
After their aged sire,

Whose well-spent life did last
Full ninety yeares and past.
But now he hath begun
That which will ne'er be done.
Crown'd with eternall blisse,
We wish our souls with his.

Votis modestis, sic flêrunt liberi.

The adjoining chapel, secured by a beautifully-ornamented screen, surmounted with funereal urns, is chiefly filled with inscriptions to the memory of the Eyre, Dingley, and other families.

On the pavement fronting these chapels, in the transept, is a large flat marble, bearing an epitaph professedly to the memory of Madam Mary Davies, daughter of Sir Jonathan Trelawny, Bart. but chiefly occupied with an account of the valour and services of her husband, Colonel Davies, who died of wounds received at the siege of Namur.

Within a recess of the transept, under the south arch of the tower, is the mausoleum of Sir Isaac Townsend, Knight of the Garter, who died in 1731. This noble memorial rises to a considerable height, and is surmounted by an elegant funereal urn, upon a pedestal tomb of white marble, enriched with foliage, and naval and military trophies, and bears on the south side the following inscription :

M. S.
ISAACI TOWNSEND, Equitis Aurati,
Qui munijs nauticis per sexaginta annos fundus est
Mari,
Per triginta quinque annos in classe regià versatus fuit;
In quâ plurimis principalibus praefuit navibus,
Navarchus dignissimus.

Terrâ,

Unus et primarijs rei-navalis procurandæ præfectis

Per viginti et quinque annos extitit,

Rei-navalis verè providus;

Utpote ubique, et mari, et terrâ,

Principi et patriæ verè fidus;

In omni vitæ studio, vir probus et integer.

Obijt vicesimo sexto die Maij, anno   { Salutis,   1731   / Ætatis,   75

Gravissimi doloris hoc posuit monumentum

Moerens vidua.

On the north side is an inscription to the memory of his Lady.

Returning from the transept to the choir steps, we observe before us, on the north side, the monument erected to the memory of Bishop Hoadly; the medallion of whom, over a group of sculpture, characteristic of his episcopal dignity and high literary talents, is considered as inimitable. Upon the pedestal supporting the design, is the following inscription—a splendid catalogue of honours and advancements:

Hic juxta sepultum est

Quiquid mortale fuit

BENJAMINI HOADLY, S. T. P.

Erat ille filius

Samuelis Hoadly,

Viri optimi et doctissimi, Eccles; Angl; Presbyteri;

Scholæ privatæ per multos annos,

Posteà scholæ publicæ Norvicensis, informatoris; et

Marthæ Pickering,

Viri Reverendi Benjamini Pickering filiæ,

Natus Westerhamiæ, in argo Cantiano.

Die XIV°· Nov. A.D. MDCLXXVI.

In aulam Sta· Cath. Cantabr. cooptatus

A. D. 1692, et ejusdem aulæ posteà socius.

In ecclesiâ S^{tæ.} Mildr. de Poultrey, Londini,
Per decem annos ab. A. D. 1701.
Concionator pomeridianus
Rector ecclesiæ S^{ti.} Petri Pauperis, Londini,
Per annos sexdecim ab. A. D. 1704.
Rector etiam ecclesiæ de Streatham, in Com. Surriæ
Per annos tredecim ab. A. D. 1710.

Episcopus Bangorensis consecratus,
Martij die 18° A. D. 1715.
Episcopus Herefordensis confirmatus,
Nov. die 3° A. D. 1721.
Episcopus Sarisburiensis confirmatus,
Oct. die 29° A. D. 1723.
Episcopus Wintoniensis confirmatus,
Sept. die 26. A. D. 1734.

Uxores duxit
1. Saram Curtis ex quâ duos filios suscepit,
Benjaminum in Med. Doctorem, et
Johannem Dioc. Winton. Cancellarium.
2. Mariam Newey, viri Reverendi
Johannis Newey, S. T. P. et Decani Cicestrensis Filiam ;
Feminas optimis animi dotibus ornatas, et
Amore summo illi conjunctissimas.
Obijt Apr. die XVII. A. D. MDCCLXI.
Ætat 85.

Patri amantissimo,
Veræ religionis ac libertatis publicæ vindici,
De se, de patriâ, de genere humano
Optime merito,
Hoc marmor posuit
J. Hoadly, F. superstes.

Against the corresponding pillar, on the south
side of the nave, is the monument erected to the
memory of Dr. Joseph Warton, Master of Winchester College, who is represented as seated in a
chair, with a book in his hand, examining a group

of boys who are standing before him. In the back ground, are busts on pedestals, inscribed with Greek characters, Homer and Aristotle. The whole is surmounted with the lyric harp; and upon the slab which forms the base of the monument, we read the following inscription:

H. S. E.

JOSEPHUS WARTON, S. T. P.

Hujus Ecclesiæ

Prebendarius,

Scholæ Wintoniensis

Per annos fere triginta

Informator,

Poeta fervidus facilis expolitus,

Criticus eruditus perspicax elegans.

Obijt XXIII Feb. MDCCC.

Ætat LXXVIII.

Hoc qualecunque

Pietatis monumentum

Præceptori optimo,

Desideratissimo

Wiccamici sui

P. C.

We now turn to a screen of the Composite order, erected at the west end of the choir, from a design of Inigo Jones, in the reign of Charles the First,[1] upon the demolition of the ancient rood loft which stood nearly upon the same spot. On each side the entrance to the choir, in recesses enriched with entablatures and pediments, are placed large bronze statues of James and Charles the First, presented to the cathedral by the latter unfortunate Monarch.

---

[1] Historical Account, 83.

From this situation we have a fine view of the grand West Window of the cathedral, which, in its early state of perfection, when glowing with the varied radiance of a thousand beautiful colours, and illumined with the full splendour of a setting sun, must have been a sight sufficient to inspire even the most callous with sensibility, the most indifferent with enthusiasm.

We now enter the choir, the stalls of which are adorned with a profusion of Gothic tracery and spire-work, carved in a variety of designs, and terminated on the south side by an episcopal throne of the Corinthian order, the gift of Bishop Trelawny, in 1706. On the opposite side, nearly fronting the throne, is the pulpit erected by Prior Silkstede, as appears from his name carved amongst the cane-work with which it is ornamented. Under the north arch of the tower we observe a rich and valuable organ, erected in 1796. The ancient situation of the organ appears to have been over the screen at the entrance to the choir, where, by its height, the perspective from the west end was entirely obstructed.[1] It was therefore removed to the place it now occupies, during the reign of Charles the First, and at the same time the ceiling of the choir was ornamented in the manner it now appears, being curiously studded with shields, bearing the arms and devices of the King and Queen, &c. the Prince of Wales, the Archbishop of Canterbury, and the Bishop and Dean of our see and cathedral.

[1] Historical Account, 83, 84.

In the centre of the whole is an emblem of the Trinity, with the following inscription surrounding it :—

SINT DOMUS HUJUS PII REGES NUTRITII, REGINÆ NUTRICES PIÆ.[1]

And near the above, on the west side, is a medallion of the King and Queen, with their faces in profile, bordered with an inscription, which is however too minute to be read from the floor of the choir.

Advancing towards the altar, we pass a plain tomb of grey marble, raised about two feet from the pavement, beneath which formerly reposed the remains of William the Second, King of England.[2] At what period his bones were torn from their sepulchre we know not ; but it appears beyond a doubt that they were disinterred, as, upon opening the tomb for plunder during the rebellion, nothing of its original charge remained except a little dust and some pieces of cloth embroidered with gold, together with a valuable ring and a small silver chalice.

The ascent and area of the altar is richly paved with coloured marble, by the liberality of Dr. William Harris, whose monumental tablet we have before mentioned. The altar is adorned with an exquisite painting by West, representing our Saviour raising Lazarus, which is classed among the masterpieces of modern art, and is placed under a canopy

---

[1] The italics, being picked out and properly arranged, give the letters M,DC,VVVVV,IIIIIIIII. equal to 1634, the year in which this and the surrounding decorations were effected.   [2] Historical Account, 30.

of wood-work, richly carved and ornamented with a profusion of foliage suspended in large festoons from the sides and front. Behind this, rises the superb screen of Bishop Fox,[1] charged with some of the most elaborate specimens of Gothic sculpture that this nation can exhibit. Until very lately, the beautiful canopied nitches with which it is decorated were occupied by a number of Vases,[2] the gift of the Rev. Dr. Harris; but these, being deemed incongruous, have been removed from the pedestals, which, in their present vacant condition, are infinitely more consistent with the original imagery of the design, than when they were occupied with a number of elegant but unmeaning Vases.

Receding a few paces from the steps of the altar, we catch, immediately above the unparalleled lace-work of the screen, the rich and varied shades of the great East Window, presenting a series of figures of saints and bishops, celebrated in the annals of the church.

We now turn our attention to the partition-walls, erected on each side of the altar and part of the choir, under the cornices of which we observe the initials and motto of Bishop Fox, by whom they were erected, as also the arms, &c. of Edward the Confessor and Cardinal Beaufort. On the top of each wall are ranged three mortuary chests, or coffins, inclosing the remains of various Princes and

---

[1] Historical Account, 69. [2] Ibid. 99.

other eminent persons, benefactors of the cathedral, and although now greatly worn and defaced, bear evident traces of their original magnificence.

The first chest from the altar, on the south side, incloses the relics of King Edred, youngest son of Edward the Elder, who was buried in the cathedral, to which he had been a considerable benefactor. The title and epitaph, which is alike on both sides of this chest, runs thus:

> Edredus Rex, obit A. D. 955.
> Hoc pius in tumulo, Rex Edredi requiescit,
> Qui has Britonum terras rexerit egregie.

The next chest on this side preserves the remains of King Edmund, eldest son of Alfred, who was crowned during the life-time of his father, but, dying before him, was interred in this cathedral. The inscription on each side is as follows:

> Edmundus Rex, obit A. D. M.
> Que theca hec retinet Edmudu suscipe Christe
> Qui vivente patre regia sceptra tulit.

The third chest from the altar, on the south side, with its parallel on the north, contains the mingled relics of different persons; and amongst them, it is conjectured, those of Cnute and his Queen Emma, of William Rufus, and of the Bishops Wina, Al-wyn, and Stigand. It appears these various remains had, by some means, become intermingled at a very early period; so that, on depositing them in the chests, it was found impossible to distinguish to whom they severally belonged. This circumstance explains somewhat of their present confused state;

but during the rebellion, these repositories having been violated by the fanatic soldiery, who used the bones as missiles to demolish the painted windows of the church,[1] they were in consequence scattered about, and many of them lost. Such of them as were recovered at the Restoration, were laid in this and the opposite chest, on each of which were the following inscriptions, now nearly illegible—on the one side:

In hac et altera a regione cista reliquæ
sunt Cnuti et Rufi Regum, Emmæ Reginæ,
Winæ et Alwini Episcorum.

On the other side:

Hac in cista A.D. 1661, promiscue recondita sunt ossa Principum et Prælatorum sacrilega barbarie dispersa, A. D. 1642.

The second or middle chest, on the north side, contains the relics of two Monarchs, viz. Kenewalch (here called Kenulph), the son of Kinegils, who founded the cathedral at the period of the Saxon conversion,[2] and those of Egbert, the great founder of the English Monarchy.

On the one side this chest is inscribed,

Kenulphus Rex, obit A. D. M. 784.

On the other,

Egbertus Rex, obit A. D. M. 857.

The epitaph, which is alike on both sides, is as follows:

Hic Rex Egbertus pausat cum
Rege Kenulpho nobis egregia munera uterq; tulit.

---

[1] Historical Account, 86.   [2] Ibid. 13.

The sixth and last chest, which is placed near the screen, on the north side, also incloses the remains of two Monarchs, viz. those of Kinegils, the first Christian King of the West Saxons, and of Ethelwolph (here called Adulphus), a great benefactor of the cathedral, and the father of Alfred. It is inscribed thus, on the one side:

Rex Kyngils, obit A. D. M. 641.

On the other,

Adulphus Rex, obit A. D. M. 859.

The epitaph is the same on both sides:

Kyngilsi in cista hac simul ossa jacent et Adulphi
ipsius fundator, hic benefactor erat.

To account for the present elevated situation of these illustrious remains, it will be necessary to advert to the circumstance recorded of Bishop de Blois,[1] the brother of King Stephen, who, in the twelfth century, collected the relics of different Princes and Prelates that had been buried in the cathedral, and deposited them in leaden coffins or chests, which he placed round the sanctuary of the church. At the time the choir was taken down and rebuilt by Bishop Fox, about the beginning of the sixteenth century,[2] there was a necessity for removing these coffins from their situation; and being found too numerous, or not sufficiently elegant for the conspicuous situation they were intended to occupy in the new works, the present ornamented chests were made, and placed over the arches of the

---

[1] Historical Account, 40.   [2] Ibid. 69.

partition wall. In four of these were deposited separately the venerable remains above described; and the remaining two were filled promiscuously with the bones of other personages, that had probably been mingled together ever since their first translation, nearly four centuries before the period of which we are speaking.

Under the middle chest, on the north side, is a table monument, half let into the partition wall, inclosing the remains of John de Pointes (or Pontissara), Bishop of Winchester, who died in 1304. The inscription on this monument is as follows:

Defuncti corpus tumulus tenet iste Johannis
Pointes, Wintoniæ Præsuli eximii, obit 1304.

On the same side, nearer the pulpit, and indeed hidden from casual observation by the seats which are placed before it, is a similar tomb, inclosing the ashes of Bishop Toclyve, who died in 1189, with the following inscription:

Præsuli egregii pausat hic membra
Ricardi Toclyve, cui summi gaudia
Sunto poli.   Obijt A. D. 1189.

We now enter the south-east aisle of the cathedral, by the door near the Bishop's throne, and advancing a few paces towards the east, the following inscription, denoting the receptacle of the heart of Bishop Nicholas de Ely, is engraved upon the partition wall of the choir:

Intus est cor Nicolai Olim Winton Episcopi,
Cujus corpus est apud Waverlie.

Adjoining the above, within a small low arch in

the wall, is the marble coffin of Richard, Duke of Beorne (or Bearne,) the second son of William the Conqueror, who met with an untimely fate while hunting in the New Forest.[1] Upon the lid of the coffin is the following original inscription, in characters of the eleventh century :

Hic jacet Ricardus Willi Septoris Regis fili et Beorn Dux.

Along the cornice which surmounts the arch, we read the following inscription, in characters of a much later period:

INTUS EST CORPUS RICARDI WILHELMI CONQUESTORIS
FILI ET BEORNE DUCIS.

Passing the low iron railing, which has lately been erected across the aisle at this spot, we reach the superb chantry of Bishop Fox, at the north-east end of the choir, the various beauties of which are almost too minute for description. In a richly-ornamented recess, under the middle arch of this splendid mausoleum, the figure of the Prelate is represented as an emaciated corpse, lying upon a winding sheet; the head supported by a mitre, and the feet resting against a scull. Above this is a small oratory or chapel, the vaulting of which is decorated with a variety of devices richly emblazoned, and mingled with the royal arms of Tudor and those of the founder, with his favourite device, the pelican. Over the scite of the altar, the different emblems of the sacrament and of the passion are supported by angels. Above these there appears originally to have been

---

[1] Historical Account, 22.

three large statues and nine small ones, the whole of which have been taken away; the pedestals and superb canopies under which they were placed, remain, however, in a high state of preservation. Upon a label, forming the base of the escutcheons, over the altar, there has been an inscription, but it having unfortunately been only painted upon the stone, has now become too much obliterated to be rendered with certainty.

We pass from this chapel to another parallel with it, much larger, but perfectly unadorned; this however appears at one time to have been the richest part of the whole fabric; as, upon this spot, a magnificent shrine of St. Swithun, made of silver and garnished with precious stones of inestimable value, was uniformly deposited.[1] The doors, at the extremities of the west side, are those by which it communicated with the high altar, immediately at the back of which it is situated.

On the north side of this chapel we enter the chantry of Bishop Gardiner, corresponding in situation and dimensions with that of Fox, but far different from it in every other respect. The architecture, which is a singular mixture of the Gothic and Ionic, is executed with considerable beauty, but has been much defaced. On the pavement, till lately, was the tomb-stone of King Edmund, the son of Alfred, whose remains are now contained in one of the mortuary chests already de-

---

[1] Milner, ii. 58.

scribed. The following inscription, in Saxon characters, was upon the stone:

+ HIC JACET EDMUNDUS REX ET ELDREDI REGIS FILIUS.

The rest of the pavement in this chapel, together with the iron bars which secured the open-work of the arches, have been destroyed, probably out of hatred to the memory of a Prelate whose bones torn from their sepulchre,[1] and whose monument, defaced and in a state of premature dilapidation and decay, seems to furnish a striking proof of retributive justice.

Returning into the south aisle, through the centre chapel and Fox's chantry, we observe, near the east end, the stone coffin of William de Basynge, a Prior of the cathedral, who died in 1295. This coffin has, with its parallel, been lately removed to its present situation, from the south transept, where it occupied a space at the bottom of the steps leading to this part of the church. The lid is ornamented with the figure of a cathedral prior; and upon the slanting ledge near the top, the following inscription is yet visible:

Hic jacet Willelmus de Basynge, quondam
Prior, istius Ecce cujus anime propicietur
Deus et qui pro aia ejus oraverit III annos
C. et XLV. dies indulgencia percipiet.

Further east, on the left hand, is the stately monument of the celebrated Cardinal Beaufort, which is considered as one of the most sumptuous in the

---

[1] Milner, ii. 59.

kingdom. The roof of the chantry is decorated with a profusion of pinnacled canopies and nitches, and is supported by clustered columns of Purbeck marble, the insides of which, terminating in an elegant fan-work, form the vaulting of the chantry. The low ballustrades surrounding the area of the tomb, are of grey marble. The tomb, also of marble, was originally adorned with a number of shields, bearing the arms and devices of Beaufort, whose effigy, in his cardinal's habit, lies upon the top. Round the ledges of the slab, which support the figure, there appears to have been two fillets of metal, bearing an inscription long since totally destroyed.

Against the south wall of the church, on our right hand, we turn to the monument of Sir John Clobery, a native of Winchester, and Colonel of a regiment in the Parliamentary army, who, from his epitaph, appears to have borne some considerable share in the events which paved the way for the restoration of Charles the Second. This memorial is graced with a full-length figure of the worthy Knight, in the military costume of his time, standing erect, under an Ionic arch, decorated and surrounded with the various insignia of war. The whole effect of this it would be impossible to describe; but if the object of those who erected it in its present situation, was to afford a practical illustration of the sublime and the ridiculous, they seem to have fully attained it.

Upon a marble tablet below the figure, we read the following epitaph:

M. S.

JOHANNIS CLOBERY militis,

Vir in omni re eximius,

Artem bellicam

Non tantum optime novit,

Sed ubiq; felicissime exercuit

Ruentis patriæ simul et Stuartorum domûs

Stator auspicatissimus

Quod Monchius et ipse

Prius in Scotiæ animo agitaverant

Ad Londinum venientes

Facile affectum dabante;

Unde

Pacem Angliæ, Carolum Secundum solio,

(Universo populo plaudente)

Restituerunt.

Inter armorum negotiorumq; strepitum

(Res raro militibus usitata)

Humanioribus ulteris sedulò incubuit

Et singulares animi dotes

Tam exquisita eruditione expolivit

Ut Athenis potius quam castris

Senuisse videretur

Scd, corpore demum morbo languescente

Se tacitè mundi motibus subduxit

Ut cœlo, quod per totum vitam

Ardentius anhelavarat unicè vacaret.

Obit anno { Salutis,   1687,
           { Ætatis sue,   63.

Hoc monumentum charissime defuncti

Relicta, ceu ultimum amoris indicium

Poni curavit.

A short distance from this monument is a flat stone, with the following inscription to the memory of Baptist Levinz, a Prebendary of this cathedral, and Bishop of Sodor and Man, who died in 1692:

BAPTISTA LEVINZ,
S. T. P.

Episcopus Sodorensis et hujus Ecclesiæ Prebendarius,
Patri Gulielmo Levinz de Eventia, in Comit. Northampt.
Armigerus ortus :
Oxoni Collegio B. M. Magdalenæ educatus ;
Patriæ suæ, Academiæ, Ecclesiæ, et seculi, ornamentum ;
Ob integritatem et sanctimoniam vitæ, morum gravitatem
Et candorem, et virtutes vere Christiânus ;
Olim spectabilis, semper memorandus ;
Naturæ et gratiæ dotibus illustris ;
Corporis elegantis, vultis decori, mentis eximiæ ;
(Nusquam splendidius habitavit philosophia.)
Literaturæ, quæ humanæ quæ divinæ, omni
Genere instructus ;
Theodoxæ religionis præco atq; propugnatur
Validissimus, Deo probatus operarius ανεπαγχυντο.
Episcopale munus modeste
Admissit, prudenter, et benefice administravit :
Primævos et apostolicos pastores imitatus, et
Qualem posteri imitentur.
Vixit.
Multus idoneus ; omnibus dilectus ;
Bene de alijs merendi studiosus, et apprime gnarus ;
Erga egenos liberalis, simulq; rei familiaris providus ;
Hospitalis sine luxu, et inter lautitias abstemius ;
In templo, juxta ac privatis in œdibus deum.
Assiduæ et sincere veneratus ;
In precibus et jejunijs, frequens, cœli appetens,
Febre correptus, bonus servas et fidelis
Domini sui guardium ingressus este
Die XXXI Januarij,
An. Dom. M.DC.XCII.   Ætat suæ, 49.
Viro optimo desideratissimoq;
Mariæ uxor dilectissima.
H. M.   M. P.

Before us, against the wall of the south-east turret, recently stood the mutilated bust of Bishop

Ethelmar, the half brother of Henry III. who died in France, in 1260. His heart, which he is represented as holding in his hands, was buried by his desire in our cathedral, as we shall presently have occasion to notice.

Three enclosed chapels form the eastern extremity of the whole fabric. The one immediately before us, called Langton's Chantry, is fitted up with oak, carved and decorated in a peculiar stile of richness and elegance; but seems unfortunately in an almost irreparable state of dilapidation. The carving, with which it is covered, consists of vine leaves and fruit, armorial bearings and devices, and a motto, " 𝕷𝖆𝖚𝖘 𝖙𝖎𝖇𝖎 𝖈𝖗𝖎𝖈𝖙𝖊"—the whole surmounted with a rich open cornice and spire-work. In the centre is the altar-tomb of Thomas Langton, Bishop of Winton, who died in 1500, which seems to have been ornamented with brasses, but at present is more conspicuous for the traces of violence with which almost every part of it is covered. The ceiling of this chapel is curiously decorated with rebuses and devices, amongst which are allusions to his Name and his See.

The middle chapel, dedicated to the Blessed Virgin, was originally of equal length with the two adjoining, but appears to have been altered to its present dimensions by Prior Silkestede, whose name we observe amongst the tracery of the vaulting. The upper end of the chapel is decorated with the remains of a series of ancient paintings, in compartments, relating chiefly to the miraculous intercession of the Virgin Mary on various occasions; but these have been so greatly defaced at different times, that, although many of the figures are still perfectly visible, the subject of some of them it is impossible to trace. In this chapel the ceremony was performed which united our bigotted Queen Mary with the no less intolerant Philip of Spain; and the wood-work of a chair, in which the Queen sat on that occasion, is still remaining near the altar.

Upon the pavement, on the north side of the latter, we read the following inscription, over the intended sepulchre of Dr. Layfield, a Prebendary of the cathedral, by whom the chapel was new paved in 1705:

Anno { Sal. humanæ 1705.
      Ætate suæ   58.

Carolus hunc posuit Lapidem Lafieldus inanem,
Præsenti exequias dum parat ipse sibi.
Si tamen hic nolet Deus illius ossa jacere
Tum teneat vacuus nomen insane lapis.

Leaving the Lady Chapel, we observe, immediately before the entrance, a long coffin-shaped tomb of grey marble, raised above the pavement, without any inscription or ornament. Beneath this monument it is conjectured are deposited the remains of Godfrey de Lucy, Bishop of Winchester,[1] who died in 1204, and by whom the whole of this part of the church was rebuilt.

A few paces from the west end of De Lucy's tomb, upon a raised slab, lies the figure of a crusader,

---

[1] Milner, ii. 63.

armed cap-a-pie, in a hauberk, with sword and shield, the latter of which is quartered with armorial distinctions. This mutilated figure has been lately removed from one of the side arches on the north of the choir, and from an inscription, said to have been formerly visible upou the monument, appears to have covered the remains of William, Count of the Isle of Wyneal, or Winnal.[1] Upon a slab, which originally might have formed one of the sides of his tomb, and in its late situation occupied the back ground of the arch under which the figure laid, the royal arms of England, France, Castile, and Leon, were enchased upon shields.

Adjoining the above is a large flat stone, covered with the traces of a profusion of brass ornaments, under which lie the remains of Thomas Silkstede, Prior of the cathedral, who died in 1524, and to whose works we have more than once alluded in our description of this part of the church.

We are now opposite the centre of the transverse wall or screen, which forms the eastern boundary of the chapels at the back of the altar, and separates the works of De Lucy from those of Fox. Along the front of this screen are a range of niches with rich embossed canopies and pedestals, upon which the images of our Saviour and the Holy Virgin, with those of the following illustrious personages, seem to have been placed, in the order of their respective names, as they are inscribed along the base of the pedestals :

---

[1] See Fourth Walk.

Kyngilsus Rex.   Scs Birinus Epc   Kynwaldz Rex.
Egbertus Rex.   Adulfus Rex.   Elured Rex fili ejz
Edwardz Rex senior   Adhelstanz Rex fili ejz

Sca Maria. + Dominus Jesus.

Edredus Rex.   Edgarus Rex.   Emmæ Regina.
Alwynus Epc   Ethelred Rex.   Scs Edwardz Rex fili ejz
Cnutus Rex.   Hardecnutus Rex filius ejus.

Immediately below the pedestals of our Lord and the Virgin Mary, which occupy the centre compartment of the screen, is the entrance to the Holy Hole, or vault, devoted to the reception of the relics of those persons whose eminent sanctity in life had procured them the character and attributive honours of saints after their decease. This is a small arched door-way, beyond which is an opening to the extent of five feet by six, and on each side of the arch the following inscription runs along the lower part of the screen:

Corpora sanctorum sunt hic in pace sepulta
Et meritis quorum fulgent miracula multa.

This entry is supposed to have led down a staircase into the crypt immediately under the high altar and sanctuary; and being, as we have observed, the place destined for the reception of relics, and the interment of persons of eminent sanctity, seems to have derived the appellation of " The Holy Hole." It appears that an attempt was made to obtain an entrance into it in the year 1789,[1] but upon removing the masonry which closed the entry, the crown of the arch above was found to have been destroyed,

---

[1] Milner, ii. 72, note.

and the whole passage so entirely choaked up with rubbish, that there was a necessity of abandoning the undertaking. It having, however, lately been thought proper to make a second attempt, the exterior stone-work was removed, and the passage laid open to its present dimensions.

At the north-east extremity of the screen, and parallel with the coffin of Prior Baysyng, is a similar tomb, without any inscription or ornament, except a processional cross which is carved upon the lid. This cross, however, must not be taken as data whereby to judge of the remains deposited beneath it, as the lid itself has been but lately removed to its present situation from one much-less conspicuous, which it occupied in the north transept. The particular remains inclosed in the coffin it seems impossible now to trace: but it is not improbable, from the ornaments of the lid which originally covered it, that it may have belonged to a prior of the cathedral.

Retracing our steps from the screen, along the centre aisle, we turn on the left to the superb chantry and tomb of Bishop Waynflete, who died in 1486. The spire-work which surrounds and covers the roof of this monument, is supposed to be equal, if not superior, in exuberance of ornament and beauty of finishing, to any structure of the kind in England. The area of the tomb, which in the opposite chapel of Beaufort is left open, is in this inclosed with a light arch-work, crowned with an exquisite facia of vine-leaves and fruit. The figure of the Bishop lies over the tomb in the episcopal habit, and is represented as in the act of prayer, emblematically offering up his heart, which he grasps between his hands. There also appears to have been a fillet of brass or other metal round the edge of this tomb; but, like that round the monument of Beaufort, it has been entirely destroyed.

At the north-east end of this chantry, we approach the chapel of the Guardian Angels, which till lately was inclosed with a screen of carved oak, somewhat like that of the Lady Chapel, with which it is parallel. This, however, has been removed, and its place supplied by a low iron railing. At the east end of the chapel a richly-ornamented slab, which we have before mentioned as having originally formed part of the tomb of the crusader, has been recently erected, and, in its present situation, adds at least to the *beauty* of the chapel, in which there is little else to notice *except* a splendid monument, which occupies the whole of the south side, and is erected to the memory of Richard Weston, Earl of Portland, Lord Treasurer of England in the reign of Charles the First. The figure of the Earl, cast in bronze, lies upon a superb base of veined marble, about the centre of the monument; and over it, in a range of nitches, were marble busts of some branches of his family. The inscription beneath is as follows:

Depositum
RICHARDI WESTON, Comitis
Portland, Magna Angliæ
Thesaurarii, quo munere Fungi
Cæpit, anno Regis Caroli

Quarto, idq; simul cum vita
Exuit, Anno prædicti Domini
Nostri Regis Decimo, Annoq;
Domini Redemptoris, 1634, Decimo
Tertio die Martii.

On the opposite side of the chapel is a tabulary monument, with the following memorial of Bishop Mews, whose mitre and crosier are suspended against one of the adjoining columns:[1]

M. S.
PETRI MEWS, LL. D.
Nuper Episcopi Winton,
Qui a Studiis Academicis,
Iniquitate Temporum violentur abreptus,
Pro Rege, pro Patriâ, pro Religione,
Militiæ se dedit :
In quâ intermeratam in Ecclesiam et Monarchiam fidem,
Abunde testatem fecit,

---

[1] Upon opening a vault immediately below this chapel, in the course of the year 1815, the leaden coffin of the Earl of Portland was discovered upon the pavement, bearing upon a tablet of brass, the following inscription :

Depositum
Illustrissimi D. D. RICARDI WESTON,
Comitis de Portland, Baronis de
Nayland, Magni Thesaurij
Angliæ, Serenissimo Regi Carolo
A Secretoribus Consiliis et Nobilisimi
Ordinis Garteriani Comilitoris.
Obitj 13 Mar. 1634.
An. ætatis suæ 59.

And nearly oppostite the above, a small flat stone marked the grave of Bishop Mews, by the following short record :

H. S. E.
PETRUS MEWS,
Winton Epus.
Obijt IX Nov[ris.]
1706.

Carolo I$^{mo.}$ Martyre Perduellium Armis oppugnato:
Idem Proscripto Carolo II$^{do.}$ Exillj Comes:
Quo Reduce, Redux,
Intermissa priora Studia feliciter resumpsit,
Et magnorum in Regiam familiam meritorum premia tulit:
Primo ad sedem Bathon. et Wellen. A. 1672.
Deinde ad Wintoniensem evectus, A. 1684.
Vir invictâ constantiâ et magnanimitate præditus,
Lenoribus tamen virtutibus conspicuus esse maluit,
Propensa erga amicos Benevolentiâ,
Effusâ erga egenos Liberalitate,
Indiscriminatà erga omnes Humanitate,
Anno demum ætatis suæ LXXXVIII$^{vo.}$
V^{to} id Novemb. A. D. 1706,
Vir misericors sublatus est,
Denuo in die supremo restituendus.

Edwardus Butler, LL. D.
Coll. S. Mariæ Magdalenæ,
Oxon. Præses et Registrarius
Principalis Diocesis Winton,
Gratitudinis ergo posuit.

Leaving the chapel, we observe, against the north wall of the church, a handsome monument of free-stone, consisting of a rich pediment, supported by pillars of the Corinthian order, over an oval tablet decorated with figures and foliage. Upon the top of this design, which is of considerable height, are coloured shields of arms; and the tablet bears the following inscription, in capital letters:

HIC SITUS EST
THOMAS MASONIIS
Jo. Massoniis, Equitus aurati filius insigne
exemplum inconstantis conditionis rer. humanar.
in quem cum certatem natura et fortûnat suas
dotes cumulato congessissent usus et industriæ
in eo amabilissimos mores eruditionem multa. rer.

supra ætatem cognitionem et variarum linguarum
Literaturam produxissent adeo ut ad felicissimum
vitæ cursum nihil illi defuisse videretur immatura
Mors tantæ spei indolem invidens orbi tam clare
Lucentum faculam crudeli ausu extinxit cum
exephebis vix dum excessissit ato ; adeo tam rari
ingenii omnes amœnitates tot benignissamæ naturæ
suavissimos flores tantam spem tam pia et justa vota
mœstissimor parentum dies una hora una
momentum annum abstulit. . . . Anno ætatis XVIII.
Salutis MDLIX. die mensis Julij XXIII.

Moestiss parens unico orbatus filio illi
et sibi in spem Resurrectionis
Pos.

Nearly opposite the centre of Waynflete's chantry, is a flat stone over the remains of Mr. Peter Symonds, founder of the alms-house called Christ's Hospital, of which we shall hereafter have occasion to speak. The inscription upon it, which is nearly illegible, concludes with the following lines :

His merit doth inherit life and fame ;
For whilst this city standes, Symonds his name,
In poore men's hearts shall never be forgotten ;
For poores prayers rise, when flesh lies rotten.

At the west end of the above, on a low raised tomb, is a mutilated figure of black marble, the head of which is decorated with a small mitre. It appears doubtful as to the remains over which this figure was originally placed in the north aisle of the church ; but it is conjectured, from the situation it there occupied, to be the monument of Peter des Roches, or de Rupibus, Bishop of Winchester, who died in 1233, and was buried in this cathedral.

Beyond this, and parallel with the coffins at the east end of the transverse screen, is a low slab, adjoining the north wall, supporting a figure, which, from the appearance of the robes, and the situation it formerly occupied, as the lid of the coffin now covered with the more comely production of the north transept, is supposed to have formed part of the monument of a Prior of the cathedral; but from its extreme mutilated condition, without either head or feet, it is impossible to speak with any degree of certainty as to the individual remains it may have covered.

We are now opposite the outside of Gardiner's chantry, consisting of a range of Gothic arches crowned with a Doric frieze and cornice, supporting the arms and devices of the founder. In a recess, about the centre of the north side, his effigy is exhibited as a skeleton, and bears unequivocal proof of the violence and indignity with which it has been treated. Proceeding further westward, we observe the tomb of Hardicnute, the last Danish Monarch of England whose body was interred in this cathedral; upon a small tablet near the centre of the tomb is the representation of an armed galley; and on another tablet adjoining it, the following inscription:

Qui jacet hic regni sceptrum tulit

Hardicnutus Emmæ Cnutonis gnatus

Et ipse fuit.   Ob. A. D. 1042.

Near the north door of the choir is the following

S

inscription upon a tomb containing the heart of Bishop Ethelmar, who died at Paris in 1261, and whose bust we have already mentioned :

Corpus Ethelmari, cujus cor nunc tenet
Isted Saxum Parisijs morte datur tumulo
Ob. A. D. 1261.

We now leave the north-east aisle, and descending a flight of steps are once more among the ponderous and lofty architecture of the transept. On the left hand, under the stairs of the organ gallery, is a small chapel which has been recently opened, called the Chapel of the Sepulchre. Towards the east end is represented in colours, the descent from the Cross; and below it, the laying of our Saviour in the Tomb; on the south side appears the descent into Hell; and in another compartment, the appearance to Mary Magdalen in the Garden. The vaulting of the chapel is also covered with the fragments of a variety of ancient paintings, consisting of portraits of saints, and other subjects connected with the life and sufferings of Christ.

The north transept, in which various inditia of altars still remain, was also originally decorated with scriptural paintings, the figures of saints, &c. Beneath the window at the end of the east aisle is a rich Gothic arch of considerable size, which has probably formed the canopy of a tomb, though there are not now any other vestiges of one remaining upon the spot. The west aisle, till lately, consisted of two chapels, which were shut up from the body of the transept, and used as workshops for the people employed in the repairs of the cathedral.

Under the arch which connects the north aisle with the transept, we observe a rich mural monument of the Rivers family. The tablet bearing the epitaph is crowned by a pyramid of grey marble, charged with shields emblazoned with armorial distinctions.

Opposite the side steps of the choir is a beautiful monument erected to the memory of James Morley, Esq. and Ann, his wife, composed of rich Parian and Sienna marbles, ornamented with a weeping willow over a large funereal urn, in front of a pyramid crowned with a cinerary vase.

Under the second arch from the choir is the plain tomb of Bishop Morley, inclosed with iron rails, and having the mitre and crosier of the bishop suspended over it against the adjacent columns of the nave.—The epitaph is as follows:

In spe resurrectionis ad vitam æternam
GEORGIUS EPISCOPUS WINTONIENSIS hic jacet,
Qui post quam pro Rege et Martyre Carolo Primo
Et cum Rege et exile Carolo Secundo,
Exilium in partibus transmarinis hic, illic,
Duodecim plus minus annorum exegisset,
Redux cum Rege tandem in Patriam suam,
Munificentia magis Regia, quam illo sui ipsius
(Tam in sublimibus in Ecclesiæ gradibus) patri merito
Primùm ex uno Canonicorum, Ecclesiæ Christi
Oxoniensis factus est decanus ; breviq; postea
In ecclesiæ Vigorniensis præsulatum est
Evectus ; tandemq; (sic volente Deo et Rege)
In hujus inclytæ Wintoniensis Ecclesiæ

Episcopatum est translatus : et jam plus
Quam Octogenarius, hoc sibi Epitaphium
Scripsit, et huic sui deposito apponi jussit.

Obijt verò anno Domini MDCLXXXIV,
Mensis Octobris die XXIX°. Anno
Ætatis suæ LXXXVII ; postquam
In hâc Episcopali Cathedra
Sederat annos XXII, mensis quinq;

Upon one of the columns adjoining the tomb of Bishop Morley, is the following epitaph engraved on a plate of brass, equally curious for its information and the style in which it is conveyed :

A MEMORIALL

For this Renowned Martialist Richard Boles, of y^e Right Worshipfull Family of the Bolses in Linckhorne Sheire, Collonell of a Ridgement of Foot of 1300, who for his gratious King Charles y$_e$ First did wounders att the Battell of Edge hill.   His last Action, to omitt all others, was at Alton, in this County of Soughthampton, was surprized by fiue or six thousand of the Rebells; which caused him, there quartered, to fly to the Church with neare fourescore of his Men, who there fought them six or seauen Houres; And then the Rebell breaking in upon him, He slew with his Sword six or seauen of them, and then was slayne himselfe, with sixty of his Men aboute him.

1641.

His gratious Soueraigne hearing of his Death gaue him his high Comendation, in y^s pationate expression,

Bring me a Moorning Scarffe, i haue lost
one of the best Comanders in this Kingdome.

Alton will tell you of that famous fight
Which y^s. man made, and bade this world good night,
His verteous life fear'd not mortalyty ;
His body must, his vertues cannot die.

Because his bloud was there so nobly spent:
This is his Tombe, that Church his Monument.
Richardus Boles, Wiltoniensis in Art. Mag.
Composuit posuitque Dolens
An. Dni. 1689.

Under the third arch is the monument of Dr. Matthew Comb, who died in 1748. This memorial consists of a sarcophagus, supporting a beautiful funereal urn, decorated with a garland of flowers, in front of a pyramid adorned with sepulchral lamps.

The next intercolumniation presents a heavy unintelligible design, overloaded with a profusion of clumsy and grotesque ornaments, probably *intended* as an imitation of Corinthian architecture. The inscription has been merely painted on a marble slab in the centre of the monument, and is entirely oliterated, or the stone has been turned; consequently there is nothing by which we can be guided in an endeavour to trace to whose memory it may have been raised, while at the same time we are consoled in our ignorance by a recollection of the taste which influenced its erection.

The next object of our attention is the monument erected to the memory of Sir Villiers Chernock, Baronet, who died in 1779. On one side of an urn, under a drooping willow, is the figure of Justice, with her attributes; on the other, is Charity, giving clothes to some naked children. In the execution of the design, considerable objection has been excited, by the introduction of metal among the ornaments.

We now come to what has been termed the puzzle of Antiquaries—the Ancient Cathedral Font. This stands under the centre arch of the north aisle, and consists of a square block of black marble, hollowed in the centre, and supported by a pedestal and four small columns of the same material. It is covered on the top and each of the sides with sculptures, which, as they seem to defy any satisfactory attempt to explain their meaning, so, by their rudeness, they bespeak their antiquity. That the workmanship is Saxon, and the subject represented has relation to the acts of some early saint of the church, seem to be allowed on all sides; but the particular application, where so many of the learned have differed, is a matter of considerable difficulty to decide upon.

Under the window, opposite the font, is an elegant monument erected in memory of Edward Montagu, Esq. and Elizabeth his wife, a lady, to whose memory we cannot do greater honour, than by repeating the eloquent language of the Historian of Winchester: " Here lies the glory of her sex, the late Mrs. Montagu, whose benevolence and charities the poor will long remember, and whose genius, displayed in the vindication of its favorite poet, the English nation will never forget."[1] This memorial consists of a tablet of white marble, with fluted columns, supporting a funereal urn; on the one side of which is seated Justice, and on the other

---

[1] Milner, ii. 99.

Wisdom, with their several attributes.   Upon an oval in front of the urn, a Genii appears, extinguishing his torch; and the whole is finished by a pyramid of veined marble rising to a considerable height.   The epitaph is as follows:

Here lies the body of
EDWARD MONTAGU,
Grandson to the first Earl of Sandwich ;
Who, after serving his country in Parliament,
With disinterested fidelity,
Retired to a life of study and contemplation ;
Preserving, to the latest hour of a long life,
The most perfect use of his understandiug and his senses
He died on the 20th May, 1775, in his 81st year.

Also,
Of ELIZABETH MONTAGU, his wife,
Daughter of Matthew Robinson, Esq.
Of West Layton, in the county of York ;
Who, possessing the united advantages
Of beauty, wit, judgment, reputation, and riches,
And employing her talents most uniformly
For the benefit of mankind,
Might be justly deemed an ornament
To her sex and country.
She died on the 25th of August, 1800, aged 81.

Likewise
Of JOHN MONTAGU, their son,
Who died in the year 1744, aged 15 months,
And was buried at Burniston, in Yorkshire,
From whence his body was removed to this place,
Aeording to the will of his mother.

Against the pillar, on the west side of the above, is a neat monumental design, erected in memory of Colonel James Morgan, consisting of an urn raised upon a low column, before which a female bends in the attitude of Grief and Resignation; on each side of the urn are implements and trophies of war; and in the back ground, the figure of an elephant denotes the region to which the deceased, in his professional character, more particularly belonged.

Under the seventh arch, is a monument in a similar stile of architecture to that under the fourth, which we have already noticed for its singularity and ugliness. The epitaph, which is curious for its triteness, runs thus:

A UNION OF TWO BROTHERS FROM AVINGTON.

The Clerks'

family were, grandfather, father, and son, successively Clerks of the Privy Seal. William, the grandfather, had but two sons, both Thomas's; their wives, both Amy's; and their heirs, both Henry's; and the heirs of the Henry's both Thomas's. Both their wives were inheritrixes; and both had two sons and one daughter, and both their daughters issuless. Both of Oxford, both of the Temple, both officers to Queen Elizabeth and our noble King James; both Justices of the Peace; both agree in arms, the one a Knight, the other a Captain.

Si quæras Avingtonum, Petas Cancellum.

Impensis Thomæ Clerk, of Hyde.

1662.

Under the ninth arch, is a mural tablet and pyramid erected to the memory of the Lady of Major Poole, who died in 1779, and her father, who died in 1763. The pyramid is crowned with a cinerary vase; and there are also two others at the base of it, inscribed with the names of the Major and his Lady.

The next and last monument in our progress, is one erected, in 1810, to the memory of Dr. John Littlehales, a physician of this city, and which affords a valuable and striking illustration of the undying honour attendant upon a life of active benevolence and virtue. The design is a bass relief of the Good Samaritan, well executed by Bacon. Below a tablet, bearing the epitaph, is a small Cross upon an open book, in which is written,

The blessing of him that was ready to perish came upon me.

Job, c. xxix. v. xiii.

The whole is composed of a beautiful white marble upon a black ground, and has, from its situation, a very striking effect.

The epitaph, which is not the least pleasing part of the design, is as follows :

Near to this place are deposited the remains of
JOHN LITTLEHALES, M. D.
Fellow of the Royal College of Physicians, London,
and formerly of Pembroke College, Oxford.
His eminent professional talents, by the blessing of Divine Providence,
were successfully exerted, with a generosity so distinguished,
and with beneficence to the poor so diffusive and unwearied,
amidst a very extensive practice,
that his decease was an event most deeply
regretted and lamented.
The principal Inhabitants of Winchester and its Neighbourhood
have erected this Monument,
as a public record of their affectionate gratitude,
to the memory of their Friend and Benefactor;
But, from the Saviour of the World,
whose faith he adorned by a life devoted to Christian benevolence,
he will receive his final reward.
He departed this life the 2d of January, 1810,
aged 57 years.
T

Immediately before us, at the west end of the north aisle, is a tribune or gallery, which appears to have been used as a station for the minstrels who performed in the cathedral, in addition to the choir, upon occasions of extraordinary magnificence and solemnity. The Reformation, among other more important changes, by putting an end to those circumstances of external pomp and splendour with which the celebration of the great festivals of the church were accompanied, rendered this gallery useles, as far as its original purpose extended; it has, however, been long appropriated as a court for for transacting the ecclesiastical business of the diocese, and where the registers of the bishops, from the year 1280, are deposited.

We have not hitherto taken notice of the numerous memorials, both ancient and modern, which cover the nave, as well on account of their general comparative want of interest, as that by so doing we should have materially interrupted the course of our progress round the church. Among these various subjects are, however, the grave-stones of the Norman Prelate Walkelyn, by whom the tower and some part of the present church was originally built; of Bishop Horne, by whom it was subsequently despoiled of some of its most venerable and interesting features; and of Prior Kingsmill, the last superior of the Monastic Foundation, and the first Dean of the Reformed Establishment.

Quitting the church by the door at the end of the north aisle, we observe in the rugged wall which forms the southern boundary of the burial ground, the mutilated arches of windows and doorways originally belonging to the Carnarie, or Bone-house of the cathedral; the west end of this wall terminates in a round mass of flint and strong mortar, which from its appearance may probably be the remains of the fortifications erected by Ethelbald round the cathedral, to protect it from the ravages of the Danes in the ninth century. [1]

Upon the large buttress at the south west corner of the cathedral, we perceive, at some height, the following anagram:

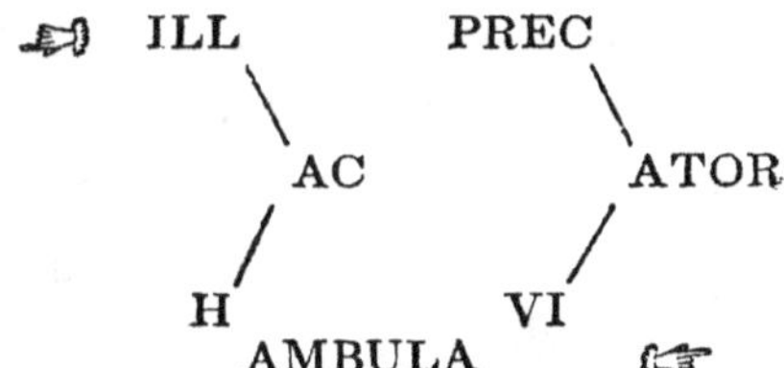

And, in the short passage before us, called the Slype, through which we now proceed, an arched stone, built in the wall, bears the following:

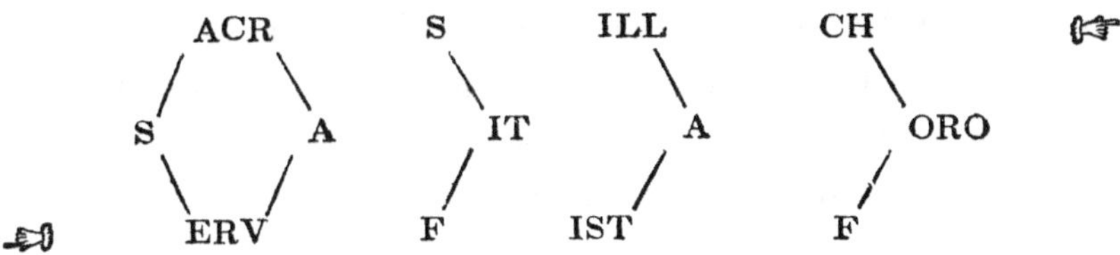

Passing the last mentioned inscription which was originally placed over the eastern boundary of the

---

[1] Historical Account, p. 12.

passage, and was, with the former, intended to commemorate the accommodation afforded by opening this communication between the Close and the City, we enter upon the scite of the ancient Cloisters, which, with the Chapter-house, and various other buildings of the Priory, were destroyed by Bishop Horne in 1563. Before us, at the south end of the transept, is a passage which formerly communicated with some of the domestic offices of the establishment and the rooms above, which are now used as the cathedral library and the school room of the choristers. The original entrance to the chapter house appears in the ornamented Gothic door-way on the right of this avenue, and the scite of that structure may be still traced, in a series of small arches, on the north and east sides of the Dean's kitchen garden.

At the south-east extremity of the cloisters the residence of the Prior was situate, of which the great hall now forms the principal apartment of the deanry, as appears from the ancient windows on the west side, the centre of which is adorned with the arms of Charles the First and his royal Consort.[1]

Most of the surrounding buildings of the Close, are of comparatively modern date, and constitute the prebendal residences attached to the cathedral.

We quit the Close, on the south side, by a firm and lofty gateway of great strength, the doors of

----

[1] Historical Account, p. 84.

which are probably the same that were erected in 1264, shortly after the gate-house and surrounding buildings had been destroyed by fire.[1] At the distance of a few paces from this gate, we reach the ancient postern of St. Michael or Kings-gate, over which is the parish church of St. Swithun, erected in its present situation by King John, in the beginning of the thirteenth century, at which time the communication under it with the southern suburb of the city was opened.[2]

This little edifice, curious for its exalted situation, is entered by a modern staircase on the west side of the gateway, and consists of a single aisle, neatly fitted up with a double row of seats. The font, which stands under the window at the west end, is the most prominent feature of its antiquity now remaining; but near the window on the north side, is a small unadorned nitch, and under it a label charged with the arms of the see, having below them the remains of an inscription, which upon a close examination, appears to have been at one time highly coloured, and from the style of the letters is probably of an early date.

Descending from the church, we proceed for some distance along St. Swithun-street, until we reach a neat building erected and endowed in the year 1607, as an asylum for six old men, four boys, and a matron, by Peter Symonds, a native of Winchester, whose grave we have noticed in our account of the

---

[1] Milner ii. 128. [2] Wavel, i. 208.

cathedral.[1] The objects of the foundation, upon which eleven persons appear to be comfortably maintained, seem to be fully explained by the following inscription, upon a large stone, over the entrance:

CHRIST'S HOSPITAL,

Which was founded
in the year of our Lord,
1607,
By PETER SYMONDS,
a Native of Winchester,
and afterwards a Mercer
in the City of London.
The Endowments of this House
are applied to the maintenance
of Six Old Men, One Matron, and Four Boys;
and also to the assistance
of One Scholar
in each of the two
English Universities.

THE NAME
of such a Benefactor
is remembered with gratitude
by Posterity.

The only singularity attached to this institution, is the dress of its members, which is of light blue, and exhibits, in appearance, the fashion of the times in which the hospital was established.

Passing up Symonds-street, as it is called from this hospital, to the south-west corner of the cathedral burial-ground, a short street on the left hand brings us once more into St. Thomas's-street, in which the parish church similarly named stands

---

[1] Ante 128.

before us on the right. The existence of this church may be traced as far back as the year 1282, at which time we find it mentioned in the Bishop's Register, under the name of St. Petrochus; and at that time it appears to have consisted of three aisles, one of which was taken down in the reign of Queen Elizabeth, at which time the church was new founded, and dedicated to St. Thomas. The altar is situated under the east window of the north aisle, and is lofty; and the church in general is said to have been considered as the neatest, if not the largest, in Winchester.[1] Setting aside a modern attempt at decoration, the church has certainly an air of neatness and of original beauty: as, for instance, the varied mouldings of the second arch from the east end, which, with its parallel in the north wall, still preserve its original Saxon features in a great degree unimpaired. Among the various monuments which meet our observation in this church, is an ancient one, at the east end of the south aisle, consisting of a neat pediment, supported by columns of free stone, adorned with arms, and bearing in the centre the following inscription:

Beati Mortui Qui

R.   B.

Obijt 23° die Martie, A°· D°· 1573.
Cum. Septem. Denos. et. Quinos. vixerat. annos.
Urbis. Ventane. Clatro. bis. munere. major.
Burtonum. Rapiunt. Crudelia. Fata. Richardu.
Conjux. Jona. manet. celebs. Wilielmus. et heres.
Janaq; nata. Patris. chari. sua. pignora. vivent.

In Domino Moriuntur.

---

[1] Wavel i. 187.

Upon a flat stone, near the south entrance to the church, is the following inscription, which, though brief, we have thought sufficiently expressive to insert :

Here lies JOHN PURDUE,
the honest College Woodman,
who died December the 7th, 1736,
aged 70 years.

Besides the above, there is not in this church any monument sufficiently interesting to notice; and, quitting its enclosure at the gate by which we entered it, a few paces northwards brings us into the High-street, where we shall terminate our First Walk.

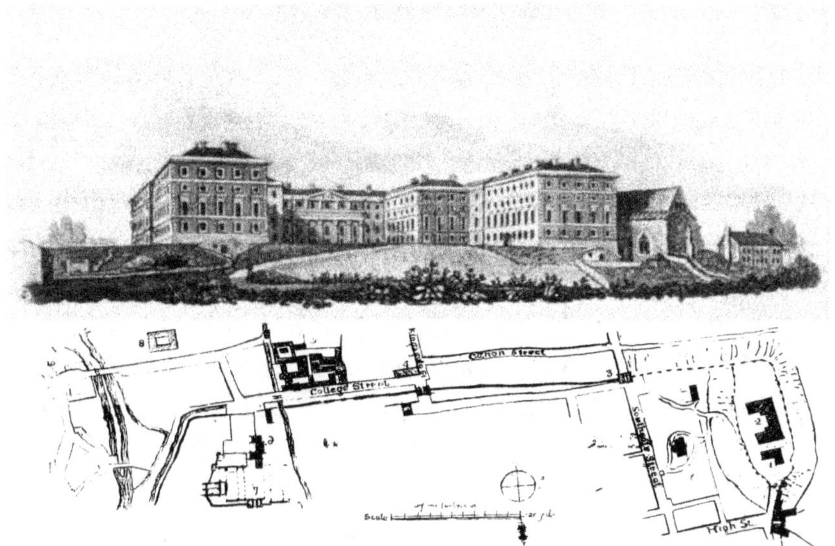

1. The Chapel of the Castle.—2. The Barracks.—3. The Barrack Gate.—4. Scite of the Nuns' Hospital.—5. The College of St. Mary.—6. Bishop Morley's Palace.—7. Wolvesey Chapel.—8. The Ruins of Wolvesey Castle.—9. Scite of St. Elizabeth's College.—10. The Wharf Bridge.—11. Footway to St. Catherine's Hill.

The Second Walk.

WE shall commence our Second Walk, like the First, from the West Gate of the City, which we now leave on the right hand, and ascend towards the Chapel of the Castle of Winchester, used as the County Hall. This Chapel, now the only remaining vestige of the buildings connected with our fortress, has an exceedingly plain and uninteresting appearance; but from its antiquity, as well as the purpose to which it is now applied, will necessarily become an object of curiosity and attention. The interior is divided by clusters of columns into three aisles, and is 110 feet in length, 55 broad, and very lofty; but much of the effect is lost by the divisions that have been made at each end, in order to form the Assize Courts for the county, which are held here in the spring and summer of each year. Its chief attraction, independent of these circum-stances, is the Round Table, as it is called, of King Arthur, which is suspended over the Judges' seat at the east end of the structure, and is decorated with the full-length portrait of that Monarch, and the names of his twenty-four Knights, as they have been collected from the early romances; perhaps, if the same data be referred to with regard to the history of the Table itself, we shall not exceed the limits of probability and reason. But upon this subject we have already expressed our opinion and our autho-rity;[1] and we shall now dismiss the Round Table with the remark, that whether it be considered as the off-spring of fiction, or an actual relic of the warlike ban-quets of chivalry, it seems, at best, but an improper object with which to ornament a court of civil justice.

Leaving the Hall, we enter, on the left hand, the inclosure of the Barracks; before speaking of which, we shall advert to the ancient Castle of Winchester, upon the scite of which they were built.

The Castle of Winchester was erected by William the Conqueror, in 1068,[2] for the protection of this his capital city, and the depository of the treasures and records of his kingdom. The whole area of the

---

[1] Historical Account, 83. [2] Ibid. 27.

structure seems to have occupied about 850 feet in length, north and south, and about 250 in breadth; of this space the keep occupied a square of about 100 feet, and was situated upon a mount near the south end of the fortifications, which were connected with those of the city by a strong wall following the slope of the ditch.[1] The keep was also flanked with a tower at each of the four corners, and a fifth stood over the entrance which faced the south. The main gate of the castle fronted the west, and stood near the centre of the corresponding part of the present building; having, directly opposite to it on the other side of the ditch, a barbican or turret of considerable strength; the whole extent of the walls were likewise crowned at convenient distances with square towers for its defence; and, in addition to these, was the extensive fosse surrounding the whole, which in some parts was 100 feet deep and as many broad.

In treating of the events connected with the Castle of Winchester, we have but an unpleasant duty to perform; for the most conspicuous traits of its history are those of violence and suffering. Thus we find, that in 1069, in the dungeons of this Castle, Stigand, Archbishop of Canterbury, breathed his last; a victim to the resentment of the impetuous Monarch by whom it had been recently erected. Here too, in 1075, Waltheof, Earl of Northampton, from the same cause, fell beneath the ignominious

---

[1] Milner, ii. 180.

hand of the public executioner. From this fortress, in 1141, the heroic Matilda, daughter of
Henry the First, by a stratagem bordering upon romance, escaped in safety from the besieging forces
of the Usurper Stephen. Towards the latter part of
the reign of John, the banners of France for a short
time floated victoriously over the towers of our castle. Again, during the triumphant reign of the
First Edward, in one of the strongest dungeons,
and loaded with irons, languished the venerable
Bishop of St. Andrew's, taken prisoner by the English in 1307, whilst fighting in defence of his unhappy
and almost subdued country. At the Castle of Winchester it was that the Parliament sat, which in
1327 devoted to a shameful death the noble and virtuous Edmund of Woodstock, uncle to Edward the
Second. In the hall of this Castle Henry the Fifth
received, in 1415, the Ambassadors of France, and
retorted the defiance of its Prince with the merited
indignation of insulted majesty. Upon the same
spot, in 1522, the voluptuous Henry the Eighth,
with his Imperial guest Charles the Fifth, were
entertained; and here, in 1554, did his daughter,
the unhappy Mary, await the arrival of Philip, her
destined husband.

Independent of these circumstances, and the natural course of events connected with our Castle, as
being for a long series of years one of the most important fortresses in the kingdom, there is little to

---

[1] Historical Account, 84.

record.   At length, after repelling the attacks of hostile armies, and the more slow but not less destructive ravages of time, during a space of six centuries, this important and interesting fabric was destined to receive, from the hands of a rebellious army under Oliver Cromwell, the blow which levelled its venerable towers with the dust.[1]   This personage, no less famous for his skilful and masterly exercise of the power and energies of the nation, than for the consummate hypocrisy and cunning which placed him at the head of it, had no sooner gained possession of the Castle, in 1645, than he undermined and blew up, with the exception of the chapel, the whole of its fortifications and buildings.   In this state of desolation it therefore continued, until 1682, when Charles the Second having fixed upon its scite for the erection of a royal mansion, every vestige of the old building was demolished, in order to clear an area for the proposed work, in the building of which the greatest part of the ruin was used.   The first stone of the palace was laid on the 23d of March, 1683,[2] by the King himself, who, during the remainder of his reign, spent much of his time in this city, for the purpose of inspecting and accelerating the progress of the work.   His death in 1685, put an immediate stop to the building; and after a considerable period, during which it remained in a neglected and unfinished condition, the first public use it seems to have been applied to, was that

---

[1] Historical Account, 69.   [2] Ibid. 99.

of a Depôt for prisoners of war, during the hostilities which commenced with France, in 1756.[1] Shortly after the rupture with that country, in 1779, one of our cruisers having taken the St. Julie, an hospital ship belonging to that nation, the sick men, together with the crew, were conveyed to this prison, and thus brought into it a destructive pestilence which swept off its wretched inhabitants in great numbers.[2] This disorder, notwithstanding its ravages within the prison, did not extend itself generally amongst the inhabitants of the city, although many persons connected with the Depôt fell victims to the contagion in different parts of it.

In the year 1792, it underwent a transition, somewhat more congenial with its original design. It had been intended as the abode of royalty, and it now became the seat of royal benevolence, being converted into an asylum for the refugee clergy of France, who, preferring a conscientious exile to the alternative of witnessing the destruction of their altars, found a shelter upon the hospitable shores of this country, and were, during a long period, relieved and supported by its voluntary bounty. At one time it appears that no less than 1000 of these unfortunates were resident in this mansion, and their conduct evinced the most exemplary propriety and gratitude; the only and best return in their power for the obligations they were daily receiving, as well from the Government as from the Nation at large.

---

[1] Wavel, ii. 151   [2] Milner, ii. 177.

In 1796, the exigencies of the times rendering it necessary to form a regular military station in this part of the country, Winchester was considered as the most eligible situation for a Depôt, and the refugee clergy were in consequence removed to different parts of the interior, and the King's House (as it is called) converted into a Barrack, in which from two to three thousand men have been lodged with perfect convenience.

The edifice, which is surrounded on the south-east and west sides by the remains of the deep fosse of the castle, is built of a red brick and Portland stone, and forms three sides of an irregular quadrangle, enriched, in the centre of each front, with columns of the Corinthian order. The principal front, which is on the east side, consists of a range of lofty pillars, with a pediment bearing the King's arms, and even in its present condition, so infinitely inferior to the original design from which it was erected,[1] presents on every side an appearance truly royal and magnificent.

Descending from the height on which the Barracks stand, by the footway on the eastern side, we proceed, in a south-eastward direction, to the gates which terminate the inclosure, and enter Southgate-street near the spot on which stood the South Gate of the city, from whence, a few paces southward bring us to the end of Canon-street, through which we shall shape our course towards the College.

---

[1] See an engraved View of the Palace from a drawing by Sir Christopher Wren, in Milner's Hist. Win. i. 433.

About the center of Canon-street, on the north side, we pass the Winchester Female Asylum, instituted in 1815, by a few benevolent individuals, and supported by voluntary contributions. This establishment is calculated for the maintenance and education of 24 girls, from the age of 13 to 16, who, on leaving the Asylum, are provided with situations and encouraged according to their merit. The economy and direction of the institution is under the immediate superintendance of its benevolent patronesses and supporters.

Crossing at the east end of Canon-street, we enter College-street, on the south side of which, near its junction with King's-gate-street, stood an ancient Hospital, supported by the Monks of St. Swithun, for the relief of sick persons, who were attended during their infirmities by Nuns, from whence it was called the *Sustern Spytal.* Though it does not appear that there were any endowment of lands or other property for the support of this Hospital, beyond the charitable gifts of the Priory, and the casual benevolence of strangers; yet it was among the first to perish, of the many similar institutions with which this city was adorned, at the period of the Reformation.

Proceeding eastwards we shortly arrive at the venerable gateway of St. Mary's College, of Winchester, founded by William de Wykeham, Bishop of Winchester, in 1387, upon the scite of a Grammar school, at which, when a boy, he had received his education.[1] This Institution, which he endowed for a Warden, 10 Fellows, 3 Chaplains, 3 Clerks, a Master, an Usher, 70 Scholars, and 16 Choristers, was completed in the space of six years, and taken possession of by the Warden and Scholars on the 28th of March, 1393 ; and the establishment so formed, has continued, during a course of more than four centuries, to flourish, unimpaired, amidst all the storms which have proved so fatal to the surrounding institutions of a religious, literary, or charitable nature; and even at that more desolating period of our history which filled Winchester with uninhabited ruins and premature decay, a special clause in the Act of Suppression, protected this foundation from the insatiate grasp of avarice and extortion, and transmitted to posterity, the generous intentions of its Founder, in all their original excellence and splendour.

Entering the gateway, over which we observe the image of the Blessed Virgin, the chosen patroness of Wykeham, we reach the first or outer court of the College, the eastern side of which is formed by a comparatively modern erection for the residence of the Warden ; the remainder of the court is occupied by a brewhouse and various out offices of the College.

Passing under the lofty tower on the south side of the court, which is ornamented on each side with the statues of the Founder, the Virgin, and the

---

Historical Account, p. 46.

x

angel Gabriel, we are struck with the uniform neatness of the buildings by which the second court is formed, varied only by the magnificent architecture of the Chapel and Hall which occupy the south side.

The area of this court is about 32 yards square, and is thus bounded: on the east and north sides, are the dormitories and the chambers of the Fellows. The room over the gateway is called, from the purpose to which it is applied, the Election Chamber, and was originally used as the chief apartment or hall of the Warden. The west side of the court is occupied by the kitchen and some domestic offices, and the south side is, as we have before observed, formed by the Chapel and the Hall.

The Chapel of the College, which we enter by a spacious porch at the west end, is 102 feet in length, and 33 broad, and is ornamented with a beautiful altar piece of the Salutation, by Le Moine. The windows, which remain nearly in their original perfection, are well worthy the attention of the curious, particularly that at the east end, which occupies the entire space in height, from the altar to the roof of the Chapel, and glowing with all the brilliancy of original genius, pourtrays the genealogy of our Saviour. The roof, which is divided into large compartments of rich tracery, is formed of wood wrought in imitation of stone, and by its loftiness, united with the deep glow of the stained windows, casts an air of solemn grandeur upon the whole, which, however, is not well supported by the modern wainscoting and stalls that surround the Chapel, and which, with the superb screen at the west end, were erected during the Wardenship of Dr. Nicholas, in 1681.[1] These objects, considered in themselves, are extremely beautiful and rich; but, like the episcopal throne of Trelawny in the Cathedral Choir, do not at all assimilate with the objects by which they are surrounded.

In the Ante-chapel, through which we approach the above, remain a few of the monumental brasses

---

[1] Wavel, i. 93.

that originally decorated the pavement of the inner chapel previous to its alteration at the above-mentioned period. Of these, the most remarkable and interesting, seem to be the following.

At the foot of the stairs, on the right side of the entrance to the inner chapel, is a large stone with an effigy, and the following inscription in brass, of which, from its situation, a part only can now be read :

Hic tegor, hic post fata Whitus propona jacere,
  Scriptor Johannes Carminis ipse mei.
Sin alibi sors est putrescere, qui meus esset
  Tunc patior tumulus fiat ut alterius.

Ne sine honore tenax sine nomine linqueret heres
  Id timui, exemplis turbor et inde novis.
Ingrati Heredes ! phas nil sperare sepulto
  Ore tenus, putei Spes in Amicitia.

Nec mihi fama tamen de marmore quæritur
  Sed spes magna piis ponitur in precibus.
Hoc custode avet hic, hoc preceptore avet ille.
  Hocq; puer puero (dixerit alter) eram.

Parce deus Socio, custodi parce magistro,
  Hic avet, ille avet hoc, hoc etiam alter avet.
Septem annos docui, que lux postrema docendo
  Stata pre essendi munere prima fuit.

Mutavit mihi non minuit fortuna Labores,
  Curaq; non modicis rebus ad aucta mihi.
Nunc subeat lector quid sancta est atq; salubris
  Res pro defuncto fratre rogare deum.

Southward of this, upon an adjoining stone, is a brass, with the following inscription, which, like most of the other epitaphs inserted, is in Old English characters:

Epitaphium JOHIS LEFFE, in jure Civili Doctoris.
Nominis hic quid habet (Lector) si forte requiras,
A folii ductu nomine nomen habet.
Wintoniæ studuit simul Oxoniæ, ut tulit ætas,
Doctore hæc vidit, disciplum illa habuit.
Sede in utraq; fuit veræ pietatis amator,
Se de alia pretium nunc pietatis habet.
Judicium si forte Deus suspenderit, ut sit
Judex propitius, Lector, habeto preces.
Obijt anno ætatis suæ 66,
An. Dni. 1557, Augusti 19.

Before us, at the south end of the recess, is the elegantly-designed monument of the Rev. Humphrey May, a Fellow of the College, who died in 1657, with the following inscriptions, upon tablets, against the sides of a raised pedestal supporting a large marble urn :

In front,
M.
HUMPH. MAY,
Hujus Coll. Socii, quia rarum virtutis
Exemplar posterorum interest non extingui
hæc urna. D.

On the east side:
H. M. Natus Rawmeriæ in agro
Sussex. Cal. Apr. An. Sal.
cɔiɔcxiii.

On the west side:
H. M. Denatus Wintoniæ in Coll.
B. Ma. prid. Cal. Sep. An. Sal.
cɔiɔclvii.

Against the stairs, on the north side of the chapel, are two effigies in brass; below one of which is the following inscription to the memory of John Morys, the first Warden upon the foundation :

Hic jacet Magister JOHES MORYS primus

Custos istius Collii qui obijt die undecim millia

Virginum, anno Dni millessimo ccccxiii, et anno

Regni Regis Henrici quinto primo, litera dominical

A. cujus anime propicietur Deus.

There are also a variety of other inscriptions and monumental tablets against the walls of this chapel; and round the north and west sides of it are ranged the ancient stalls of the inner chapel, but without any part of the rich pinnacled canopies which in their original situation most probably adorned them; having, as in the cathedral, the small shelving seat, called the Miserere, the various designs beneath which are highly curious, as well from the beauty of the carving as the ludicrous figures which some of them present.

Leaving the Ante Chapel, we proceed by the porch into the Cloisters, at their north-west extremity. This solemn and striking memorial of past times, forms a square of 132 feet, and is ornamented with bold Gothic arches having quatrefoiled mullions, and terminated by a circular roof. The cloisters, with the adjoining chapel, having been for more than four centuries the usual burial-place of the society, present us with a number of monumental inscriptions, some of which, as being more particularly interesting, we shall insert.

Immediately at the entrance is a small brass, set in the wall, with the following inscription to the memory of Mr. John Dolber, a Fellow of the College in 1560.

Epi. mi. JO. DOL. Socii defunt.
3 Aprilis, 1560.
C austri pro foribus Dolbern cerne sepultu
Umbraru assessor janitor ille loci est.
Non malus ; ille fuit qui verba novissima dixit
O bone Christe precor te miserere mei.
Sanctorum assessor vel cœli janitor ut sit
Fune pias Christo lector amice preces.

A few paces beyond this, on the same side, is a second brass, with the following :

EDMUNDE HODSON, Clerk, and Fellow of
this College, died the vii[th] of August, 1580.
Who so thow arte, with loving harte,
Stonde, read and think on me,
For as I was, so nowe thow arte,
And as I am so shalt thow be.

Continuing along the west cloister, we perceive against the wall, the following inscription upon brass :

Epit. WILL. ADKINS, in Artibus Magistri et Socii
istius Collegii.
Nolle tun nihil est ad magni velle tonatis,
Juvitusq; licet nunc Gulielme jaces.
Ingenio tam lætus eras quam corpore obesus,
Commodus, et multa, non sine teste, fide.
Nunc te Xps habet, habeasq; oxpe precamur
Nec tibi qui moritur decinat esse tuus.
Obijt XVIII. die Decembris. An. M.D.LXI. cujus aie
Deus propicietur. Amen.

Opposite the third arch of this cloister is a beautiful monumental tablet of white marble, lately erected, bearing the following :

M. S.
Integerrimi et amicissimi viri
A Joannes Oglander, Baronetto,
Oriundi
Rev[d.] HENRICI OGLANDER, S. T. P.

Qui Ingenuo Gratique Præditus Animo
Per hoc Marmor voluit Prossteri
Se Filurimum Debuisse
Gulielmo de Wykeham,
Et Duobus Collegiis ab eodem institutis
Quorum serie continuata.
Obijt
Die Mensis Martis Decimi Sexto,
Anno {Domini M.DCCCXIV.
{Ætatis suæ LXX.

Beyond this we observe, upon a brass, the following inscription :

THO. DAVISON, obiit 20 Julii, 1586.
Hic nunc denique Davisone putres,
Triginta socius perennis annos,
Vivens ipse tibi nimis severus,
Expirans alijs satis profusos.

From hence we proceed to the east end of the south cloister, before we meet with any object particularly deserving of notice. At this spot the superb mural monument of the Rev. Charles Scott attracts our attention, being composed of a rich variety of beautiful marbles, in front of which a tablet bears the following epitaph :

CAROLUS SCOTT, A. M.
Hujusce Collegii Socius,
Et Paræciæ de Compton Rector,
Obijt 13º die Oct. 1762.
Ferè nonagenarius,
Morum integerrimus,
Amicitiarum egregiè tenax,
Multiplici scientia instructus,
Theologiæ et matheseôs præter alias,
Summis in ecclesiâ dignitatibus haud impar,
Literato in hoc otio,
Bene latere maluit

Quippe inter Wiccamicos ascribi
Honestissimum duxit :
Utrique Collegio,
Sane huic amplissima,
Pii gratique cordis legavit
Monumenta.
Nil prius in animo fuit votusque,
Quam ut indies fiant auctiora
Hæc literarum hospitia ;
Ut artes et scientiæ,
Pura fides et morum sanctitas
His, tanquam suis sedibus
Faustissimè perfruantur.
M. S.
CAROLI SCOTT,
Hoc marmor voluit,
ANNA FLETCHER,
Gratitudinis ergo,

Upon the base of this monument, a group of Children or Genii are represented weeping over various emblems of the sciences, and pointing to an oval tablet bearing the profile of the deceased; and the whole design, together, forms the most finished modern ornament of the Cloisters.

Our next object is a brass in the East Cloister, with the following inscription :

GULIELMUS TURNER,
Hujus Coll. Clericus, obijt 14 die
Martii An. Dni. 1644.
Olim cantica (musicæ peritus)
Dulci voce dedisti, et arte multa ;
At nunc longe anima pelis fruente
Edis dulcius hæc peritusq;

Advancing northwards, we find, near a modern door-way, the following inscription upon a brass in the wall:

Epita. Mri. RO. WATTO, Socii hujus Collegii,
Defunct 13 Jan. 1596.
Postquam transegi centum vel circiter annos,
Longa mihi sed non curva senecta fuit.
Languor inexhaustos quassans paralyticus artus
Huic animam cælo, tradidit ossa solo.

And beyond this, is a similar memorial for Mr. Thomas Lark, a Fellow of the College, viz.

Epitaphium Magistri THOMÆ LARK, nuper
Socii istius Coll. ob. 16 Maij, 1582.
Qui præmor hoc tumulo dicor prænomine Thomas,
Cognomen fecit dulcis alauda mihi.
Bis septem menses, ter septem præsbyter annos,
Hic colui, cujus nunc fruor, ore deum.

In the North Cloister we observe, among others, the sepulchral brass of Mr. John Clerke, a Fellow of the College, with the following:

Epita. JO. CLERKE,
Clausus Johannes jacet hoc sub marmore Clerkus,
Qui fuit hic quondam presbyter et socius,
In terra roseos solitus stillare liquores,
In cælo vivis nunc quoq; gaudet aquis.
Obit x die mensis Junii, 1571.

In traversing the Cloisters, we meet with a number of mural monuments of various degrees of beauty in point of design and execution; but the one which more particularly attracted our attention, was a memorial, erected near the north end of the East Cloister, for a Reverend Dr. Ballard, consisting merely of a plain pyramid of black marble, with a tablet at the base, bearing an inscription, and supporting a funereal urn. There was nothing perhaps in this to justify our expression of the idea, but it struck us that the unaffected simplicity of this design formed the *most expressive* memorial, and conveyed more forcibly to the imagination the object it was designed to commemorate, than all the more splendid and costly efforts of the statuary art with which our cathedrals and churches are incumbered, and which seem, by a superabundance of allegorical design and richness of decoration, to have reduced the pious tribute of affectionate grief *to* a mere vehicle for perpetuating the name of the Artist.

The Library of the College is situated in the centre of the area of the Cloisters, and was originally erected and endowed as a chantry by John Fromond, a liberal benefactor to both of Wykeham's Colleges, in 1430, about thirty-seven years after the erection of the College itself.[1] At the period of the Reformation the chaplain was removed, and the building remained unappropriated until 1629, about which time it was converted into a Library, by the liberality of Dr. Pinke, Warden of New College. The exterior appearance of this edifice is nearly similar to that of Wykeham's erection; and the curving of the arches, and tracery of the ceiling within, are formed upon the same general design as the corresponding works of that Prelate in the cathedral. The area of this room is thirty-six feet by eighteen ; it is well furnished with books, among which are some valuable works of the earlier ages, as also some miscellaneous curiosities. The east window is richly ornamented with stained glass; and the whole presents an elegant and highly-finished appearance.

Returning through the chapel-porch into the second court of the College, we ascend, by a flight of stairs at the south-west corner, into the Refectory or Dining Hall. This room, which is sixty-three feet in length by thirty broad, is exceedingly lofty, finishing in a rich open roof, of which the timbers are curiously carved and arranged. Along the sides are fixed tables and benches for the scholars; and at the upper end of the room is a raised floor for the table of the Warden and principal

---

[1] Milner, ii. 143. Wavel, i. 128.

officers of the foundation. At its opposite extremity, separated by a screen, is the buttery-hatch, &c. and in the centre a large hearth or fire-place, that part of the roof immediately over it being higher than the rest, with apertures at the sides to discharge the smoke. The whole appearance of this room is exceedingly grand and finished, and, after a lapse of ages, preserves its original features in a very striking degree.

Descending the Hall-stairs, we enter on the right hand, a narrow passage conducting us into a fourth court, of which the magnificent edifice built for the School-room, forms the south side, and the back of the cloisters and the hall, the north and east. The School-room, which is modern compared with the rest of the College, was built by a subscription among the Wiccamists, in 1687, and appears to have then cost 2592*l*. 18*s*. 3*d*. Over the entrance on the north side, is a noble statue of Wykeham, presented to the Society, by the father of Cibber, the Laureat, in 1692, with the following inscription along the base:

M. S.

GULIELMI DE WYKEHAM,

Episcopi Wintoniensis,

Collegii hujus Fundatoris,

Statuam hanc e metallo conflandam

Atque heic sumptu suo ponendam curavit,

Ex conjuge affinis suâ,

CAIUS GABRIEL CIBBERUS,

Statuarius Regius.

MDCLXXXXII

Entering the School-room, which is, perhaps, the largest, if not the handsomest, in the kingdom, being 90 feet long, by 36 broad, and of a proportionate height, with a rich and elegant ceiling; we perceive at the east end, the following tablet of the laws to be observed by the Students :

TABULA LEGUM PÆDAGOGICARUM.

IN TEMPLO.—Deus colitor. Preces cum pio animi affectu peraguntor. Oculi ne vagantor. Silentium esto. Nihil profanum legitor.

IN SCHOLA.—Diligentiâ quisque utitor. Submissè loquitor secum. Clarè ad Præceptorum. Nemini molestus esto. Orthographicè scribito. Arma Scholastica in promptu semper habeto.

IN AULA.—Qui mensas consecrat clarè pronunciato. Cæteri respondento. Recti interim omnes stanto. Recitationes intelligentèr et aptè distinguuntor. Ad mensas sedentibus omnia decora sunto.

IN ATRIO.—Ne quis fenestras saxis pilisve petito. Ædificium neve inscribendo neve insculpendo deformato. Neve operto Capite neve sine socio coram Magistris incedito.

IN CUBICULIS.—Munda omnia sunto. Vespere studetor. Noctu quies esto.

IN OPPIDO AD MONTEM.—Sociati omnes incedunto. Modestiam præ se ferunto. Magistris ac obviis honestioribus Capita aperiuntor. Vultus, gestus, incessus componuntor. Intra terminos apud Montem præscriptos quisque se contineto.

IN OMNI LOCO ET TEMPORE.—Qui Plebeius est, Præfectis obtemperato. Qui Præfectus est, ligitimè imperato. Is ordo vitio careto : Cæteris specimen esto. Uterque a pravis omnibus verbisq; factisq; abstineto.

Hæc, aut his similia, qui contra faxit, si quando deferantur, Judicium damus.

Feriis exactis Nemo domi impunè moratur. Extrà Collegium absque veniâ exeuntes tertiâ vice expellimus.

At the opposite extremity of the room, upon another tablet, are the following devices and inscriptions :

AUT DISCE.	A Mitre and Crosier.	The expected reward of learning.
AUT DISCEDE.	{ An Ink-horn, a Case of Mathematical Instruments, & a Sword. }	The emblems of those who depart and choose a Civil or Military life.
MANET SORS TERTIA CÆDI.	{ A Scourge. }	The lot of those who will qualify themselves for neither.

The benches, which stand in groups of nine or ten in a frame, are fixed in parallel lines down each side of the room, about five feet from each other, and serve as well for seats as to support the moveable studies, which in the language of the School, are called *Scobs*, and of which each boy possesses one. These boxes are uniform in their size and construction, and afford, when the outer lid is raised, a sort of screen from the noise or interruption of the adjoining student; they contain also pens ink and paper, with such books as are requisite for the particular study of the person to whom it belongs.

Behind the School-room, is a spacious meadow allotted as the play-ground of the scholars, and on the west side of it, but in a separate meadow at a convenient distance, stands the Infirmary of the College, built during the reign of Charles the First, by Warden Harris, for the use of the students, in case of sickness.

Returning from the play-ground into the second Court, we are shewn, against the wall of a passage leading to the kitchen, a sort of monster, represented partly as a human being, and partly as a hog, a deer, and an ass; and which, by a stretch of ingenuity, is compared by some verses adjoining it, to the similitude of a Faithful Servant; and such it may be, yet we cannot help observing here, that the venerable, and we might say sacred, walls of the Foundation of Wykeham, are but little honoured by the preservation of a picture, better calculated to excite a shudder of disgust, than to convey any possible idea of humour or utility to those who waste their time in looking at it.

We will now say a few words, for the information of our readers, relative to the course of proceeding at the College Election, which occurs annually about the middle of July, the usual period of the visitation of the Warden and Fellows of New College, Oxford, to whom this foundation is subservient both in government and discipline.

Upon the arrival of the Visitors from New College, on the Tuesday in the election week, they are received at the middle gate by the scholars, one of whom welcomes them in a Latin oration. They then proceed to the Election Chamber over the gate, where, in obedience to their office as Visitors, they inquire into the government of the College, and hear any complaints that may be preferred. This formula being over, they act in the remaining business as electors, conjointly with the Warden, Sub-warden, and Head Master of Winchester College. The following morning the examinations commence, and last for two days; the scholars examined being usually the twenty-four seniors of the school, divided into three classes. These examinations being finished, the boys who are candidates for admission to the College present themselves, and are also examined. On the evening of the last day of these trials, the rolls are formed, and the elections commence. Of the candidates for New College, there are usually three descriptions, viz. 1st, Boys of the Founder's kin, two of whom, if properly qualified, are set at the head of the roll;—2d, Students of eighteen or nineteen, who are called Superannuates, and who leave the school directly after the election;—and, 3d, the remainder of the Senior Students who have been examined; any of whom, by distinguished merit and abilities, may obtain a place on the roll above the Superannuates. These affairs being concluded, the vacation commences; and the same evening the celebrated song of *Dulce Domum* is sung in the courts and school-room of the College, by the boys, accompanied by a full band; the whole producing an effect indescribably beautiful and interesting.

The words of this song are as follows :

Concinamus, O sodales !
Eja ! quid silemus !
Nobile canticum !
Dulce melos, domum !
Dulce domum, resonemus !

CHORUS.
Domum, domum, dulce domum !
Domum, domum, dulce domum !
Dulce, dulce, dulce domum !
Dulce domum, resonemus !

Appropinquat ecce ! felix
Hora gaudiorum :
Post grave tedium
Advenit omnium
Meta petita laborum.
Domum, &c.

Musa, libros mitte, fessa,
  Mitte pensa dura,
Mitte negotium
Jam datur otium,
  Me mea millito cura.
            Domum, &c.

Ridet annus, prata rident;
  Nosque rideamus.
Jam repetit domum
Daulius advena:
  Nosque domum repetamus.
            Domum, &c.

Heus! Rogere, fer caballos;
  Eja, nunc eamus.
Limen amabile
Matris et oscula,
  Suaviter et repetamus.
            Domum, &c.

Concinamus ad penates,
  Vox et audiatur;
Phospore! quid jubar,
Segnius emicans,
  Gaudia nostra moratur?
            Domum, &c.

Contiguous to the College, on the west side, is a spacious quadrangular building, forming the lodgings, &c. of the boys not upon the foundation, of whom there are generally upwards of one hundred under the immediate care of the Head Master. There is also a spacious hall, fifty feet in length and thirty in breadth, in which the Commoners dine; and adjacent to it an extensive cloister, for their accommodation.

From this survey of the College, we now proceed a short distance towards the east, which brings us opposite the entrance of the Episcopal Palace of the Bishops of Winchester. This, we shall however pass by, for the more important object presented by the Ruins of Wolvesey Castle, which adjoin it on the north-east.

This edifice, the once stately residence of our Bishops, was erected by Henry de Blois, in 1138, upon the scite of a palace built by Kinegils, the first Christian King of the West Saxons, about five centuries before that period, upon a scale of incredible grandeur and magnificence.[1] Its strength must also have been considerable; as we find, that during the war between Stephen and the Empress Matilda, which occurred shortly after its completion, De Blois, shutting himself up within it, was enabled to withstand a siege against the forces of the Empress, whose cause he had abandoned, and whose partizans were at length forced to retire from before

---

[1] Historical Account, 11.—May not the numerous fragments of columns built into the massy walls of this venerable ruin, be part of the identical palace erected by Kinegils, and afterwards given by his son Kenewalch to Agilbert, the successor of St. Birinus, shortly after the conversion of the West Saxon kingdom ? Surely the moralist and the antiquary are alike concerned in the inquiry ; for although the remains of 1200 years may appear insignificant, as matters of general antiquity, yet how infinitely more interesting than the collected treasures of Imperial Rome itself, would be even one solitary stone which we might trace to have been appropriated to a purpose connected with the very infancy of Christianity in these islands ! In the former we concern ourselves merely as matters of useful study and general historic knowledge ; in the contemplation of the latter, we are interested as men, as Christians, as countrymen ; treading upon the very same ground with those by whose hands the hoary pile was raised, over the mouldering relics of which the violence of accumulated ages has not been able to draw a veil.

it.[1] Upon the accession of Henry the Second, this, as well as all the other castles of our Bishop, were dismantled; and it was still further weakened by the Barons, during the turbulent reign of Henry the Third. From the latter period we therefore do not find Wolvesey mentioned as a place of any strength, although it continued to be the ordinary residence of the Bishops of Winchester, and as such subsisted in splendour during a course of five centuries, when, upon the surrender of this city to Cromwell, in 1646, it was totally demolished, and reduced to a heap of uninhabitable ruins.

The remains before us are conjectured to have belonged to the Keep, and seem to have extended about 250 feet east and west, and 160 north and south.[2] The north and east sides, which form the principal part of the ruin, are built of large flints faced with a thick coating of hard mortar, giving the whole an appearance of free-stone. Two projecting towers on the east side preserve exteriorly much of their original appearance; the evident remains of a staircase, communicating with that at the south-east end, still exist; and a small watch-room at the summit, retains much of its original condition. From the level of this apartment, a shaft, of about four feet wide by eight feet long, runs parallel with the whole depth of the tower, having on each side of it a clear facing of hewn stone. There is no visible communication by this shaft (so far as

---

[1] Historical Account, 29.   [2] Milner, ii. 146.

it was cleared from the rubbish with which it was choaked) with any place below; yet, unless such is the case, its object in this situation is not easily to be accounted for, and unfortunately permission could not be obtained to prosecute the inquiry. On the north side of the ruin, a low gateway still remains, the pointed arch of which is in excellent preservation,[1] as are some of the rich mouldings and circular arches of the windows, which we observe at a considerable height on the south and north-east sides of the ruin.

Turning from the contemplation of these magnificent remains, we observe, to the south, the Episcopal Chapel of Wolvesey, which is comparatively of modern date; and, except for the train of ideas associated with its situation, is not sufficiently interesting to excite further notice.

Adjoining the chapel, stood the noble building, erected in 1684, as an episcopal residence, by Bishop Morley,[2] who did not however live to witness the completion of his munificent design. It was therefore, after some delay, finished by Bishop Trelawny, who succeeded to the episcopal throne of Winchester in 1706, and, when complete, formed one of the most beautiful modern edifices within the city. Unfortunately for Winchester, after the decease of the latter Prelate, in 1721, it became neglected, and thenceforward was suffered to continue in a rapid progress towards an early and at last an

---

[1] See Vignette, on the Title-page   [2] Historical Account, 71.

irretrievable decay. Accordingly, some few years since, the greatest part of the palace was taken down, and the present structure, which formed the west wing of the original design, was adapted to the necessary purposes of the whole. This itself is a plain and neat building; but the grounds and offices belonging to it, on the south-west side, still remain unappropriated and in a state of neglect.

Returning from hence into the street, we pass the north-east end of the garden belonging to the Warden of Winchester College, near the southern extremity of which is a meadow that formed the scite of the College of St. Elizabeth, of Hungary, founded, as we have before mentioned,[1] by Bishop Pontissara, in 1301, for a Warden, six Priests, three Deacons and Subdeacons, and a certain number of Students. This establishment, after subsisting little more than two centuries, was suppressed at the Reformation, at which time it appears to have been valued at 112*l.* 17*s.* 4*d.* per annum. In the scramble for religious property, so universal at the period in question, it seems to have fallen into the hands of Sir Thomas Wriothesley, afterwards created Earl of Southampton, from whom it was purchased by Dr. John White, Warden of St. Mary's College, for 360*l.*; the situation it occupied being convenient for the use of Wickham's College; but so invete- rate appears to have been the feeling of the times against even the mere shadow of a foundation de-

---

[1] Historical Account, p. 40.

voted to religion and literature, that in this, as in many other instances, one of the conditions of sale was, that its walls should be levelled with the ground by a stipulated time. In consequence, the various buildings of which this College consisted, were, with its church, destroyed to their foundations. In a meadow adjoining St. Elizabeth's College, on the east side, there appears also to have been an ancient chapel dedicated to St. Stephen; but this establishment, like many others with which Winchester was once enriched, retains no other vestige of its existence than a name.

Continuing our progress over the Wharf-bridge, we have a pleasant walk to St. Catherine's Hill, about half a mile from the City, near the summit of which, the bold entrenchments of a Roman camp are still visible. There seems formerly to have been a small chapel upon this Hill, dedicated to St. Catherine; but we find that it was suppressed, and its endowment appropriated by Cardinal Wolsey to the use of his new colleges at Ipswich and Oxford, during the short time he held the Bishopric of Winchester.

From this Hill, in summer the daily resort of the Collegians, we have an extensive prospect of the surrounding country, with all its beautiful variations of hill and dale, enriched with the luxurious windings of the river Itchen; below us on our right hand is the Cathedral, rising in massive grandeur over the surrounding buildings of the city, crowned at its western extremity by the intended residence of

Monarchs; while immediately before us in the valley,
the interesting towers of St. Cross raise their venerable heads amidst the sheltering foliage of the adjoining meadows; nor can we imagine a finer contrast
to the calm ideas, associated with the contemplation of such a scene, than that afforded by a group
of trees on the opposite hill, which mark the spot
from whence a fortunate Rebel succeeded in throwing consternation and dismay into our ancient and
loyal city, and which still preserves the memory of
its disgrace, by the designation of " Oliver's Battery."

1. The County Hospital.—2. Scite of St. Mary Kalendar.—3. The Market-House.—4. St. Maurice's Church.—5. The City Bridewell.—6. The Passage to the Central Schools.—7. The Schools.—8. The Silk Mills.—9. St. John's House.—10. East Gate House.—11. St. Peter's Cheesehill.—12. The Weirs.

The Third Walk.

WE shall commence our Third Walk eastward from the Cross, in the High-street. Immediately before us, on the right hand, is the Piazza, or Pent-house as it is more generally called, the effect of successive encroachments upon the High-street, and of which, its only good quality is, that it may be used as a dry walk for the inhabitants in wet weather. Proceeding a few paces along this Piazza, we cross over to Parchment-street, in which formerly stood the churches of St. Martin and St. Lawrence, of neither of which is there now any vestige. Near the centre

2 A

of this street stands the noble and commodious Hospital for the county of Hants, of which we have before spoken as established in 1736.[1] This institution is supported by voluntary subscriptions and benefactions, and is under the superintendance of a Committee chosen from among its patrons, aided by the professional talents of the most eminent medical characters in Winchester, who regularly attend it in rotation. There is also a resident apothecary, &c. and its domestic economy is under the immediate controul of visitors elected by the Committee.

Returning from the County Hospital into the High-street, we pass the two Meeting-houses of Dissenters of separate denominations, one of which has been but recently opened. Nearly opposite the centre of the Piazza, we traverse the scite of the parish church of St. Mary Kalendar, which appears formerly to have been a principal ornament of the High-street. A little beyond the Pent-house, on the right hand, is a commodious Market-house, erected in 1772, previous to which time the Cross and Piazza we have just passed formed the scene of traffic between the inhabitants and market people. Our next object of attention is the ancient parish church of St. Maurice, originally a Priory dedicated to St. Peter, which after flourishing for several centuries, was dissolved by Henry the Eighth, in 1539.[2] The church, at present, consists of two aisles, one on

---

[1] Historical Account, 77.   [2] Wavel, i. 191.

the north side having been taken down shortly after the above event. The entrance is by a passage at the west end, in which we observe a specimen of the Saxon arch in good preservation ; but the interior of the church has not any feature peculiar to itself, or differing from the usual ornaments of a parish church. Above the altar, which is neat, is the large east window of the north aisle, retaining but few traces of its ancient beauty and appearance; and upon a pier of the adjoining window on the north side, a brass, set in the wall, bears the following inscription :

FRIDESWIDE, first wife to CHARLES NEWBOULTE, Citizen, and twice Maior of this Cittie of Winchester, was by her second Husbande, George Johnson, Minister of God's Worde and one of the Masters of the Colledge, layed in the Grave and covered with the same stone of her former Husbande; by whose syde lyeth their daughter Dulcabella Johnson ; shee lived right christianly with the first XIIII. and with the later XXI yeares, being of the age of LIII. Shee chearefully embraced a bitter death in assurance of a better resurrection,
July XXVII. Ano Do.
MDCXXVI.

And in regarde of Humane Frailty might say
Betwixt twooe Stayes at length I fell to the Ground,
From me the Lay—I from the Churchman fell ;
Whose shall I be at the last Trumpet's sound ?
Nor Church nor Layman's, for in Heaven dwell
Nor Wife nor Husband ; but all triumph there,
All beare Palm branches, and all Crownes doe weare.

Her vertues and her Husbands love contende,
With this harde brasse, which shall have the last end.

Passing a flat stone with a brass bearing the following interesting memorial of four infants, who seem to have been the only children of a Mr. John Bond, and are interred at the east end of the north aisle :

M. S.

In præ immaturam mortem IIII infantulorum

Intra tres Annos et Natorem et heu !

rursus.

Denatorum Epitaphium.

Quatuor Infantes urnâ conduntur in ista,

Extinctus vita et limine quisq; suæ

Jana dies bis quinque videns macro bia dici

Præ reliquis poterat, tempora si muneres

Anna dies Quatuor ; tantum tres Anna secunda,

Vixit Joannes vagiit, et moritur.

Nempe igitur possent, quam vere dicere ut hora

Vita fugax ! oritur demoriturq; cito.

Io. BOND. Pater. M. P. A°. D^ni· cɔɔɔcxɪɪ.

we reach at the south-east end of the church, a large mural monument, enriched with shields of arms, aud bearing upon a tablet of free stone, supported by pillars, the following curious. epitaph :

Post Tenebras Spero Lucem.

Behold here lyeth the corps of him, that was an ancient wight,
Whoe lyved fower score yeres and nyne, John Mychelborne he hight;
This man, when seabenth day was come, of latest moneth sabe one,
Departed from that lyngeringe lyf, which here he had of lone.
It was the latest day of lyf, whiche he did here retepne,
It was the first oure noble Quene, began her eightene raigne ;
A man of good and honest fame, and eke of gentle blod;
Not void of skyll, and counsell sage, to do his country good ;
Of Sussex soile both borne and bred, beloved of eche man soe
That uone of him can speke but well, no not his mortal foe
So that althow his corpes full colde, in earth belowe doeth lye
Heat God no doubt hathe plast his sowle in Heaven that is soe high.

No. 7. An Dni 1575.

If the pleasing and unaffected simplicity of the above is not amusing, the following may, perhaps, be so, but it must be for a very opposite reason :

To the memory of
WILLIAM WIDMORE.
He was (which is most rare)
A friend without guile,
An Apothecary without ostentation.
His extensive charities in his profession
Entitle him to be called,
The Physician of the Poor.
Let other inscriptions
Boast honours, pedigree and riches,
Here lies an honest Englishman,
Who died the 19th day of June,
1756,
Aged 63.

Along the south side of the church, are a number of inscriptions on brass, which do not appear sufficiently interesting to repeat ; and of the various modern tablets, &c. with which the church is plentifully furnished, there are none worth describing, if we except that, bearing the last-mentioned epitaph, and which consists of a pyramid of black and white marble, charged at the summit with a coat of arms. This memorial, undoubtedly the most elegant of any in the church, is of considerable size, but is buried among pews in the most obscure situation of the whole fabric.

At the western extremity of the north aisle, we ascend a few steps into a low narrow room over the porch, called the Vestry, said to have been originally used as a Confessional ; but the only vestige of Popery now visible about it, is a small image of St. Michael, removed to its present station, from the body of the church, at the period of the Reformation.

Some distance further, on the same side of the street, we pass the City Bridewell, erected in 1800. Immediately in front of this prison, is the scite of the collegiate church of the Holy Trinity, founded by some merchants of Winchester in the 11th century, as a general charnel-house for the city. A short distance along the adjoining street, which here branches off towards the south, stood the Royal Abbey of Benedictine Nuns, dedicated to St. Mary, founded by Alswytha, Queen of Alfred the Great, in 900. Of this foundation, whose name is now almost its only memorial, we have already spoken in our Historical Account.[1] It appears to have flourished during upwards of six centuries, in a style of eminent grandeur and magnificence, but with others of a similar nature terminated its being in the reign of our 8th Henry, and at this period has scarcely a vestige remaining of its existence.

From the end of this street, next the City Bridewell, the High-street was formerly contracted by a range of old buildings which continued in a direct line to the city gate. Upon the demolition of the latter, in 1777, or shortly after, these were removed, and the area laid open to the street, which is thereby rendered extremely spacious and convenient.

---

[1] Historical Account, 13.

Proceeding on our way towards the Bridge, a long narrow passage, on the right hand of the High-street, conducts us to the spacious building erected for the Central Schools of Winchester, which are conducted upon the principles of the Rev. Dr. Bell, and in which at present 140 boys and 190 girls receive a gratuitous and serviceable education. These establishments were formed in 1812, under the immediate patronage of the Bishop of Winchester,[1] and are supported by voluntary subscriptions and donations from the inhabitants of the city and neighbourhood. The management of these schools is under the superintendance of a committee of Ladies and Gentlemen, chosen from the subscribers, by whom visitors are appointed to inspect and examine into the conduct and progress of the whole.

On the opposite side of this passage, are the extensive Silk Mills, established in Winchester some years since, from which a considerable number of the lower classes derive a comfortable maintenance.

Returning by the passage into the High-street, which we shall now cross to the north side, we shortly reach St. John's House, the public banqueting-house and assembly-room of Winchester. This was originally founded as an hospital, and dedicated to St. John the Baptist, in 934, by St. Brinstan, a Bishop of Winchester. The edifice having been destroyed, during the subsequent ravages of the Danes in our city, it was, in 1304, re-erected and

---

[1] See Reports of the Hampshire Society for the Education of the Infant Poor.

endowed by John Le Devenish, a magistrate of Winchester, for a charity of the most benevolent and useful description.[1]   But this, among crowds of less useful charities, was destroyed by the Act of 38 Henry the Eighth, by which, in conjunction with the rapacity of the commissioners, it was stripped of its possessions, and even of the miserable furniture provided for the use of the poor objects who were to have been relieved by it. We find, however, that after much difficulty the Corporation succeeded in procuring the restoration of the bare walls for a public hall and magazine. In the subsequent reign of Mary, it was again endowed as a charity, but upon a far more limited scale than before, by Richard Lambe, Esq. who erected suitable habitations behind the main edifice, for six poor widows of citizens, and appropriated sufficient funds for their support.

The chief apartment of this structure is, in length, 62 feet by 38, and 28 feet high, and is fitted up in a stile of elegant neatness, from a benefaction of a Colonel Brydges, in 1749, the portrait of whom is suspended against the south side of the room. Its chief ornament is, however, the beautiful whole-length picture of Charles the Second, given by that Monarch to our Corporation when he accepted the freedom of the city, in 1682. The other portraits which adorn this truly noble chamber, are those of William Paulet (Earl of Wiltshire), created Marquis of Winchester by Edward the Sixth, and of

---

[1] Historical Account, 41.

Paulet St. John, Esq. Below the last-mentioned portrait is the entrance to the coffee-room, &c. much inferior in size and appearance to the principal chamber; but, like it, decorated with several portraits, among which are those of Bishop Morley, and Richard Lambe, Esq. the last founder of the charity. A sort of Chronological Table is also suspended against the west end, containing a list of the most important events relating to the history of the city; some of which, as there stated, are, if not total fictions, at least extremely doubtful and uncertain.

Descending from these apartments, we turn, on the right hand, into a little court behind the main building, in which are the Alms-Houses of the widows, supported upon Lambe's foundation, as before stated. Against the wall of a cloister, on the south side of the court, is an old sculpture representing the head of John the Baptist upon a charger, which is supposed to be of great antiquity, and till lately was suffered to occupy a situation in the dusthole, where it might as well have remained, as have been placed where it is, hidden amongst a parcel of lumber, and disfigured with cobwebs and whitewash.

Leaving St. John's House, and its ancient chapel on the east side, now used as a free-school, the last edifice of any note within the limits of the city, is Eastgate House, belonging to the Mildmay family, the grounds of which formed the scite of the church and convent of the Dominicans, or Black Friars, founded by Peter Des Roches, or De Rupibus, Bishop of Winchester, in 1230, and of which apparently not a vestige now remains.

From hence, proceeding eastward, we cross a neat stone Bridge of a single arch, erected in 1814, over the river Itchen, which terminates the boundary of the city, and enter the Soke or Borough of Winchester, at one time more populous and extensive than the whole city itself.   At the end of the street from the bridge, a footway leads to the summit of St. Giles's Hill, which in this part overhangs the city in a stile of abrupt grandeur.

Ascending the Hill, there is a fine view of the surrounding country, with the principal street of the city, in a direct line before us, open throughout its whole extent, and terminated at the west extremity by its ancient and only remaining gate.

Upon this Hill was formerly held the great Fair of St. Giles, first instituted, for a single day, by William the Conqueror, and granted to his cousin, Bishop Walkelyn, and his successors, Bishops of Winchester.   William Rufus extended its duration to three days, Henry the First to eight, Stephen to fourteen, and Henry the Second to sixteen; during which all the shops of the city were closed, and no business was allowed to be transacted within the distance of seven leagues in every direction.[1]   On the evening preceding the commencement of the fair, the Mayor of the city gave up the keys to an officer appointed for that purpose by the Bishop, who did

---

[1] Milner, ii. 211.

not resign them until the fair was ended. During a considerable period this mart continued to flourish, and was the constant resort of merchants from every part of the kingdom, and even from beyond the seas; but in the reign of Henry the Sixth it began to decline; and since that period, various causes co-operating with the decay of the city itself, have reduced it to its original limit of a single day.

Upon the extensive downs adjoining this Hill, in an eastern direction, the ruins of a Hospital, dedicated to St. Mary Magdalen, and supposed to have been erected and endowed by Bishop Toclyve, in the latter part of the twelfth century, stood till within these few years. This Hospital, like that of St. Cross, seems to have been founded chiefly for the support of aged and decayed persons; and after losing the chief part of its possessions at the period of the Reformation, received its final blow in the reign of Charles the Second, when its unfortunate inhabitants were obliged, by a royal mandate, to resign their dwelling, which was thereupon converted into a place of confinement for Dutch prisoners of war, and its former occupiers dispersed in various parts of the city.[1] After answering the purposes of Government in this manner for some considerable time, during which every species of wanton mischief seems to have been used to its injury, it was again delivered up to the use of its rightful inhabitants, but in such a state of ruin and

---

[1] Wavel, ii. 164, &c.

desolation that it was impossible for them to return to it. This fact appears to have been stated
in a petition to the King, representing the damage
which the society had sustained, and praying relief.
By the estimate which was made of the necessary
expence of rebuilding the hospital, it seems that the
sum of 650*l.* only was requisite; but to the eternal
shame of the Government, 100*l.* only were allowed![1]

After so disgraceful a return for the obedience
and sufferings of this unfortunate society, the structure was necessarily abandoned to its fate; and remaining in a desolate condition for a considerable
period, was at length, in 1788, taken down, and
almost every trace of its existence upon the spot,
has been subsequently destroyed.[2]

Returning towards the city from the Hill, by the
path we ascended, we reach, on the left hand, the
principal street of the Soke, called Cheesehill-street,
a few paces along which, on the west side, brings us
to the ancient church of St. Peter Chusull, which
we find mentioned in the Bishops' Register as early
as 1282; and there is little doubt but it existed at
a period considerably earlier. This edifice, which
now forms almost a regular square, consists of two
aisles; one on the north side having most likely been
demolished at the time, similar alterations were effected in the other churches of our city at the latter
end of the sixteenth century. The whole appearance of it on the inside is barely neat, and entirely

[1] Wavel, ii. 207.   [2] See the Vignette to this Walk for an Interior
View of this Chapel.

without decoration, except at the east end of the south aisle, where we observe some canopied nitches for images. The rich foliage of one on the north side of the window, corresponds much, in point of design and execution, with the beautiful workmanship of De Lucy, over the pedestals of the Saxon Monarchs in the transverse screen of the cathedral.

Upon the floor of the seat now used as a vestry, immediately under the above canopies, is a large flat stone with a brass, bearing the following short inscription:

𝔒rate pro aie 𝔐argarite 𝔘uedale.

The similarity of this name with that of Wykeham's patron, Nicholas Uvedale, to whom it is perhaps not improbable the person here interred might have been related, seems a sufficient reason for repeating the otherwise uninteresting memorial; for who is there living that has witnessed the incalculable benefits to posterity which have sprung from the benevolent genius of that truly great man, and does not revere the name of him who first drew the gem from its native obscurity, and by his patronage and munificence encouraged those splendid talents, by the exercise of which his *protegee* became an honour to his age, and a lasting benefactor to his country?

The whole east end of the church seems formerly to have been divided from the rest by a wooden screen, a part of which still remains; both the windows at this end also retain some traces of their original state, particularly that of the main aisle. The design of the whole appears to have been very simple.

There are no epitaphs or inscriptions in this church that appear worthy of repeating, except the one we have before given. Leaving it, therefore, by a door under the massive tower at the south-east end, we return over the City Bridge, at the foot of which, on the left hand, is a pleasant footway called the Wires, which at some distance branches off to the right, and conducts us into College-street, having in the course of our path the rapid and clear stream of the Itchen on our left hand, and the venerable ivy-crowned walls that formed the outer fortifications of Wolvesey Castle on our right.

1. The Bridge.—2. Old Barrack.—3. St. John's Church.—4. St. Martin's Church, Winnall.—5. Dane Gate, or Bourne Gate.—6. North Wall of the City.—7. Area of supposed combat between Colbrande the Dane, and Sir Guy of Warwick.—8. St. Peter's Chapel.—9. Benedictine Convent.

The Fourth Walk.

WE commence our next tour from the Soke Bridge, and passing on the left hand a dirty avenue called Water-lane, shortly reach St. John's-street, along which we shall direct our course towards Winnall.

About the centre of this street, on the east side, an old building of flint and square stones will probably attract our notice, to which its only claim is, that it was erected for and used as a Barrack previous to the appropriation of the King's House to that purpose. It is now used as a store-house.

A little beyond this, on the opposite side of the street, is the ancient church of St. John upon the Hill, which, from its style, appears to have been erected about the time of the Conqueror;[1] and although it has undoubtedly received considerable repairs, still retains the most evident marks of antiquity of any of the parish churches of Winchester.

Upon entering this church, it is impossible to avoid being struck with the unaffected neatness and simple grandeur pervading the whole edifice, which is divided by massive low pillars into three aisles of equal dimensions, having the whole of the east end parted off by a light screen of Gothic archwork. The whole of the windows preserve some remains of the rich glass with which they were formerly adorned, and by their style afford a plain demonstration that the church retains its original form and magnitude. The subject of the painting in the great east window, seems to have been the miracles of St. John, the patron of the church, whose portrait still remains in the centre compartment. While speaking of these paintings, we cannot avoid calling the attention to a small mutilated portrait preserved in the second compartment of the east window of the south aisle, which for beauty of finishing and liveliness of expression is, perhaps, not to be excelled. The area of the altar, exceedingly plain, is divided from the corresponding parts of the side aisles, by a continuation of the screen, so as to

---

[1] Wavel, ii. 212.

form, as it were, three separate chancels, in each of which we observe, on the right, the ancient Piscina, an evident proof of the existence of three distinct altars. At the east end of the north aisle is a very rich altar-tomb, bearing shields in compartments, charged alternately with the emblems of the Passion, and the letters 𝕿 𝕾. There appears to have been a label round the edge of the tomb, similar to that on those of Wykeham and Edyngton, in the cathedral; but it has been long torn away, and with it every apparent identity of the remains over which it was placed.

The lower part of the tower is open to the church at the west end of the south aisle, and is remarkably strong, being principally built of lime-stone cased with flint and other durable materials. It appears, from a date on the south side, to have been repaired about 1685, and on the same side is an excellent clock, presented by Charles the Second probably about the like period.

We leave this church almost with a feeling of reluctance, so well does its interesting simplicity accord with our ideas of an edifice devoted to the purposes of Christian worship. In place of a motley confusion of monumental sculpture and too often undeserved eulogy, the walls are chiefly adorned with texts of scripture illustrative of the purpose for which they were raised. In place of an ill-judged profusion of expensive ornament, useful only at best to draw the mind from the undisturbed contemplation of our religious duties, there is nothing in the circuit of this church on which the eye can gaze, or the mind can dwell, that will not convey with it a striking reference to those great objects on which, in such a place, our attention and our feelings should be alone employed.

Having quitted the enclosure of the church, we proceed, in a northward direction, to the junction of the roads at the end of St. John's-street, near which formerly stood a huge Cross, called Bubb's or Bubby's Cross,[1] and which from its elevated situation must have been conspicuous to most parts of the city. Passing this spot, we continue by the high ground towards Winnal, and in our progress have an uninterrupted view, over the meadows, of the north side of the city, with the suburb of Hyde, and all that now remains of its celebrated Abbey. Near the end of this lane, at its descent, we enter the little parish of Winnal, or Wynal, the church of which, dedicated to St. Martin, stands before us on the left hand, and is a small edifice of stone, plentifully sprinkled with brick-work. This church, which within is little better than a small barn, is of considerable antiquity, and is named in the Registers of Bishop Pontissara, about 1282; but, like the famous knife, it has been so often repaired in all its parts, that none of the original workmanship can be traced. The walls, which are green with damp, are not varied by a single object; and the communion table, and accompaniments, are in unison

---

[1] Milner, ii. 220.

with the rest of the structure. In addition to this unpleasant account, the burial-ground which surrounds the church is so very low and damp, that the graves on being opened generally fill with water; few persons are, therefore, interred here, the parishioners having, with some others, the privilege of burial in the cemetry upon St. Giles's Hill.

Inconsiderable and mean as this place now is, there seems reason to believe that it was once sufficiently important to give a name of honour to the illustrious personage whose effigy as a Crusader decorates a tomb at the east end of the cathedral, which we are assured originally bore the following inscription :

Hic jacet Willielmus Comes de Insula
Uana als Wyneall.[1]

Although it does not immediately follow, in the absence of every other proof, that this must have been the place alluded to in the above inscription; still, when we reflect on the once exalted rank of Winchester itself, and the consequent importance of its suburbs and vicinity, added to the fact that it is by no means improbable this place, lying immediately upon the river, might originally have been insulated, there does not perhaps appear any very striking objection to the claim of honour above stated in its favour.

From St. Martin's Church we return by a kind of street on the right hand in a south-west direction,

---

Gale, 32.

towards the city, which we now enter by the remains of an ancient postern called Dane Gate, or Bourne Gate. Passing through this, we have on our right hand, for a considerable distance, the remains of the north wall of the city, which in some places seems to retain its original height, and somewhat of its former appearance, and in others is intermixed with repairs of more recent date. At a short distance on the north side of this wall, viz. in the meadow called Denemarck, or Hyde Mead, we behold the spot immortalized as the scene of the famous combat between Sir Guy of Warwick and Colbrande the Danish giant, of the circumstances attending which we have before expressed our opinion.[1]

We now pass the ends of the three Brook-streets, which like the other parts of our city were once conspicuous for the churches and religious establishments with which they were occupied. In Middle-Brook-street the Poor-House for the united parishes of Winchester and its vicinity is situated, where the poor find a comfortable asylum. Quitting this, we shortly arrive at the northern extremity of St. Peter's-street, along which we shall shape our progress towards the High-street. About half way down, on the right hand, we reach the Catholic Chapel of St. Peter, erected in 1792, near the scite of an ancient church dedicated to St. Peter Marcellus. This chapel, which is fitted up and decorated in the usual stile of edifices devoted to the

---

[1] Historical Account, 14.

service of the Catholic religion, seems, however, by the splendour of its ornaments and the elegance of its design, to be greatly superior to the generality of chapels of the like nature. But leaving the minutiæ of its decorations to the abler descriptive pen of one more intimately connected with the subject, to whose elaborate and scientific work we beg to refer our more interested readers,[1] we shall content ourselves with merely adverting to those objects within its precincts more particularly connected with the general subject of our pages.

The first object in the neighbourhood of St. Peter's Chapel that should engage our attention, is the beautiful Saxon Doorway forming the principal entrance, which was removed, upon the demolition of the chapel of the Hospital of St. Mary Magdalen, where it formed the western entrance,[2] to its present situation. In reference to the probable erection of this porch in its original situation, by Bishop Toclyve, in the twelfth century,[3] the following inscription is cut upon a stone over the centre of the arch :

D.   O.   M.

Ædificat: MCLXXIV.

A. D.

Reædificat: MDCCXCII.

Immediately within this portal, in the wall of the avenue, are various fragments from the ruins of Hyde Abbey, consisting of capitals of columns, and bosses of groins, representing foliage and animals, curious for their design and valuable for their ex-

---

[1] Milner, ii. 240.   [2] Wavel, ii. 156.   [3] Milner, ii. 242.

cellence and antiquity.   Near them is a bust from the fortifications of the Castle; and upon the ground beneath a huge Druidical altar-stone,[1] weighing nearly two tons, brought hither (where it is alike a memorial and a contrast) from some other part of the city.

The Chapel, which is a light Gothic building 75 feet long and 35 in height to the summit of the pinnacles, stands immediately at the end of a short avenue; and within the porch, against the right-hand wall, we observe a marble tablet, originally erected by the Emigrant Clergy of France in their chapel at the King's House, at the time it was appropriated for their accommodation.   The inscription upon the tablet is as follows:

FAVENTE DEO OPT. MAX.

Diu sospes et incolumis,

In suorum decus ac delicias,

In exteriorum admirationem et perfugium,

Vivat

GEORGIUS III.

Mag. Britan. &c. Rex piisimus !

Æterno pacis beneficis gaudeat !

Jugi pietatis, scientiæ, et opum laude

Efflorescat,

Nobilissima Gens Britannica,

Quæ

Politicarum immemor querelarum,

Clerum Gallicanum

Innumeris calamitatibus oppressum,

Patriis sedibus expulsum,

Terris et alto jactatum,

Almæ parentis instar

---

[1] Milner, i. 10. ii. 243.

Hospitali gremio excepit benignissimè,
Fovit tenerrimè,
Protexit studiocissimè,
Voluntariâ cunctorum regni ordinum subscriptione
Aluit generossimè.
Sit etiam longùm felix,
Præstantissimus Senator Britannicus
JOHANNES WILMOT,
Publicæ munificentiæ
Unà cum selectissimis
Et integerrimis viris,
Dispensator prudentissimus!
Hæc ardentibus votis
A supremo rerum moderatore
Efflagitat Clerus Gallicanus
Per Universas
Britannici imperii plagas dispersus.
Hæc imprimis, anhelanti pectore,
Ad aras supplex provulta,
Impetrare studet indesinenter
Ejusdem cleri pars non exigua,
Regalibus istis in ædibus,
Insigni munere, collecta,
Quæ
Hoc leve gratissimi pignus animi
Ad perpetuam rei memoriam,
Exaratum voluit.
Anno reparatæ salutis M,DCC,XCIII.
Atque XXXIII Georgii III.
Altius hæc animis, quam marmore sculpta
Manebunt.

Returning into St. Peter's-street, we shortly pass,
on the opposite side of the way, an extensive building called the Convent, inhabited by English Nuns
of the order of St. Benedict. The females at present composing this establishment, amount in number to about thirty, and came from Brussels at the

period of the French Revolution. Here, in addition to their conventual duties, they conduct a ladies school upon an extensive scale and of the most respectable nature.

Lower down, on the opposite side of the street, is all that now remains of an edifice designed by Sir Christopher Wren for the residence of the Duchess of Portsmouth, the favourite mistress of Charles the Second, and built by him about the same time that he was raising the magnificent palace at the west end of the city, of which we have already spoken. Till lately, a bust of the celebrated beauty for whom the house was erected stood over the entrance; this was however removed at the time the house was reduced to its present size in 1815.

Beyond this, a few paces brings us into the High-street, where we shall terminate our **Fourth Walk.**

1. The Gaol.—2. The Theatre.—3. Scite of the Palace of Henry the Second.—4. Staple Gardens.—5 Scite of the North Gate.—6. Ruins of Hyde Abbey.—7. Church of St. Bartholomew.—8. The County Bridewell.—9. Hyde School.—10. Hermit's Tower.—11. The Obelisk.—12. The West Gate.

The Fifth Walk.

OUR Fifth Walk commences at the south end of Gaol-street, next the George Inn, from whence, a few paces brings us opposite a magnificent structure, erected in 1805, under the direction of Mr. G. Moneypenny, as a frontispiece to the County Gaol.[1] The building before us contains, therefore, merely the Keeper's house and offices, and the apartments of the debtors; the prison appropriated to the felons being a detached brick edifice immediately behind, built upon the plan of the philanthropic Howard,

[1] See the Vignette to the Fourth Walk.

whose regulations are adhered to in the government of it. The effect of the grand front, which is built of white brick, enriched with rusticated coins, &c. of Portland stone, in a stile of massive ornament, is, however, totally lost, from the contracted situation in which it is placed.

Immediately opposite the Gaol is a small building, erected about 1790, for a Theatre, and possesing all the requisite qualifications for a place of public amusement but two, namely, cleanliness and convenience. The performers, generally speaking, are of a respectable cast, and are occasionally assisted in their endeavours " to hold as 'twere the mirror up to nature," by one or other of the more celebrated votaries of Thespis from the metropolis.

Beyond the Theatre, a gentle curve near the end of the street, conducts us by a narrow lane towards the scite of a Palace erected by Henry the Second, respecting which little more remains on record than the fact of its having once existed. Upon the same spot, about two centuries afterwards, the merchants of Winchester built their extensive warehouses for wool, upon the establishment of the staple at this place in 1353.[1] This, however, being suddenly removed to Calais in 1363, the various buildings, for want of means to employ them, were suffered to fall into decay, and at this time, like the royal seat, upon the foundations of which they stood, not a single trace remains of their existence.

---

[1] Historical Account, 45.

A short distance from the end of the lane leading to Staple Gardens, the North Gate of the city was situated, built most probably in a similar stile of fortification with the West Gate, and defended on the outside by a wide and deep moat. Nearly adjacent to the gate, on the south side, the church of Allhallows was situated, and on the north side, or, as some say, upon it,[1] stood a similar edifice, dedicated to St. Mary.[2] Beyond this, a few paces brings us into Hyde-street, on the east side of which we shortly reach all that is now left of Hyde Abbey.

---

[1] Trussell's MSS. l. i. p. 26.

[2] It may appear singular that each of the fortified entrances to our city should have so closely adjoined edifices devoted to the peaceful exercise of divine worship; but it should be remembered that Winchester was ever a religious city, and at one time must have been no less celebrated for the number of churches with which it was enriched, than for its early importance and antiquity. In, or shortly previous to, the year 1282, forty-seven churches and chapels, besides those attached to the great monasteries of St. Swithun, St. Mary, and Hyde, were standing within the walls of the city, or in its immediate vicinity; we are not therefore surprised at reading that " passinger$_s$ cowld noe way enter intoe y^s cittie, ether through any of the gates, or the single posternes, but of necessitye, ether they must goe under a church, or so close unto a church, or some oratorye, that they might not touch, at ye entrance hereunto, any thing so soone as the walls of sutch places. The testimonyes whereof are at this tyme, (i. e. 1620,) by the ruwynes of the churches, and sutch places, as for instance, whosoever then came in at the Northgate, must come under the church of St. Marye, builte uppon yt gate, and close by the church of St. Allhollows, builte close within the wall, both of wch were burnt downe in ye tyme of king Stephen, att ye entrye of Henrye de Bloyes, the kyng's brother, thatt way: Yf they came through King's-gate then likewise under the church of St. Swythyn's, builte over that gate, and which is att y^s day used as a parish church; Yf through Westgate, then close to a chapple builte without ye walls, but adjoined to ye gate, parte whereof is their yet standing, or by the church of St. Peter's, Whitebread, builte on

Of the original foundation of the Newan Mynstre, or Abbey of St. Grimbald, on the north side of the cathedral, by Alfred the Great, in 890, and the subsequent removal of its monks to Hyde Meadows, in 1110, we have before spoken.[1] Scarcely had its fraternity got settled in their new and magnificent abode, than they appear to have fallen under the displeasure of Henry de Blois, Bishop of Winchester, whose behaviour to them was so oppressive that from forty members they were in a little time reduced to ten.[2] The Bishop's anger seems to have been excited by their opposition to his ambitious design of erecting the abbey into a bishopric, and then, by subjecting it and the see of Chichester to his jurisdiction, have advanced his diocese of Winchester to the archiepiscopal dignity. Independent of this,

---

the same side of the waye, but within the gate ; but that with the former peryshed in y[e] flames ; Yf they came through the East-gate, they came close to the walls of the church of the White-fryars, builte within the cittie, on the north side of the High-street, their, and ruwyned in y[e] tyme of the suppression of sutch places, intended for holy devotion, and then by the chapple of St· John's their yet standing, wch in these dayes is made useful for some pious purpose; Yf any came through the South-gate, then they must needes goe by the church of St. Mary Ode, built within the cittie, on the west side of Gould-street, some parte of the ruwynes whereoff be yet apparant their, but whether y[s] church peryshed in the flames with the other, or was battered downe as standing betwixt Maude the Queen besiedging, and Maude the Empresse, besiedged, is verye uncertayne, but aboute that time y[t] was ruwyned ; Nay, yf the entrance hadd been through Durngate postern, (though no ordenary way) yet itt must needes have beene close by the walls of the church of the Black-fryars, a moste curious piece of workmanshipp of full square black flint, as yet remayneth visible in the ruins thereoff."—Trussell's MSS. l. i. p. 26.

[1] Historical Account, 13, 24.   [2] Dugdale's Monasticon, i. 501.

there appears (notwithstanding the removal of the monks of St. Grimbald from the neighbourhood of St. Swithun's Priory) to have been a sort of latent jealousy between the members of the two foundations, which, as it had often burst into a flame while contiguous to each other, so it was not entirely eradicated by their separation.[1] The heavy consequences of De Blois' resentment were speedily followed by the ravages of civil war, which, in 1142, extending throughout the kingdom, our city became one of the earliest and most devoted of its victims; and in the course of its desolating fury, the Abbey of Hyde was burnt to the ground, and with it a great part of its treasures perished in the flames.[2]

The general effects of these various calamities had hardly subsided, before the monks found a munificent friend and patron in Henry the Second, during whose reign the Abbey was rebuilt with great magnificence, and shortly became, as well from the rank of its Abbot as from the great revenues belonging to it, one of the most distinguished monasteries in the kingdom.

---

[1] This jealousy may not perhaps be improperly attributed to the number and importance of the various relics which the monks of the Newan Mynstre possessed, and which enabled them to maintain a sort of rivalry with their more ancient neighbours in the only point upon which they could least bear competition. Thus, at the removal of the former to Hyde, they appear to have carried with them, among other illustrious remains, those of the great Alfred and his Queen Alswytha, as also those of King Edward the Elder, King Edmund, the Abbess St. Eadburgh (grand-daughter of Alfred), and St. Grimbald, the first Superior of the Newan Mynstre, and subsequently the Patron to whom it was dedicated; persons all eminent for their sanctity, and the veneration in which their shrines were held by the people.

[2] Historical Account, 30.

After continuing to maintain a pre-eminent rank among the religious establishments of England during several centuries, the æra of the Reformation arrived; and the general havoc that immediately followed fell heavy upon Hyde Abbey, reducing it in a very short period from the hospitable abode of charity and religious magnificence to a heap of solitary ruins.[1]

The Church, the hallowed scite of which is now occupied by the County Bridewell, appears, in its prosperity, to have been cruciform, and extended in length from east to west about 240 feet.[2] Of this edifice not a stone remains; and with regard to the extensive ruin, which till within even a few months past existed on the south-west side, it would perhaps at this time be deemed presumptuous to offer an opinion, either as to its general form or the purpose to which it might originally have been appropriated. Its situation certainly was that of the domestic offices of the monastery; and in an old building on the south side, an immense arched chimney and fire-place seemed to indicate the situation of the Abbot's kitchen. A large building lately used as a barn, adjoining the north gate of the monastery, which still remains,[3] was conjectured to have once

---

[1] Henry Lord Wriothesley, afterwards Earl of Southampton, to whom the buildings of Hyde Abbey were given, in the early part of Edward the Sixth, demolished the greatest part of them for the sake of the materials, which he found useful in erecting his magnificent seat at Stratton, in this county.   [2] Wavel, i. 14.   [3] See the Vignette to this Walk, for a View of the North Wall and Gateway of the Monastery.

formed a part of the Abbot's hall; and in various parts of the ruin, the richly-ornamented arches of windows, &c. remained in tolerable preservation. In a small garden on the south-east side, a beautiful Gothic arch of large dimensions has been nearly buried in the adjoining wall; this, probably, from its situation, might have formed the entrance to the gardens of the monastery; but like the extensive buildings of which the monastery consisted, these also have long been sacrificed to what is termed improvement. And now, as if any vestige of the existence of this venerable pile, associated as it necessarily is with the recollection of him, whose violated tomb will remain an invisible, and silent, but lasting record of the ingratitude of Winchester—as if a single trace of this was necessarily an object of reproach to the contrasted habits, and perverted feeling, which dictated the erection of a gaol over his grave, in the eighteenth century—even the few frail morsels that escaped the first desolators, have at length fallen victims to the caprice of their perhaps less bigoted but certainly not less destructive successors.

Was there no other record of the mutability and weakness of earthly grandeur at this moment existing in our once powerful city, the favoured residence of Kings, and for ages the capital of England, the Ruins of Hyde Abbey would alone be a lesson speaking volumes to us. The burial-place of the immortal Alfred being at this moment occupied by a receptacle for crime; the stately abode of mitred Abbots levelled with the dust, and mingled with the filth and rubbish of a cow yard!

Upon this subject, so *peculiarly interesting* to Winchester, as being connected with the *honoured* memory of a Prince who, to the splendid title of Deliverer united the more glorious one of Father of his Country, we trust the insertion of the following extract from the Archæologia will not be deemed impertinent:

" You will lament with me the failure of my researches, and feel some share of the same indignation, when I inform you that the ashes of the great Alfred, after having been scattered about by the hands of convicts, are now probably covered by a building erected for their confinement and punishment.   And when you are told that this occurred so lately as the year 1788, and that no one in the neighbourhood, led either by curiosity or veneration for his remains, attempted to discover or rescue them from this ignoble fate, your surprise will not, I think, be less than my own."

Plan of the Foundations of Hyde Abbey Church, taken 1787.

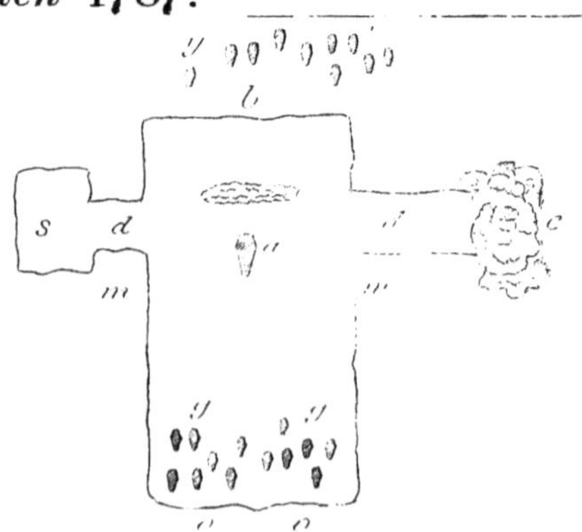

The foundations were laid in strong beaten clay, to the depth of four feet. The point *a* appeared to be nearly the centre of the clay, taken from north to south, of which there was about fourteen yards on each side, viz. from *a* to *m* and *m*. From *a* eastward to *b*, was supposed to be about twenty-four yards; and from thence the rubbish and foundations extended some yards further. About *d* and *d*, there were two paths of clay nearly six feet wide; one, ending to the north, in a spot in which the clay was laid in a squarish form as at *s*, and about which there were also ruins of foundations. This is conceived to have been the sacristy; the other path to the south, at the termination of which much rubbish is to be seen, *c*, probably led to the cloisters, and apartments of the monks, which in all monasteries it seems were uniformly to the south of the church.

" About *a* was also found a stone coffin cased with lead both within and without, containing some bones and remains of garments; the lead in its decayed state sold for two guineas, the bones were thrown about, and the stone coffin broken in pieces. There were two other coffins, and no more, found in this part, which were also broken, and buried as low as the springs. At *h* there were remains of a solid basis of masonry, and fragments of small columns of Purbeck marble. Might not this have been part of the high altar, or of the tomb of Alfred near it?[1] Possibly the two other coffins contained the remains

---

[1] " The bones of Alfred, King of the West Saxons, and of Edward his son and King, were translated from the Newan Minstre, and laid in a tomb before the high altar at Hyde. In the which tomb there was of late found two little tables of lead, inscribed with their names."—Lel. Itin. iii. 102.

of his son Edward and his Queen Alswytha. Farther west, as at *g g*, more stone coffins were found, and the clay extended to *o o*. The situation and number of the coffins denote this to have been the nave of the church. Farther east than *b*, were great numbers of stone coffins, and some rather more south just beyond; but in this part there was no clay; and from its being beyond the traces of the foundations, it may be concluded that it was the church-yard."[1]

Returning into Hyde-street, a few paces brings us near the inclosure of the parish church of St. Bartholomew, supposed to have been originally erected about the same period or rather earlier than its more magnificent but less fortunate neighbour, within whose precinct it stood. The present edifice seems for the most part to have been built with materials afforded by the ruins of the Abbey in 1541, except near the east end of the south wall, which, from its general appearance and the two ornamented nitches of the second window, may probably be a part of the original fabric. This church has been greatly repaired at various times; and at present consists of one large aisle, with a plain gallery at the west end. Its original form appears to have been that of a cross, forming a nave and transepts, but in the course of the various alterations it has undergone, the transept on the north

---

[1] From a paper entitled, " Enquiries, &c. concerning the Tomb of King Alfred, at Hyde Abbey, Winchester. By H. Howard, Esq."—Archæologia, v. xiii. p. 309.

side only remains; and from the limited scale upon which the whole seems to have been erected, is little better than a large closet; yet in this closet, however improbable it may appear, almost totally hidden from the sight and hearing of the greater part of the congregation, we find the altar.

The unaccountable singularity of this mode of disposing of the chancel, seems the more surprising when we observe its proper situation, at the east end of the church, totally unappropriated, and the wall, under which it should be placed, decorated with a very neat table of the Ten Commandments.

There are several inscriptions on the ground; but except the following, none calculated to excite attention or interest; this is upon a brass in the middle of the aisle, and is as follows:

Sum pulvis, qui carne fuit vestitus amœna
Disce tuos casus, hac qui Discurris amice
Edmundum dixere meum Poore, nomen at illud
Extinxit suprema dies mens bibit in ævum.

1599.

Near the west end of the north wall are the two following inscriptions upon tablets of black marble, intersected by the gallery but adjoining each other, viz. upon one,

M. S.

JACOBI GUALTERI a Paisij

Hujus Ecclesiæ Vicariæ

Et infra sepulta Petris

——— veritatis causa susceptum semper memorandu

Omnibus virtutibus splendidi
——vero et patienta splendissimi

. . . .

. . . .

. . . .

Solis uxoris et filiæ mœrentibus non satis
Obdormivet in Domino
2° die Augusti anno salutis 1699 et suæ 64.
Exilij 14°
Beatus ille cui Auxilio est Deus Jacobi cujus
Spes est in Domino Deo suo.——Ps. 146.
Dominus servat Peregrinus Papillum et
Viduam statuminat.——v. 9.

Upon the other tablet,

Infra jacet
JACOBUS GAULTERIS a Paisij
Ingenuus Eruditus Juvenis
Genabo in Gallia Oriundus

. . . .

. . . .

. . . .

——juxta Civitatem Collegio tanta
humanitate tanq; cum munificentiæ exceptus est liberi
tam generosa cura educati ut exilium ejus fœlix
dici potuerit dum obsequantissi filium exemptum
luget Pater necesse habeat quam curam de se Deus
gesserit cum mente revolvere ne forte de Dei
armore dubitet tam prædicare ut ægritudinem levet
efficax enim doloris lenimentum est——Divini nominis celebratio.
Eodem tumulo conduntur Reliquæ
Annæ Matris Prædicti Jacobi quæ ob:
Aug^{ti} 14° 1710.

Leaving the church, we observe at the south-east
end of the burial-ground the neat and commodious
building erected for a County Bridewell, in the
front court of which are several stone coffins, discovered some time since in making a saw-pit in the

middle court of the prison; and about the walls and avenues are some curious fragments of ornamental masonry that have been collected from the adjacent ruins.

Returning from the contemplation of these various objects, so eminently calculated to impress us with the opposite ideas of Piety and Guilt, we pass, in our way towards the city, Hyde Abbey School, conducted by the Rev. C. Richards, and long considered as one of the first classical seminaries in the kingdom. Upon arriving once more near the scite of the North Gate, we proceed under the tottering remains of the city wall to its north-west extremity, where are the ruins of a small bastion called the Hermit's Tower, the prospect from which is extremely beautiful and extensive. Hence, continuing our Walk round the enclosure of a young plantation immediately beneath the ruin, we ascend a short lane, once crowded with buildings and echoing with bustle and activity, now divested of every trace of habitation, and silent as are those who occupied them, having an immense fosse and the picturesque ruins of the city wall on the one side, and on the other some small paddocks and a garden. At the end of this lane stands an Obelisk, erected in 1759, to commemorate the dreadful visitation of the plague, which in 1666 almost reduced the city to a heap of solitary ruins. Upon the spot occupied by this obelisk the markets were held; and the huge stone that forms its base is the same on which the traffic was conducted, as we have stated in a former part of our Work. The height of this memorial is about 24 feet, and an inscription on the sides explains the object of its erection. From hence, a style on the opposite side of the road will conduct us to a field called Oram's Harbour, near which the deep entrenchments thrown up for the defence of the city during the civil war of 1644, are still distinguishable; and returning to the road by the Obelisk, a few paces will again bring us to the West Gate of the city.

1. King's Gate, with the Parish Church of St. Swithun.—2. St. Michael's Church.
3. Scite of the Carmelite Convent.—4. Scite of the Parish Church of St. Faith.
—5. Hospital of St. Cross.—6. The Friary.—7. Scite of the South Gate.

The Sixth Walk.

WE shall commence our Sixth and last Walk from the north end of King'sgate-street, near the ancient Postern of that name, a notice of which will be found in a former part of our Work.[1]

At short distance along King'sgate-street, a passage on the right hand conducts us toward the parish church of St. Michael, which, like most structures of a similar nature in Winchester, still retains some traces both of antiquity and mutilation.

[1] See First Walk, p. 141.

This church is also mentioned in the registers of Bishop Pontissara, anno 1280, and most probably had existed for some considerable period before that time. It is chiefly built with a mixture of flint and square stones, and is divided by five low pointed arches into two aisles, having at the west end of that on the south side, a plain tower, over one of the windows of which, the date, 1582, appears very legible, being probably the time of its erection or repair. Passing along the interior, we observe on the north side of one of the arches dividing the aisles, some traces of an ancient staircase, which till of late years communicated with a small room over the altar, supposed to have been used as a confessional.[1] This room, whatever was its purpose, has been destroyed, and the space occupied by it thrown into the height of the chancel. There are some few pieces of stained glass remaining in the east window; but with the exception of a single head, nothing sufficiently perfect to be understood. The edifice upon the whole is extremely neat; and by the erection of two galleries, has been rendered very commodious, but has not any claim to our attention beyond the usual characteristics of a parish church.

Of the various monumental inscriptions that surround the interior of the building, the three following appear most deserving of notice.

Upon a small black marble tablet against the north wall of the church:

---

[1] Wavel, i. 205.

CONSTANTIA PHILIPPI TAYLOR,
Conjux charissima, 19. 9bris
Anno salutis 1656, ætat 50.
Animam Deo resignavit.

Mori nequis mortua licit : nam geminum erit
Tibi monumentum ; marmor et virtus tua :
Marmore perennior : necem victura quæ,
Te vicit; et quâ sis secunda nemini.

Against the east wall of the north aisle is a rich oval tablet of white marble, adorned with armorial bearings, supported by a base of seven sculls. In the centre of the tablet we read the following inscription:

M. S.
Septem Liber^m
Elizabethæ, Franciscæ,
Gulielmi, Mariæ, Georgii,
Annæ, Caroli,
Qui omnes susquiennes, præter
Gul^m qui Octaviensis decessere
HENRICUS } BEESTON.
ANNA }
P. P. Mœsti P.
CIƆIƆLXXV.
Talium est Regnum Cœlorum.
Mat. xix. xiv.

Against the south wall of the chancel, near the entrance to the vestry, we observe a plain black stone, surmounted by a small shield of arms, and bearing the following:

M. S.
Hic propter ossa MILLESENTÆ,
Matris, suæ charissimæ
Corpus recumbit filiæ
Katherinæ, nuper conjugis
JOHANNIS RICHARDS, Clerici,

2 F

Vir qualis illa fæmina
Prudens, pudica, provida,
Sincera, pietate, ad Deum.
Ad pauperes benefica,
Tenella mater liberis
(Quos tres reliquit masculos)
Non proximorum amantior
Aut proximis dilectior
Consumpta pthysi mortua est
Die Decembris ultimo
An. Dn. cɪɔ. ɪɔcLɪɪɪɪ. Ætat suæ 31.
Mœrens maritus posuit.

Returning into King'sgate-street by the before-
mentioned passage, we stand opposite a wall inclosing a piece of ground called College Mead, the scite
of a Carmelite Convent, founded in 1278,[1] and
which, at the dissolution of religious houses, was
given, with the adjoining land, to Wykeham's College, to which, from its contiguity, it doubtless formed a valuable acquisition.

Continuing our Walk southwards, we shortly pass,
in a meadow at the end of King'sgate-street, the
scite of the parish church of St. Faith, which, with
others, was destroyed to its foundations in the early
part of the sixteenth century, in consequence of the
excessive poverty and depopulation of their respective parishes, by which they had been reduced to little better than mere ruins. Of these, the church
of St. Faith appears to have been one; and it is not
perhaps an idle conjecture to suppose that the numerous inequalities of the surface, visible at the north-
west end of the meadow in question, may have

---

[1] Milner, ii. 150.

been occasioned by the yet remaining foundations of it.

Continuing our progress by the path through the meadow, we approach at a short distance the principal object of our Walk.

The Hospital of St. Cross, near this city, was founded in 1136, by Henry De Blois, Bishop of Winchester;[1] who, by his charter of institution, required that thirteen poor decayed men, past their strength, so that without assistance they could not maintain themselves, should have continual habitation in the Hospital, and be provided with proper clothing and necessaries, and a daily allowance of good and wholesome provision; but in case it should happen that any one of the persons so appointed should recover his strength and means, then such person to be respectfully discharged, and another proper object admitted in his stead. Besides the thirteen resident brethren, one hundred other poor, of good character and the most indigent that could be found, were to be provided daily with a substantial dinner, having permission to carry away with them such surplus provision as might remain after all were satisfied. Other charities were also provided, to be distributed amongst the poor in general, as the revenues of the foundation should be able to bear; the whole of which at that time amounting to about 250*l.* per annum, derived as well from the Founder's own private fortune as from a donation

---

[1] Historical Account, 32.

of several valuable rectories, &c. belonging to his diocese or under his patronage, were made applicable to the use of his charity.

The domestic management of the establishment appears to have been confided to a Master and Steward, who, with other inferior officers and servants, were supported upon the foundation, under the superintendance of the Master and Brethren of the Hospital of St. John of Jerusalem, who were appointed by De Blois as guardians and administrators of the whole.

It appears that the Brotherhood of St. John, at a very early period, misconducted themselves in the management of the Hospital; which was thereupon, after some difficulty, surrendered, through the mediation of Henry the Second, into the hands of Richard Toclyve, Bishop of Winchester, the successor of De Blois; and this prelate, considering the revenues of the charity as sufficient for the maintenance of many more poor than were originally limited, directed, that beyond the number appointed by the Founder, one hundred other poor should be also daily fed at the hospital, with the same privilege and allowances as the former.[1] This extension of the charity does not however seem to have been of very long continuance, and the out-pensioners were shortly after reduced to their original number.

The purposes of the charity having in the course of years been greatly abused, and the intentions of

---

[1] Historical Account, 33.

the illustrious Founder entirely perverted by the avarice and rapacity of several of its successive Masters, who seem to have considered their office as a situation of profit rather than of trust, and to have converted to their private use great part of the funds designed for charitable purposes only, it was, in the course of the fourteenth century, after much difficulty, brought back to its original purpose, by the management and indefatigable perseverance of our memorable prelate William de Wykeham, who not only recovered the various possessions which had been alienated, and restored the charity to the complete enjoyment of its original rights, but also seems to have considerably repaired the various buildings of the Hospital, which had been long suffered to remain in a state of dilapidation.

In 1444, Henry Beaufort, Bishop of Winchester, having, according to the usage of the times, resolved to dispose of a considerable sum of money in the furtherance of piety and charity, seems to have preferred improving the foundation of De Blois to the alternative of becoming a founder himself.[1] He therefore made a very great addition to its endowment, which at this time consisted of manors, &c. of the yearly value of 500*l.* and appointed that, in addition to the number of persons upon the first establishment, there should be also maintained two priests, thirty-five brethren, and three sisters, who were to act as nurses to the sick and infirm part of

---

[1] Historical Account, 50.

the community. For the accommodation of these persons he considerably enlarged, and in great part rebuilt, the original buildings of the Hospital; and to the establishment thus formed, he appears to have given the title of **Domus Eleemosynaria Nobilis Paupertatis,** or the Alms House of Noble Poverty.

The establishment of St. Cross, thus re-modelled and improved, seems, however, as in the early part of its history, to have soon fallen into the hands of men who made their authority subservient to their personal interest rather than to the benefit of the charity confided to their protection. In addition to these causes of decay, were the spoliations which it underwent during the eventful struggles of the rival factions of York and Lancaster; in the course of which its revenues were curtailed and possessions alienated, by the adherents of the former party, as a mark of their enmity to the family of the Cardinal. So complete indeed seems to have been the work of despoliation at this period, that by an instrument of Bishop Waynflete, dated the 2d of August, 1486, (within forty years after the death of the Cardinal,) it is stated, " that time and the insatiable malice of men having entirely stripped the charity of the secular estates annexed to it by Beaufort, so that it was then impossible his pious and charitable intentions could be fulfilled, the Bishop (i. e. Wayneflete), from a sense of duty and other laudable motives impelling him, and with a view to uphold the design of his predecessor, so far as it might be supported by the produce of that part of its endowment which remained, therefore directed, that in room of the forty persons appointed by Beaufort, there should in future be only one chaplain and two brethren, with necessary portions and allowances for their maintenance."[1]

From this period the charity thus curtailed seems to have continued in an almost uninterrupted exercise of the benevolence of its successive founders and benefactors, until the æra of the Reformation, when great part of its remaining possessions were sequestered and alienated. Henceforth, therefore, in place of the regular maintenance of forty-two persons resident within the Hospital, besides the one hundred poor who were fed daily by its liberality, the charity has consisted but of thirteen resident Brethren, with a Master, Steward, and Chaplain. There are, however, one hundred poor who still receive sixpence a week each, and at stated periods a certain portion of bread is distributed in the forecourt of the hospital; while, in addition to these pitiable fragments of its ancient hospitality, the porter is daily furnished with a quantity of good bread and beer for the refreshment of such poor travellers as may apply at the gate for that assistance.

After these preliminary observations, we shall advance to a survey of the Hospital itself; a scene alike grateful and instructive as an establishment, which, even in its present mutilated condition, does honour to the country that owns it, and reflects a lustre upon charity itself, by the comfort and re-

---

[1] Life of Bishop Waynflete, p. 77.

spectability with which the objects of it are sur-rounded.

We approach the Hospital by the north entrance, having on the left hand, after passing the outer gate, a low range of buildings which formerly constituted the hall or apartment wherein the hundred out-pen-sioners were served with their daily portions, and thence called **The Hundred Mene's Hall.** This, however, has long since been converted into stabling, wherein are lost all traces of its former condition. On the opposite side of the court is the kitchen and other offices belonging to the Hospital; and, before us, the spacious gateway and tower erected by Car-dinal Beaufort, as also part of the refectory, form the principal objects of our attention; of these, the first-mentioned is naturally the most prominent.

This structure consists of a lofty square tower decorated with Gothic niches, in two of which there seem to have been originally statues of the Cardinals Beaufort and De Blois,[1] the centre being adorned with a large cross, towards which they

---

[1] It may appear presumption, in the total absence of all positive proof, to offer an opinion in opposition to an historian and antiquary of such celebrity as Dr. Milner ; but it is submitted, that as Beaufort, from motives of deli-cacy, chose to extend the original charity of De Blois rather than found a new one of his own, it is not at all improbable the opposite niche should have been occupied by the effigy of De Blois, the original founder, rather than by the image of St. John, which could have no possible allusion to the establish-ment, other than as being the patron of the Knights Hospitallers ; a body of men who had long been deemed unfit to have any connection with the cha-rity, and it is therefore hardly probable that their patron should, as such, have been selected to occupy the place in question.

were represented as offering their devotions; such
at least is the attitude of the figure which remains,
apparently that of Beaufort. Immediately below
these niches is the window of the Founder's Chamber, and upon the cornice under it, a series of busts
intermingled with foliage; and the Cardinal's hat,
together with the arms of the second Founder,
in the spandils of the arch, complete the decorations of the north face of the tower.

Passing forwards, we enter the extensive irregular area of the main court, bounded on the east,
west, and north sides, by the neat uniform buildings
of the Hospital, and partly on the south open to the
picturesque scenery of the adjoining meadows.

Turning to the right, a few paces brings us to a
flight of steps leading to the Refectory, which, with
the Tower on the one side and the Master's Residence on the other, occupies the south side of the
court. We enter this apartment by a porch at the
west end, separated by a screen from the body of
the Hall, which is about thirty-six feet by twenty-
four, adorned with rich Gothic windows, and having at the east end a raised floor for the table of the
officers, those for the brethren being ranged along
the sides of the Hall. Upon the whole, there is
yet much in this room to excite an interest, and to
convey an idea of its original appearance and condition; and the impression is strikingly assisted by
the rude yet ornamental display of the timbers in the
roof; by the lofty tribune or gallery at the west
end, from whence the benediction was given to the

meals of the brethren, and whence also on particular festivals the cheerful sound of minstrelsy enlivened the banquet, and in animated strains re-echoed the virtues of the illustrious Founders; and lastly, in the huge raised hearth in the centre of the Hall, round which the venerable brothers were wont to sit, and awaken the listlessness of age by the tales of youth and fondly-cherished memorials of times gone by.

At the south-east end of the Hall, a spacious staircase communicates with the Chambers of the Tower. Ascending these stairs, we enter the Founder's Chamber, a plain apartment of about twenty-four feet by twenty, but in which there is now nothing left to denote its original use or importance, or the ornaments with which it may have been decorated. Beyond this to the east, we descend into a second chamber, much inferior in appearance to the former, but varying little in respect of size. Against the north side, are still remaining some old wainscot presses carved in scrolls, somewhat similar in design to those of Silkstede, in the south transept of the cathedral, but far, very far, unlike them in condition. On the west side of the chamber, the following legend appears in raised letters upon the ach of the chimney: *R. S. Dilexi Sapienam Anno Do.* 1vo3, being the initials and motto of Roger (or Robert) Sherborne, who we find was Master of the Hospital about that time.[1] On

---

[1] Wavel, ii. 231.

the south side of this room we again descend into a gallery or range of apartments, 120 feet long by 20 wide, extending the whole length of the eastern side of the court, and having below them an ambulatory or retired walk for the accommodation of the society in wet or unfavourable weather. These apartments were it appears originally erected by Cardinal Beaufort, at the time he added to the endowment of the charity and increased the number of its objects, as an infirmary for the use of the sick brethren and the nuns appointed by his regulations to attend them; hence they seem to have been called the *Nunnes' Chambers;* a name the gallery still retains, and in this retains perhaps the only vestige which the hand of modern taste, more destructive than the ravages of time, has left to excite an idea of its original purpose and appearance. By means of a small staircase near the north end of the gallery, the convalescents were enabled to take proper exercise in the cloister, as also to attend their duties in the church with which it communicates, while on the other hand, by means of folding shutters at the south end of the range, the more infirm and bed-ridden inhabitants of the Nuns' Chambers could participate in the service of the choir without the inconvenience or danger of removal.

Returning from the gallery through the first-mentioned chambers, we descend by the staircase of the tower into the great court of the Hospital, having the uniform range of buildings composing the Lodgings of this little society on our right hand. On our left is the Ambulatory, or Cloister, of which we have just spoken ; and before us the venerable Church of De Blois, in all its original beauty, projects considerably into the area of the court, and by the irregularity adds greatly to the interest which the beautiful simplicity of the buildings, aided by a partial view of the adjoining meadows, and adorned with a profusion of stately timber, is eminently calculated to produce.

The Church of St. Cross, which may be called a cathedral in miniature, with its various appendages of nave and side-aisles, choir, transepts, and lateral chapels, appears to be the workmanship of Be Blois, and is certainly the most complete of all the various buildings connected with the foundation; and were there no other vestiges of his liberality and taste at this moment existing, the specimens of both, which this edifice affords us, would be sufficient to convince the most prejudiced that he possessed them in an eminent degree. To attempt a minute detail of the various beauties which present themselves, would alone require a volume. We shall therefore confine ourselves to a mere general description, and invite the reader to supply our deficiency by the more satisfactory alternative of occular inspection.

We enter the Church by the north transept, immediately under the folding lattice of the gallery or Nuns' Chambers. In this transept there is little to excite the attention of the cursory observer; and from hence, a few paces brings us into the choir, immediately below the tower, which is intended as a lanthorn to it, being ornamented with galleries, and open to a considerable height above the vaulting of the nave. The length of the church, from the altar to the west door, is 160 feet, and its breadth, including the transepts, 120.

The principal ornaments of the choir are a number of large semicircular arches which surround it, and, intersecting each other, produce a range of beautiful pointed arches, enriched with all the variety of Saxon and Norman ornament which the sculptors of that age appear to have been acquainted with, and admitting through the intersections the light of the first tier of windows round the altar. The second or upper tier is formed by the usual pointed arch, and is also adorned with the like variety of ornament, which even extends to the very ribs of the roof. On each side of the altar are rich stone screens of Gothic spire-work, the workmanship of one on the north side being most elaborate and beautiful; but these screens are evidently the additions of a later period than the rest of this part of the church, inasmuch as we find the upper part of the designs have been broken away, to reduce them to a proper size for the pointed arches under which they stand. The altar itself is in unison with the surrounding objects of a church where unassuming neatness and simple elegance are the most prominent features. On each side of the choir is a semicircular range of stalls in wainscot, ornamented with a variety of carving, amongst which a series of medallioned busts form the pendants of the canopies. On the desk of one

of the stalls a variety of fanciful letters are cut, pur-
porting to be the initials and names of officers belonging to the choir in 1575, among which are those
of a chaunter and singing-men; at present, however, there are no such officers attached to the
foundation.

Immediately before the steps leading to the altar,
are three large flat stones lying parallel with each
other, and bearing inscriptions, of which that upon
the southernmost is as follows:

Hic quod mortale erat deposuit

Qui parte sui meliore inter immortales vivit

Hic jacet GULIELMUS LEWIS

Quem in totus jacerat, virtus ad superos enexit

Theologiæ Doctor Insiquis

Qui quam verbo Docius Theologiam Christianam.

Moribus felicius expressit

Constanti enim in Deum pietate

Fide in Regem inconcussa

Sincera in omnes caritate floruit

Utramque expertus fortunam

Utraque major

Quia nec elatus prospera, nec adversa dejectus

Hujus Hospitalis Sancœ Crucis Magister et Rector,

Et Cathedralis Ecclesiæ Wintoniensis Canonicus

Tot magnu titulis virtutibus tamen major.

Cœlo maturus ibi ut æternum vineret

Vinore inter mortales desiit

Die viiº mensa Julii, anno 1667.

The next, or central stone, bears the following:

H. S. E.

Quod mortale fuit

ABRAHAMI MARKLAND, S. T. P.

Rectoris Ecclesiæ de Meonstoke,

Ecclesiæ Cathedralis Winton Canonici,

Et hujus Hospitali Magistri,

Cui per annos 34.
Pari vigilantia ac munificentiæ præfuit
Locum ipsum hortorum amænitate
Et elegantie ornavit
Fratrum egenorum stipendia auxit
Quos animo paterno rexit
Et exemplo suo ad pietatam formavit
Cætera sacerdotalis muneris officia
Summa cum laude exercuit
In conscionibus frequens, facundus flexanimus
Morum suavitate
Et propensa erga omnes humanitate
Conspicuus.
Post vitam per lxxxiii annos
Æquabili integritatis tenera decursam
Cœlo maturus in Christo obdormivit
Jul. xxix. A. D. 1728.

The next, on the north side, bears the following inscription :

H. S. E.
Optima Fæminæ
CATHERINA,
Filia EDWARDI PITT,
De Stratfieldsea, Armigeri,
Conjux Abra. Markland, S. T. P.
Eccl. Cath. Wint. Præbendarii,
Et hujusce domus Magistri,
Quæ ad sacram squaxin fertinans
Humanæ pietatis portæsa
Ad celestem se contulit
Morte subita nec tamen improvisa
Non tam apoplexia
Quam ecstasi correpta
Suavem ac humilem castam ac pudicam.
Magnam, ac nobilem, piam ac divinam.
Animam efflavit,
A. D. 1695.

Between the stone bearing the last-mentioned inscription and the one preceding, are two small slabs, recording the grave of two of the children of the deceased Abraham and Catherine Markland.

From hence, a few paces towards the west brings us to a large flat stone, ornamented with a sepulchral brass, and bearing the following inscription:

Orate pro aie dni Thoma Lawne, Rectoris de Mottisfount, qui obiit anno die mensis Maij, Ao. Dn. M. Quingentissimo xbiij°· Cujus aie propicietur Deus.

Immediately before us, under the west arch of the tower, is the sepulchral brass of John de Campden, Master of St. Cross in 1383, a memorial no less curious for the design than for the excellent state of preservation in which it remains. This record of mortality consists of a large flat stone, surrounded near the edges with a broad fillet of brass, connected at the ends with escutcheons, bearing alternately emblems of the Trinity and armorial devices. Along this label we read the following:

Credo qd redemptor meus bibitdrin nobissimo die de terra surrecturus sum et rursum circumdabor pelle mea et incarne mea bidebo Deum saluatorē meū quem bisurus, sum ego ipe et occuli mea conspecturi sunt et non alius reposita est hec spes mea in sinu meo.

In the centre of the above is a large brass, representing a person in the secular habit, having on his right side the following prayer, upon a label issuing from his mouth:

Jhu cū benis judica noli me codepnat

On the left side of the figure, upon a similar label,

Qui plasmasti me miserere mei.

And upon a tablet, forming the base of the design, is the following:

Hic jacet Johannes de Campeden, quondam custos istius Hospitalis cujus anime propicietur Deus.

Quitting the enclosure of the choir, we observe the rich west window, erected at the expence of the late Rev. Dr. Lockman, Master of St. Cross, which, among a variety of figures and devices, pourtrays the arms of the present Royal Family, of the Hospital, and of the Donor, together with those of the two Cardinals, De Blois and Beaufort.

Turning to the right, we perceive under the first window from the transept, a rich and curious arch in the north wall, having beneath it, upon a flat coffin-shaped stone, the following inscription in modern letters, the old stone with the original Saxon characters, having been lately removed:

Petrus de Sancta Maria,
ob: 1295.

A few paces from this tomb, near the first pillar, is the Font, which, however, has nothing in its appearance to deserve notice, save an idea attached to its erection, it having most probably been placed in its present situation in the early part of the sixteenth century, about which time the adjacent parish of St. Faith, having, from depopulation and other causes, become unable to maintain its church, the parish appears to have been annexed to the church of St. Cross, which consequently became entitled to the usual privilege of a regular parochial church.

In the line from the west door to the entrance of the choir, are a variety of flat stones with brasses, &c. bearing inscriptions; but none of these being of particular interest, we shall not occupy our pages by repeating them.

Under the middle window of the south aisle, is an elegant mural monument, erected to the memory of Charles Wolfran Cornwall, Esq. Speaker of the House of Commons in 1780. This memorial consists of a beautiful Sarcophagus of Sienna marble, under a pediment of the Doric order, ornamented at the base with the Speaker's mace, upon a rich embroidered cushion, &c. Below this, upon a large white tablet, we read the following inscription:

Near this place lieth the body of
The Right Honourable CHARLES WOLFRAN CORNWALL,
Son of Jacobs Cornwall, Esq.
Of an ancient family in the county of Hereford.

Having been educated at the College near Winchester,
And removed from thence to New College, Oxford,
He applied himself to the study of the law,
But was diverted from proceeding in the course of this profession,
For which he was eminently qualified,
By being appointed a Commissioner for examining German Accounts, 1763,
Which trust he so discharged
As to merit and receive a reward from the Public.
He became a Member of the House of Commons,
In the 13th Parliament of Great Britain, 1768,
And served in the succeeding Parliaments of 1774, 80, and 84.
He was appointed one of the Lords Commissioners of the Treasury, 1775;
Chief Justice in Eyre of the Royal Forests North of Trent;
And one of his Majesty's Most Honourable Privy Council, 1780.
In the Parliament assembled in that year
He was chosen Speaker of the House of Commons,
And re-chosen to the same office, 1784.

Endued with a strong and correct understanding;
Having a perfect knowlege of the privileges and functions
Of the great Assembly in which he presided;
And a sincere attachment to the Constitution of his Country,
He filled the high office, of which he died possessed,
With ability, with dignity, with impartiality.
In private life,
While an accurate memory, a perspicuity of thought and expression,
A peculiar pleasantry of conversation and agreeableness of manners,
Rendered his society highly engaging,
He was endeared to the persons more nearly connected with him,
By the warmth and constancy of his affection and his friendship.

He was born June 15, 1735,
And died January 2, 1789.

He married, 1764,
ELIZABETH, daughter of CHARLES JENKINSON, Esq.
(Lieutenant-Colonel of the regiment of Horse-Guards Blue,)
And son of Sir ROBERT JENKINSON, Bart.
Of Walcot, in the couuty of Oxford,
Who survived him,
And by whom this monument is erected,
In token of her unalterable love and esteem.

In the same grave are interred
The remains of ELIZABETH CORNWALL, his Wife,
Who died the 8th of March, 1809,
Aged 78 years.

Near the screen, on the north side of the nave, is a large brass upon a flat stone, with the following inscription:

The yere of oure Lord, M.C.C.C.C. and two,
Upon the xi day in the moneth of Feberer,
The soul of John Newles the body passid fro.
A brother of this place. resting under this stone here,
Borne in Beane Squyer, and servant more than xxx yere
Unto Harry Beauford, Busshop and Cardinall.
Whos soules God convey, and his Moder dere,
Unto the blisse of Heven that is eternall.   Amen.

There is nothing in the south transept sufficiently remarkable to excite the notice of the casual visitor; the scientific observer will however find beauties, the artist models for imitation at every step, throughout this interesting structure.

Near the scite of the altar, at the east end of the south aisle, a flat stone, with a brass, records the death of a Mr. John Wayte, a brother, who died in 1502; and in the south transept, as also in the body of the church, there are a variety of similar memorials for deceased brothers of the Hospital. Returning by the way we entered, we pass a small chapel on the north side of the choir, in which we find nothing particularly interesting except a curious piscina, and the mouldering frame-work of an ancient altar, which still remains under the east window.

Quitting the Church by the north porch, we turn on our left hand towards the meadows which adjoin the Hospital on the south and east sides, and proceeding a short distance eastwards, observe on our left hand, in the corner formed by the junction of the south transept and nave, a singular instance of architectural beauty in the union of two circular arches, forming what is called the triple arch, ornamented with a variety of enriched zig-zag and other Saxon ornaments.

On leaving the Hospital, it may not be improper to advert slightly to the accommodation afforded to its inhabitants, each of whom is furnished with three distinct chambers for his use, and also with a small portion of ground for cultivation or amusement. In addition to the daily allowance, the members of this venerable society have, upon certain occasions, a share of the fines, &c. on the renewal of leases of the Hospital lands, divided amongst them; so that it is by no means unusual for a man who has been a few years upon the foundation to have a little property at his disposal. The peculiar dress worn by the brethren on all occasions consists merely of a black open gown, having a small silver cross upon the left side.

Upon the whole, whether we consider the feeling that designed or the liberality that endowed this establishment; whether we look to it as the hospitable and happy asylum of age and infirmity; or as a splendid monument of the piety and benevolence of other times; there is throughout, an indefinable sentiment of gratification which attaches to us at first sight, and which leaves us not at our departure —we enter it with curiosity—we remain in it with admiration—and we quit it with reluctance and regret.

Returning from the survey of St. Cross, by the great road from Southampton to Winchester, we pass near the latter, on the right hand side, a part of the ancient enclosure of a church and convent of Augustine Friars, an establishment dissolved with others at an early period of the Reformation, and which now retains the appellation of the Priory, or Friary, as the almost only vestige of its existence.

Beyond this, a few paces brings us to the spot formerly occupied by the South Gate of the city of

Winchester; and having thus conducted our Readers through a series of Walks, designed, so far as our abilities would permit, to afford an authentic Descriptive Account of a City which, in the language of one of its most public Records, " hath given place of birth, education, baptism, marriage, micholgemots, gemots, synods national and provincial, and sepulchre, to more Kings, Queens, Princes, Dukes, Earls, Barons, Bishops, and Mitred Prelates, before the year of our Lord 1239, than all the then cities in England together could do."[1]   We shall here take our leave.

---

[1] City Tables, St. John's House.

APPENDIX

No. I.

Bishops of Winchester.

☞ The line below the name of each Bishop shews the number of years he possessed the See, inclusive, and the name of the reigning Monarch.

I. Birinus,

(Anno 635 to 650.—Kinegils.)

An Italian Monk, was made the first Bishop of the West Saxons, by Pope Honorius, about the year 635, and afterwards converted Kinegils, King of the West Saxons, by whom Dorchester was appointed as his Episcopal residence. He died A. D. 650, and was buried at Dorchester.

II. Agilbert,

(Anno 650 to 660.—Kenewalch.)

A native of France, succeeded Birinus, and upon the partition of the See by Kenewalch, about 660, was made Bishop of Dorchester only, which he being offended at, retired to France, where he died.

III. Wina,

(Anno 660 to 663.—Kenewalch.)

Upon the removal of Agilbert to Dorchester, was made BISHOP of WIN-CHESTER, by Kenewalch, who expelled him the diocese about 663; upon which flying for protection to Wulfhere, King of Mercia, he purchased of that Monarch the Bishopric of London, being the first Simonist recorded in English history.

IV. Eleutherius,

(Anno 667 to 674.—Kenewalch.)

A nephew of Agilbert, after the See had been vacant four years, was consecrated Bishop in 667, by the recommendation of his uncle.   He died 674.

V. Headda,

(Anno 674 to 703.—Sigebert.)

Succeeded in 674.   This Prelate translated the body of St. Birinus from Dorchester to Winchester, and died in 703.

VI. Daniel,

(Anno 704 to 745.—Ina.)

Upon the death of Headda, was appointed Bishop of Winchester, and after exercising the Episcopal government for 41 years, resigned his See, and retired to the station of a private Monk at Malmesbury, where he died in 745.

VII. Humfred,

(Anno 744 to 756.—Cuthbert.)

Succeeded Daniel in 744, and died in 756.

VIII. Kinebard,

(Anno 756 to 780.—Kenulph.)

Was appointed to the See of Winchester in 756, and was succeeded in 780 by

IX. Athelard,

(Anno 780 to 793.—Bithric.)

Abbot of Malmesbury, who in 793, was translated to Canterbury.

X. Egbald.—XI. Dudda.—XII. Kyneberth.—XIII. Alhmund.—XIV. Wigthein.

(Anno 793 to 829.—Bithric and Egbert.)

Were successively Bishops of Winchester after Athelard; of these Wigthein died in 829.

XV. Herefrith,

(Anno 829 to 834.—Egbert.)

Succeeded Wigthein, and attending his Sovereign Egbert, to the battle of Charmouth, was slain by the Danes in 834, whereupon

XVI. Edmund,

(Anno 834.—Egbert.)

Was appointed to the See, which he enjoyed but a few months, when his death made way for

XVII. Helmstan,

(Anno 834 to 837.—Egbert.)

A Monk of the cathedral, and tutor to Ethelwolph, son of Egbert, afterwards King of England. He died in 837, and was succeeded by

XVIII. Ethelwolph,

(Anno 837.—Egbert.)

A Monk of Winchester, who, upon the death of his father Egbert, in 837, was crowned King of England under a dispensation from Leo, whereupon

XIX. Swithun,

(Anno 837 to 862.—Ethelwolph.)

Who succeeded Helmstan as tutor to Ethelwolph, was appointed to the vacant See, which he held till his death, in 862. His remains were interred at the north-west end of the cathedral burial ground.

XX. Alfrith,

(Anno 862 to 863.—Ethelred,)

Succeeded Swithun, and, in 863, was translated to Canterbury, during whose time nearly all the monasteries in England were destroyed by the Danes.

XXI. Dunbert,

(Anno 864 to 879.—Ethelred.)

Was appointed to the See in 864, and died about 879.

XXII. Denewulph,

(Anno 879 to 903.—Alfred.)

The friend and preserver of Alfred, was appointed Bishop upon the death of Dunbert, and continued in possession of the See nearly 24 years, when, upon his death in 903,

XXIII. Athelm, or Bertulf,

(Anno 903 to 909.—Alfred.)

Succeeded to the Episcopal dignity, and was, with several others, appointed, by Alfred, guardian of the realm against the Danes. Upon his death, in 909,

XXIV. 𝕱𝖗𝖎𝖙𝖍𝖘𝖙𝖆𝖓,

(Anno 909 to 931.—Edward the Elder.)

Was consecrated by Plegmund, Archbishop of Canterbury, and resigned his charge about 931, after holding the See 22 years.

XXV. 𝕭𝖗𝖎𝖓𝖘𝖙𝖆𝖓,

(Anno 931 to 934.—Athelstan.)

Upon the resignation of Frithstan, succeeded to the Diocese of Winchester, and by his mortifications and austerity, procured for himself the honours of a Saint.   He died about 934.

XXVI. 𝕰𝖑𝖕𝖍𝖊𝖌𝖊,

(Anno 934 to 946.—Athelstan.)

A Monk of Glastonbury, upon the death of Brinstan, succeeded to the vacant Bishopric.   This Prelate died in 946, and was followed by

XXVII. 𝕰𝖑𝖋𝖘𝖎𝖓, or 𝕬𝖑𝖋𝖘𝖎𝖚𝖘,

(Anno 946 to 959.—Eldred.)

Who died in 959, from intense cold, on his way over the Alps, to procure the Papal confirmation to the Archbishopric of Canterbury, which he had surreptitiously obtained.   He was succeeded by

XXVIII. 𝕭𝖗𝖎𝖙𝖍𝖊𝖑𝖒,

(Anno 959 to 963.—Edgar.)

Who remained in possession of the See till 963, when

XXIX. 𝕰𝖙𝖍𝖊𝖑𝖜𝖔𝖑𝖉,

(Anno 963 to 982.—Edgar.)

Abbot of Abyngdon, was appointed to the Bishopric, and remained 19 years.   This Prelate rebuilt his cathedral from the ground, in a style of massive grandeur, and greatly improved the buildings and offices belonging to the monastery ;[1] and among other instances of his liberality, he is said to have sold all the plate and rich vestments belonging to the church, in a time of great scarcity, and to have given the money to the poor, saying, that " the church might again be provided with ornaments ; but life lost could never be recovered."   Upon his death, in 982, his successor was

XXX. 𝕰𝖑𝖕𝖍𝖊𝖌𝖊,

(Anno 982 to 1006.—Ethelred.)

Abbot of Bath, who in 1006, was translated to Canterbury, and afterwards murdered by the Danes.

---

[1] Historical Account, 16.

XXXI. 𝕶enulph, or 𝕰lsius,

(Anno 1006 to 1008.—Ethelred.)

Abbot of Peterborough, obtained the Bishopric by simony, and after enjoying it little more than a year, made way for

XXXII. 𝕭rithwold, or 𝕰thelwold,

(Anno 1008 to 1015.—Ethelred.)

Who died in 1015, when

XXXIII. 𝕰lsin, 𝕰alsin, or 𝕰adsin,

(Anno 1015 to 1038.—Edmund Ironsides.)

A Secular Priest, was preferred to the Bishopric of Winchester, from whence, in 1038, he was translated to the Archbishopric of Canterbury.

XXXIV. 𝕬lwyn,

(Anno 1038 to 1047.—Harold Harfager.)

A Monk of Winchester, thereupon succeeded to the Episcopal dignity, and being in great favour with Queen Emma, mother of Edward the Confessor, was reported to the King, by Robert, Archbishop of Canterbury, an ambitious and intriguing priest, as having been indecently familiar with her, whereupon Alwyn was thrown into prison ; but his innocence and that of the Queen being satisfactorily established, he was restored to liberty and his See ; upon this the Archbishop fled the kingdom, and shortly after died in exile. Alwyn continued in possession of his Bishopric until his death in 1047.[1]

XXXV. 𝕾tigand,

(Anno 1047 to 1069.—Edward the Confessor.)

Chaplain to Edward the Confessor, was translated from Norwich to Winchester, in 1047 ; and in 1052, procured the Archbishopric of Canterbury ; this, with Winchester, he held until a short time previous to his death, which happened during his imprisonment by William the Conqueror, to whom he had rendered himself obnoxious by his courage, as well as by his pride and covetousness. He died in the Castle of Winchester,[2] anno 1069, upon which

XXXVI. 𝖂alkelyn,

(Anno 1069 to 1097.—William the Conqueror.)

A relation of the Conqueror, was consecrated Bishop of Winchester, and held his See during 27 years. He built the tower of the present church, and part of the transepts, &c. at his own expence.[3] He died anno 1097, and was succeeded by

---

1 Historical Account, 18.　　2 Ante, 147.　　3 Historical Account, 21.

XXXVII. William Giffard,
(Anno 1107 to 1128.—HENRY I.)

Whose appointment to the See by Henry the First, (a lay Prince,) gave rise to great disputes between that Monarch and Anselm, Archbishop of Canterbury, by whom the Bishop was to have been consecrated. The Archbishop, in this controversy, was of course supported by the Pope, (Gregory the Seventh,) and, after a long dissention, the quarrel ended by mutual concessions, and Giffard, in 1107, was consecrated to his See, which he continued in possession of until his death in 1128. During his Prelacy he erected a Palace in Southwark[1] for the accommodation of the Bishops of Winchester, during their attendance in Parliament, and which, previous to its decay, was considered one of the most magnificent structures in the city or suburbs of London.

XXXVIII. Henry de Blois,
(Anno 1129 to 1171.—HENRY I.)

Abbot of Glastonbury, and brother of Stephen, King of England, was consecrated to Winchester in 1129. This Prelate appears to have taken a most active part in the dissentions that arose between Stephen and the Empress Matilda, daughter of Henry the First, in the course of which fidelity does not appear to have been the most prominent of his virtues,[2] he siding with each party as their affairs preponderated, although in the end he seems to have departed from this principle, and to have given his brother's cause the preference. During these quarrels, Winchester suffered greatly, most part of it being burnt by the contesting armies, though in the origin of this particular misfortune the Bishop is thought to have had but too great a share. Among the most important transactions of this Prelate, the foundation of the Hospital of St. Cross is most deserving notice.[3] The Castles of Wolvesey and Farnham were also built by him, and afterwards dismantled by Henry the Second. Henry de Blois died on the 6th of August, 1171 ; and, after a vacancy of three years,

XXXIX. Richard Toclyve, or More,
(Anno 1174 to 1189.—HENRY II.)

Archdeacon of Poictiers, was consecrated to Winchester in 1174, and is conjectured to have built and endowed a College or Hospital, upon the Down on

---

1 " The venerable remains of Winchester House were laid open to public view by a fire, which occurred in August, 1814, and destroyed a long range of warehouses, magazines of corn, &c. After this event, what was presumed to have been the great hall, exhibited three conjoined entrances at the east end, and a grand circular window in the gable, terminating the wall at that point, and very curious and uncommon from its scientific intersection of triangular compartments. The tracery of the window was intricate, and the centre of the circle peculiarly beautiful ; its diameter was twelve feet, and it was probably of the age of Edward the First. A pier remained at the north-east angle of the wall, with part of a connecting arch. The range of windows in the south wall were nearly entire ; the arches mostly of a flat character and having but few mouldings, though two doors on the lower story were very elegant. Most of these remains were destroyed, or built in with the new work, on the restoration of the warehouses."—Hughson's London. vol. ii. 285.

2 Historical Account, 28. 3 Ibid. 32.

the east side of the city, dedicated to St. Mary Magdalen.[1] He died in 1189.

XL. Godfrey de Lucy,
(Anno 1189 to 1204.—Richard I.)

Son of Richard de Lucy, Chief Justice of England, succeeded Toclyve in the Bishopric of Winchester, to which he was consecrated on the 1st of November, 1189.   During his Prelacy he rebuilt the end of his cathedral from the choir eastward, and opened a navigable canal from Alresford to Southampton.   He also purchased of the King, at an exorbitant price, several manors and dignities, which he annexed to his See, the whole of which were unjustly resumed by Richard, upon his return from the Crusades.[2] Upon his death, in 1204, he was succeeded by

XLI. Peter de la Roche,
(Anno 1204 to 1238.—John.)

A native of Poictiers, a man of great ability, and unlimited authority under King John, whom, in conjunction with the Bishops of Norwich and Durham, he persuaded for some time to withstand the anathemas of the Pope. In 1214 he appears to have been made Chief Justice of England ; and during the minority of Henry the Third, had the chief management of the Government in his hands.[3] He died at Farnham, on the 9th of June, 1238, and was succeeded in his Bishopric by

XLII. William de Raley,
(Anno 1238 to 1249.—Henry III.)

Bishop of Norwich, who, after considerable difficulty, got possession of his See, being opposed by Henry the Third, who desired to have had William, Bishop of Valentia, the Queen's uncle, appointed to the Bishopric. His wishes being however rejected by the Monks of our cathedral, who were firm in the exercise of their right of election, the King commanded the Mayor of Winchester to forbid the Bishop entrance to the city, which he accordingly did, and for his interference was immediately, with the whole city, excommunicated.   The Bishop, after this spirited proceeding, found it prudent to fly the realm, until, by the intercession of Boniface, Archbishop of Canterbury, and the Pope, he obtained leave to return, and was then quietly permitted to take possession of his Bishopric.   So great, however, had been the charges to which he was put by these proceedings, that he never properly recovered the effect of them ; and, retiring into Italy with a very small retinue, died at Turin, on the 20th of September, 1249, upon which

XLIII. Ethelmar,
(Anno 1249 to 1259.—Henry III.)

A Poictievian, half-brother to the King, was elected by the Monks, upon the earnest request of Henry the Third, who came in person to the chapter-house

---

1 Historical Account, 32, 33. 113—187.   2 Ibid. 34.   3 Ibid. 37.

of the cathedral to give efficacy to his wishes.   The Monks, who had suffered most severely by their opposition to the King in the former instance, were now constrained by fear to comply with his request, and Ethelmar was accordingly elected, but never consecrated ; and having, in the course of nine years, amassed great treasures, in 1259 left the realm, and died at Paris, anno 1261.   His heart only was buried in his cathedral.[1]

XLIV. John Gernsey, or de Orford,

(Anno 1265 to 1268.—Henry III.)

Chancellor of York, after the See had remained vacant four years, was consecrated, at Rome, Bishop of Winchester, anno 1265; but shortly after his return to England was suspended by Ottobonus, the Pope's Legate, for taking part with the Barons against Henry the Third.   He died at Viterbo, in Italy, 1268.

XLV. Nicholas de Ely,

(Anno 1268 to 1280.—Henry III.)

Bishop of Worcester, was translated to this See upon the refusal of John Peckham, Archbishop of Canterbury, to consecrate Richard More, a Doctor in Divinity, who had been chosen by the Monks of our cathedral to the Prelacy.   He died in 1280, at Waverley, where he was buried, his heart only being interred in his cathedral.[2]

XLVI. John de Pointes, or Pontissara,

(Anno 1280 to 1304.—Edward I.)

Was then appointed to the See of Winchester, by the sole authority of Pope Nicholas the Third, who had began to assume the absolute disposal of all Bishoprics.   He does not appear to have been favourably inclined to the Monks of his cathedral, whose revenues he is said to have greatly diminished. He founded and endowed a College, near his Castle of Wolvesey, which he dedicated to St. Elizabeth of Hungary ;[3] and, having occupied the Episcopal chair nearly twenty-four years, died at Winchester, anno 1304, and is buried under the north wall of the Presbytery.

XLVII. Henry Woodloke, or de Merewel,

(Anno 1304 to 1316.—Edward I.)

Prior of Winchester, was elected Bishop by the Monks, in February, 1304; and in 1307 he crowned Edward the Second ; the Archbishop of Canterbury having been banished the kingdom for treason, by Edward the First. He died in 1316.

---

1 Ante, 120, 130.   2 Ante, 113.   3 Historical Account, 40. 113.

XLVIII. John de Sandale, or Kendall,

(Anno 1316 to 1319.—Edward II.)

Chancellor of England, was elected Bishop of Winchester upon the death of Henry Woodloke, in 1316. He appears to have enjoyed the Prelacy but a short time; and upon his death, at his Palace in Southwark, on the 2d of November, 1319,

XLIX. Reginald de Asserio,

(Anno 1319 to 1323.—Edward II.)

A Canon of Orleans, and the Papal Legate, was appointed by the Pope to the vacant See, against the consent of the King and the Archbishop of Canterbury; the latter of whom refused to consecrate him, which ceremony was subsequently performed by the Bishop of London. He died in 1323.

L. John de Stratford,

(Anno 1323 to 1333.—Edward II.)

Archdeacon of Lincoln, was thereupon appointed to the Bishopric, by the Pope, and, like his predecessor, against the will of the King, Edward the Second, who intended to have preferred his Chancellor, Robert Baldock, to the Prelacy. In consequence, Stratford had no sooner taken possession of his diocese, than the King caused all his temporalities to be sequestered. He was, however, after some time, permitted to enjoy his good fortune unmolested; and upon the accession of Edward the Third, was made Chancellor of England; and in 1333, upon the death of Archbishop Mepham, was translated to Canterbury.

LI. Adam Tarleton, or de Orlton,

(Anno 1333 to 1345.—Edward III.)

Bishop of Hereford, and afterwards of Worcester, was translated by the Pope to Winchester, upon the preferment of Bishop Stratford to Canterbury. This Prelate, while Bishop of Hereford, appears to have taken part with Queen Isabella, against Edward the Third, whose death he is said to have facilitated by the following ambiguous answer, given to the application of the King's gaolers, whether or not he should be made away with, viz. " *Edwardum occidere nolite timere bonum est;*" by which, if a comma is set between *nolite* and *timere*, it forbids; if between *timere* and *bonum*, it exhorts to the commission of the act. The wishes of the Queen and her partisans being well understood, the unfortunate King was accordingly sacrificed; and the ambiguity of the above answer being favourable to their design, the Queen and Bishop, to save appearances with the nation, persecuted their instruments, in this work of blood, with great severity; meanwhile, as a reward for this ingenious piece of villany, Tarleton was first translated to Worcester and thence to Winchester; in which latter See he continued until his death, in 1345, having governed the diocese nearly twelve years.

LII. 𝔚𝔦𝔩𝔩𝔦𝔞𝔪 𝔡𝔢 𝔈𝔡𝔶𝔫𝔡𝔬𝔫,

(Anno 1345 to 1366.—Edward III.)

Treasurer of England, was consecrated to Winchester in 1345, and appears to have been in great favour with Edward the Third, by whom he was made Chancellor, and at his instance elected Archbishop of Canterbury, an honour he refused to accept,[1] saying, " *Though Canterbury has the highest rack, yet Winchester has the deepest manger.*" He commenced the repair of his cathedral, beginning at the west end, in which he had made but little progress, when he was stayed by death, anno 1366. He appears, notwithstanding the avaricious inference to be drawn from the above refusal, to have been very careless of his temporalities, as he left his palaces and estates in a ruinous condition ; so that his successor recovered of his executors, for dilapidations, 1662*l.* 10*s.* besides 1556 head of neat cattle, 3876 wethers, 4717 ewes, 3521 lambs, and 127 swine, stock belonging to the Bishopric, which had been made away with.

LIII. 𝔚𝔦𝔩𝔩𝔦𝔞𝔪 𝔡𝔢 𝔚𝔶𝔨𝔢𝔥𝔞𝔪,

(Anno 1366 to 1404.—Edward III.)

Soon after the death of Edyndon, was elected, by the Prior and Convent of Winchester, to the Bishopric, upon the earnest recommendation of Edward the Third. This Prelate appears to have been a man of the most transcendant abilities and unprecedented good fortune, inasmuch as we find him raised from at best but an obscure station to some of the highest and most important offices in the kingdom. As we have before given an account of his uninterrupted progress towards honour and dignity, as also of the various good actions by which he threw a lustre even upon dignity itself, we shall not here enlarge upon his merits.[2] He died at South Waltham, on the 27th of September, 1404, having held his See thirty-eight years ; a pattern to his cotemporaries, and an example to be envied rather than equalled by his successors.

LIV. 𝔥𝔢𝔫𝔯𝔶 𝔅𝔢𝔞𝔲𝔣𝔬𝔯𝔱,

(Anno 1404 to 1447.—Henry IV.)

Bishop of Lincoln, brother to King Henry the Fourth, was translated to Winchester by Pope Martin the First, upon the decease of Wykeham, and shortly afterwards elected Cardinal of St. Eusebius. He appears to have been exceedingly rich, and was of great assistance to his nephew, Henry the Fifth, in his wars against France, in which he furnished him with money. Liberality and a generous hospitaliity stood high upon the list of his virtues ; and valour and wisdom were possessed by him in an eminent degree ; and perhaps the hand of fancy has never traced so wild and wayward a portrait as that drawn of Cardinal Beaufort, by our great Shakespeare, in which the falsehood is barely equalled by the masterly expression of it. Towards the latter end of Beaufort's life he employed large sums in re-endowing the Hospital of St. Cross, near Winchester,

---

1 Historical Account, 45, 99.   2 Ibid. 46, 95, 152.

founded by Bishop De Blois.[1]   He appears to have been thrice Chancellor of England, and, with the Duke of Gloucester, guardian of Henry the Sixth during his minority.   He died on the 11th of April, 1447, having been Bishop of Winchester forty-three years, and is buried under a sumptuous tomb at the east end of his cathedral.

LV. William Waynflete, or Pattyn,

(Anno 1447 to 1486.—Henry VI.)

Provost of Eton College, was the next occupier of the Episcopal throne of Winchester.   This Prelate had been educated first at the College of Wykeham in this city, and afterwards at New College, Oxford; whence he was preferred, for his eminent abilities and learning, by Henry the Sixth, to the Provostship of Eton.   Upon the deposition of this Monarch, his attachment to the House of Lancaster occasioned him much persecution from Edward the Fourth, notwithstanding which he founded the magnificent College of St. Mary Magdalen, in Oxford.   He died on the 11th of August, 1486, having sat thirty-nine years, and is buried in a rich chantry at the east end of his cathedral.[2]

LVI. Peter Courtney,

(Anno 1487 to 1492.—Richard III.)

Bishop of Exeter, was translated to Winchester in January, 1487, and died September 22, 1492, having governed the diocese nearly six years.   He is said to have been buried in his cathedral, but the spot is not ascertained.

LVII. Thomas Langton,

(Anno 1492 to 1500.—Henry VII.)

Bishop of Salisbury, after a short vacancy, was translated to Winchester, and died of the plague in the year 1500, immediately after his election to the Metropolitical See of Canterbury.   During his Prelacy he erected a sumptuous chantry and tomb in his cathedral, on the south side of the Lady Chapel,[3] in which he was interred, and was succeeded by

LVIII. Richard Fox,

(Anno 1502 to 1528.—Henry VII.)

Bishop of Durham, who, being deservedly in high favour with Henry the Seventh, to whom he had been of inestimable service in his attempt for the crown of England, was translated to Winchester in 1502.   So great seems to have been the King's friendship for him, that he was chosen by him godfather to his second son, afterwards Henry VIII.   After his translation to Winchester, he appears, in conjunction with Hugh Oldham, Bishop of Exeter, to have built and endowed the College of Corpus Christi, in Oxford, as also Free-schools at Grantham, Taunton, and other places. He consider-

---

[1] Historical Account, 50, 116.   [2] Ante, 124.   [3] Ante, 120.

ably repaired and beautified his cathedral,[1] and died in 1528, having governed his diocese nearly twenty-seven years, several of which he was blind. He is buried in a superb chantry, on the south side of the Presbytery, immediately behind the unparalleled altar-screen erected by him.   Upon his death,

LIX. Thomas Wolsey,
(Anno 1529 to 1530.—Henry VIII.)

Who, from an obscure rank in society, by his industry and talent, aided by good fortune, became Chancellor of England, and Cardinal Legate, as also Archbishop of York, and Bishop of Durham, Bath, and Winchester; all which Sees, with divers other ecclesiastical benefices of great value, he held in commendam, by a dispensation from the Pope.   He was translated to Winchester in 1529;[2] and by that step attained the bounds of his greatness, as he very soon after fell under the displeasure of his capricious master, Henry VIII. by whom he was suddenly deprived of his office as Chancellor, and charged with a præmunire, for assuming the legantine power in the kingdom without sufficient authority.   To this disgrace, followed by the seizure of all his possessions, Wolsey appears to have submitted himself with a meekness and humility equal to his former greatness.   After enduring extreme mortification, and even penury, for the space of a year, he was ordered by the King to retire to York, where he was soon after arrested by the Earl of Northumberland for high treason, and conducted by him towards London, on his way to which he was taken ill, and died at the Abbey of Leicester, on the 29th of November, 1530, under circumstances that justify a strong suspicion of his having been poisoned.   During the prosperity of this singularly great man, he began the erection of two magnificent Colleges, at Ipswich and Oxford, which, if they had been finished, would probably have been the most stately monuments of the age.   For the endowment of these Colleges he obtained leave of the Pope to dissolve forty small monasteries, the revenues of which he appropriated to their support; and thus opened a door for Henry the Eighth to destroy the remainder throughout the kingdom.   He appears to have taken possession of his diocese of Winchester by proxy, and has not left any memorial of his episcopal government within it.   He was buried at Leicester; and, after the See had been vacant nearly four years, was succeeded by

LX. Stephen Gardiner,

(Anno 1534 to 1551, Henry VIII. and Anno 1553 to 1555, Mary.)

The illegitimate son of Dr. Lionel Woodville or Wydville, Bishop of Salisbury, brother to the Lady Elizabeth Grey, Queen of Edward the Fourth. He appears to have been in high favour with Henry the Eighth, by whom he was appointed to the Bishopric of Winchester in 1534,[3] as a reward for the zeal and ability he manifested in the service of that capricious Prince during his controversy with the Pope.   In 1548 he was committed to the Tower, for a sermon preached before Edward the Sixth, where, after he had been confined upwards of two years, he was, in 1551, deprived of his Bishopric.

---

[1] Historical Account, 52, 114.   [2] Ibid. 55.   [3] Ibid, 55, 129.

Upon the accession of the Princess Mary, in 1553, he was restored to his Bishopric and liberty, and was also made Chancellor of the kingdom, and had the honour of crowning her on the 1st of October of the same year; and shortly after this he appears to have been possessed of greater power, both civil and ecclesiastical, than any English Minister had enjoyed, except his immediate predecessor Cardinal Wolsey. For the victims to the sanguinary zeal of this Prelate, we refer to history at large; and although towards the latter end of his time he is said to have declined persecuting the Protestants, yet his mercy appears to have extended no further than mere personal forbearance, as his prisoners were thenceforward delivered over for punishment to the jurisdiction of Bonner, Bishop of London, instead of his own. He died at Whitehall, on the 13th of November, 1555, and was buried at the east end of the choir, on the north side of his cathedral, at Winchester, in a tolerably handsome chantry, which had been prepared for him during his life-time. Bishop Gardiner appears to have been a learned and clever man, but intolerant, cruel, haughty, and ambitious; at his death he is said to have expressed great remorse for his former life, often repeating these words—" *Erravi cum Petro, sed non flevi cum Petro :*"—I have erred with Peter, but not wept with him.

LXI. John Poynet,

(Anno 1551 to 1553.—EDWARD VI.)

Bishop of Rochester, was translated to Winchester upon the deprivation of Bishop Gardiner, in 1550; but upon the accession of Mary, in 1553, was forced to quit the kingdom, and died at Strasburgh, on the 11th of April, 1556, having enjoyed his See little more than two years.

LXII. John White,

(Anno 1556 to 1558.—MARY.)

Bishop of Lincoln, upon the decease of Gardiner, was translated to Winchester, on condition that he should pay, from the revenues of his See, 1000*l.* a year to Cardinal Pole, who had sued importunately for the Bishopric, upon the ground that his revenue, as Archbishop of Canterbury, was not sufficient to maintain his dignity as a Cardinal. These terms White acceded to, and was thereupon admitted to his See in May, 1557. which he however held but for a short time, being deprived of it by Queen Elizabeth upon her accession, for refusing to conform to the religion she had established. He died at South Warnborough, in Hampshire, on the 11th of January, 1559, and was buried in the cathedral.

LXIII. Robert Horne,

(Anno 1560 to 1580.—ELIZABETH.)

Dean of Durham, succeeded Bishop White in the Episcopal government of Winchester, to which he was consecrated February 16, 1560, shortly after his return from a voluntary banishment, which he had chosen during the reign of Queen Mary. He appears to have been a learned and good man, but unfortunately too fond of improvement and mistaken in his ideas of it, in consequence of which some of the most venerable and interesting features of his church were destroyed, and the fabric itself evidently injured.[1]   Independent of this failing, he appears to have conducted himself well in his diocese, which he governed nearly twenty years, and died at Winchester House, Southwark, on the 1st of June, 1580, from whence his body was removed to his cathedral for interment.

LXIV. John Watson,

(Anno 1580 to 1583.—ELIZABETH.)

Dean of Winchester, was then appointed to the Bishopric by Queen Elizabeth, a preferment, it is said, much against his inclination ; he was however consecrated on the 18th of September, 1580, and died in January, 1583. He also was buried at Winchester, and was succeeded by

LXV. Thomas Cooper,

(Anno 1584 to 1594.—ELIZABETH.)

Bishop of Lincoln, who was translated in 1584.   He appears to have been in great esteem with Elizabeth on account of his literary talents, and was honoured with repeated marks of her favour.   He enjoyed the government of his diocese nearly ten years, and, dying on the 20th of April, 1594, was buried in the north transept of his cathedral.

LXVI. William Wickham,

(Anno 1595.—ELIZABETH.)

A Fellow of King's College, Cambridge, succeeded Dr. Cooper, in both his Bishoprics of Lincoln and Winchester, to the latter of which he was translated in March, 1595, and was removed by death on the 12th of June following, having sat but little more than two months.   He was succeeded by

LXVII. William Day,

(Anno 1595.—ELIZABETH.)

Dean of Windsor, and Provost of Eton, who was consecrated on the 26th of June, 1595, and, like his predecessor, occupied the Episcopal chair little more than two months, dying about the middle of September in the same year.[2]   In the early part of the life of Bishop Day, he appears to have been

---

[1] Historical Account, 59, 138.

[2] On the east side of the chancel of the adjacent parish church of Easton, a plain tabulary monument, erected against the wall, bears the following inscription, which, as a matter of record, is in itself perhaps sufficiently curious to deserve notice ; and from the connection of some of the persons mentioned in it, with Bishop Day and his immediate predecessor, may not improperly be inserted here.

1595.

THE RIGHTEOVS SHAL BE HAD IN EVERLASTING REMEMBRANCE.

Agatha Barlow, widow, daughter of Humfrey Welsborne, late wife of William Barlow, Bishop of Chichester, who departed this life the 13 of Auguste, anno

resident at King's College, Cambridge, where at one time, being in extreme want, he applied to his brother, George Day, then Bishop of Chichester, for relief, which that Prelate, knowing his aversion to Popery, refused him, saying, " *It is not just to support an enemy of the Church out of her own goods.*"

LXVIII. Thomas Bilson,

(Anno 1596 to 1616.—Elizabeth.)

Bishop of Worcester, was translated hither, and consecrated on the 13th of June, 1596. He appears to have been a learned and pious man, and was of the Privy Council both to Elizabeth and James the First. He died the 18th of June, 1616, having sat twenty years, and is buried at Wesminster. His successor was

LXIX. James Montague,

(Anno 1617 to 1618.—James I.)

Translated from Bath and Wells, anno 1617. The monuments of his Episcopal liberality are to be found chiefly at Wells and Cambridge, at the latter of which he was educated. He also repaired and ornamented the Abbey Church of Bath, wherein he was buried, upon his death, on the 20th of July, 1618, having been Bishop of Winchester little more than one year.

LXX. Lancelot Andrews,

(Anno 1618 to 1628.—James I.)

Bishop of Chichester, was consecrated to Winchester in 1618. He is said to have been the most popular preacher of his time, and his writings were held in great esteem by Charles the First, who commissioned the Bishops of London and Ely to collect and print his works. He remained here ten years; and on the 26th of September, 1628, made way, by death, for

---

domi 1568, and liethe buried in the cathedrail churche of Chichester, by whom shee had seven children that came unto men and wemens state, too sunns and five daughtrs; the sunns William and John; the daughters, Margarite, wife unto William Overton, Bishop of Coventry and Litchefild; Anne, wife unto Herbert Westfayling, Bishop of Hereforde; Elizabeth died anno   , wife unto William Day, now Bishop of Winchester; Frances, wife unto Toby Mathew, Bishop of Durrham; Antonine, late wife unto William Wickam disceased, Bishop of Winchester. Shee being a woman, godly, wise, and discreete from her youthe, most fayhefull unto her husband bothe in prosperite and adversite, and a companione with him in banishmente for the Gospell sake; moste kinde and loving unto all her children, and dearly beloved of them all for her ability, of a liberall mynde and pitifull unto the poore. Shee haveing lived aboute lxxxx yeares, dyed in the Lorde, whom shee daily served, the xiii of June, anno domini 1595, in the howse of her sunne William, being then Person of this Churche and Prebendary of Winchester.

Rogatu, et sumptibus, filia dilectæ,
Franciscæ Mathew.

LXXI. Richard Neile,

(Anno 1628 to 1631.—Charles I.)

Bishop of Durham, translated, anno 1628, to Winchester, where he remained but little more than three years, being, in 1631, preferred to the Archbishopric of York.

LXXII. Walter Curle,

(Anno 1632 to 1650.—Charles I.)

Bishop of Bath and Wells, was translated in 1632 to Winchester, where he remained, until ejected by the Anti-Episcopians, during the great rebellion. He appears to have been a great sufferer for his loyalty, and died in exile, anno 1650.

LXXIII. Brian Duppa,

(Anno 1660 to 1662.—Charles II.)

Bishop of Salisbury, upon the restoration of Monarchy and Episcopacy, was restored to his See, and translated to the Bishopric of Winchester, on the 24th of September, 1660, which he lived but a short time to enjoy, dying in March, 1662; upon which

LXXIV. George Morley,

(Anno 1662 to 1684.—Charles II.)

Bishop of Worcester, was translated to this See on the 14th of May, 1662, and governed it until his death, in October, 1684. During his Prelacy he built and endowed an Hospital or College, on the north side of the cathedral, for the support of ten Widows of Clergymen; he also erected an Episcopal Palace, upon an extensive scale, near the ruins of Wolvesey Castle, which he did not however live to finish.[1] Upon his death,

LXXV. Peter Mews,

(Anno 1684 to 1706.—James II.)

Bishop of Bath and Wells, was translated to Winchester, November 22, 1684. This Prelate was educated at Merchant Taylors' School, and afterwards obtained a Fellowship of St. John's College, Oxford. Notwithstanding his studies and future prospects were directed towards the church, his early inclinations seem to have pointed to a military life, and he appears to have been an active officer in the army of Charles the First, during the whole of the rebellion. Upon the death of the King, in 1648, he fortunately made his escape into Holland, and continued in the service of Charles the Second, until the Restoration, when he returned to his College, and, by favour of the

---

1 Historical Account, 71, 131.

King, obtained several ecclesiastical preferments.[1] He died at Farnham Castle, November the 9th, 1706, having governed this diocese twenty-two years.

LXXVI. Jonathan Trelawny,

(Anno 1706 to 1721.—ANNE.)

Bishop of Exeter, was translated to Winchester upon the decease of Bishop Mews, anno 1706. He appears to have been consecrated Bishop of Bristol in 1685; and, during his government of that See, was one of the seven Prelates committed to the Tower for their opposition to the measures of James the Second. He was afterwards rewarded by William the Third with the Bishop-ric of Exeter, and thence, as before mentioned, translated to Winchester, where he died in 1721, and was succeeded by

LXXVII. Charles Trimnell,

(Anno 1721 to 1723.—GEORGE I.)

Who was translated from Norwich in 1721; and upon his death, in 1723,

LXXVIII. Richard Willis,

(Anno 1723 to 1734.—GEORGE I.)

Bishop of Salisbury, and formerly Chaplain to William the Third, by whom he was greatly admired for his extempore eloquence, was translated hither, where he continued till his death, in 1734,[2] upon which

LXXIX. Benjamin Hoadly,

(Anno 1734 to 1761.—GEORGE II.)

Bishop of Salisbury, was translated to Winchester, anno 1734. During the course of a long and honourable life, Dr. Hoadly appears to have invariably distinguished himself by a firm and conscientious support of the principles of Religious Toleration. His great patron, George I. seems to have been fully sensible of his abilities; and thus we find nearly his whole life passed in an unwearied exercise of his controversial talent, and in the progressive acquisi-tion of honour,[3] the merited reward of those strenuous exertions by which he struck at the root of that direst of all evils, Ecclesiastical Tyranny. Bishop Hoadly died at his Palace at Chelsea, anno 1761, aged 85, and was suc-ceeded by

LXXX. John Thomas,

(Anno 1761 to 1781.—GEORGE III.)

Bishop of Salisbury, of whom it is alone sufficient honour to record that he

---

[1] Ante, 126.   [2] Ante. 96.   [3] Ante, 104.

was considered a fit person to be entrusted with the education of our excellent and venerable Monarch;[1] and surely if that axiom be still correct, which says, " By their fruits ye shall know them," Bishop Thomas must have been, in every sense of the word, a GOOD man. Upon the death of this Prelate, in 1781,

LXXXI. Brownlow North,

(Anno 1781.—GEORGE III.)

Bishop of Worcester, was translated to the diocese of Winchester.

---

[1] Ante, 99.

APPENDIX,
No. II.

𝕰xtracts from the 𝕽eturns

MADE TO

THE SELECT COMMITTEE

APPOINTED TO INQUIRE INTO THE STATE OF THE PUBLIC RECORDS OF THE KINGDOM.

From the Return of the DEPUTY REGISTRAR *of that Part of the* DIOCESE *of* WINCHESTER *which is in the County of Southampton.*

Public Records, folio 309.

I. THERE are in the custody of the Deputy Registrar all the original Wills proved, and Administrations granted, in the Registry of the Bishop of Winchester, in the county of Southampton, from the year 1660 to the present time; there are also Registers containing the Ecclesiastical Records of the respective Bishops of the See of Winchester, from the year 1280 to 1600, excepting one or two Registers which are not in the Registry. The Proceedings in the Consistory Court are also in the custody of the Deputy Registrar, but these are not by any means perfect.

II. The original Wills and Administrations are preserved in boxes in the Deputy Registrar's dwelling-house. The Registers above-mentioned are kept in presses, erected for that purpose, in the Consistory Court in the Cathedral Church of Winchester, and are in a place of security and accommodation. The Proceedings in the Consistory Court are also kept there.

III. They are all in very good preservation; and the Wills, Administrations, and Registers, are arranged according to the dates; the other Proceedings, being very imperfect, are promiscuously placed in the presses.

IV. To the Wills and Administrations there are complete indexes; to the Registers there is an Index, but it is by no means complete, insomuch that in making a search, every folio in each Register must be looked at. It is in contemplation for the Deputy Registrar to complete this Index, as it will be of great use. To the other Proceedings in this Court there is not any Catalogue or Index.

(Signed)

May 6, 1800.   JOHN RIDDING, *Deputy Registrar.*[1]

[1] The present Deputy Registrar is Charles Wooldridge, Esq. Winchester.

From the Return of the DEAN *and* CHAPTER *of* WINCHESTER.

Public Records, folio 341.

I. There are in the custody of the Dean and Chapter of Winchester, the several Charters, Grants, Registers, and Manuscript Books, hereinafter particularly mentioned, that is to say,

10 Nov. 23 Edw. III. a Grant of Giles Hill Fair, by King Edward III. to the Dean and Chapter of Winchester.

14 Apr. 2 Hen. V. Charter of K. Henry V. confirming the above grant.

28 Mar. 32 Hen. VIII. Charter of the Foundation of the Church of the Holy Trinity of Winchester.

1 May, 33 Hen. VIII. Charter of the Foundation of the Church of the Holy Trinity of Winchester.

3 Feb. 4 Eliz. Exemplification and Confirmation of the Charter of King Hen. V. by Queen Elizabeth.

A Book containing the Statutes of the Cathedral Church, confirmed by King Charles, in MS. containing 130 pages, signed by the King at the top of the first page, and at the bottom of every page by the Archbishop of Canterbury.

Two Books of Survey of the Possessions late belonging to the Dean and Chapter of Winchester, taken in 1649, by virtue of a commission grounded upon an Act of the Commons of England assembled in Parliament, for the abolishing Deans, and Deans and Chapters, &c. under the hands and seals of five of the Trustees in the Act named.

Authentic MS. copies of the Charter of Henry VIII. of the Statutes of the Cathedral, and of the two Books of Parliamentary Surveys ; and in the box where the Customary of Crondall is deposited, there is a memorandum that copies of the same are kept in the churches of Crondall, Yately, and Aldershot.

There are, besides, Books or Ledgers, in which are entered the Leases granted by the Dean and Chapter, some Patents and Confirmations thereof, Presentations, Installations, &c. from 1345 to the present time.

There are, moreover, Books in which the Proceedings at the different Courts belonging to the Dean and Chapter are entered, some of which are kept in the Chapter House, while others are in the custody of the Deputy Steward, for the purpose of referring to them.

II. The above Records are kept in different parts of the Cathedral Church, some are preserved in the Library, others in the Chapter House and Muniment Room, and the Ledgers in the Chapter Clerk's Office.

III. The said Records are not generally in a state of good preservation, from their being very old and some of them much defaced. The Parliamentary Surveys are in very good preservation, as are the Ledgers; and the latter are arranged according to date.

IV. There are not complete and general Indexes to the above-mentioned Records ; but to almost all the Ledgers there are complete Indexes.

6 *May*, 1800.   (Signed)   JOHN RIDDING, *Chapter Clerk*.[1]

[1] The present Chapter Clerk is James Lampard, Esq. Southgate-street, Winchester.

From the Return of the WARDEN *and* FELLOWS *of* ST. MARY COLLEGE *of* WINCHESTER, *in Oxford, commonly called New College.*

Public Records, folio 357.

I. They have in their custody the original Charter of Incorporation, granted to William of Wykeham, the Founder of the said College, by King Richard the Second, and confirmation of the same by many succeeding Kings of England; with various Royal Licences, to enable the College to obtain, by purchase or otherwise, property in Land, particularly one of the latter sort, granted by his late Majesty, King George the Second, in the xivth year of his reign.

    Original Grants, or authentic Copies of Grants, made by King Henry the Second, and other Kings of England, to Aliens and others, of Lands and Tenements since conveyed to the said College, and now its property.

    The Chartulary, in part at least, if not the whole, of the Priory of Newenton Longueville.

    Royal Mandates, of divers dates, to Sheriffs and others, concerning Proceedings at Law respecting parcels of the College Property.

    Copies of Records of Judicial Proceedings in the King's Courts at different periods, with Exemplifications of Inrolment, touching the Private Possessions of the College.

II. They further inform the Select Committee, that the documents aforesaid are kept in the third story of a square tower, consisting of four stories, each cieled with a strong arch of stone.

III. That the said instruments are all in a state of good preservation, and deposited partly in two oak chests and partly in drawers, arranged according to the title of the estates to which they respectively refer.

IV. That the College has no complete general catalogue, schedule, or repertory, nor as yet any particular index to the said instruments.

V. But that a considerable portion thereof, perhaps the whole collection, has been transcribed into the Registers of the Society, so as to facilitate the finding any instrument which it may be necessary to consult.

(Signed)   SAMUEL GAUNTLETT, *Warden of New College.*
March 26, 1800.

From the Return of the DEPUTY CLERK *of the* PEACE *for the* COUNTY *of* SOUTHAMPTON.

Public Records, folio 287.

I. The several sorts of Public Records, Rolls, Instruments, and Manuscript Books and Papers, in the custody of the Deputy Clerk of the Peace of the said County, consist of eighteen volumes in manuscript, containing the Orders of the General Quarter Sessions, from the year 1690 to the present time, and the Inrolments of many Deeds and other Matters directed by the several Acts of Parliament; also of many Rolls of Awards under Bills for inclosure of Common Fields, and Plans of different Navigations, which have taken place within the last fifty years.

II. The building in which the above Records are lodged adjoins the County Hall, (commonly called the Castle of Winchester,) and is public property, is in complete repair, very commodious, and perfectly secure.

III. The Records before-mentioned are in a good state of preservation, and the Books arranged according to their dates; the other Rolls are kept in a large box, without any order.

IV. There are no complete or correct general catalogues or calendars, schedules or repertories, or particular indexes, to each sort.

(Signed) PETER KERBY,
Deputy Clerk of the Peace for the County
May 14, 1800. *of Southampton.*[1]

1 The present Deputy Clerk of the Peace is Thomas Woodham, Esq. Winchester.

From the Return of the Society *of* Antiquaries, *dated Somerset House, March* 24, 1800.

Public Records, folio 386.

" —— A MS. on vellum, in quarto, in curious old binding, with a border of red velvet, being the Domesday Book for the City of Winchester, made in the reign of King Henry the First, dated A. D. 1148."

Extract of Return from the Record Office *of the* Chapter House, Westminster.

Public Records, folio 41.

" Return of Commissioners, 12 Hen. VIII. of the whole number of Men, in each parish in Hampshire, capable of bearing arms, distinguishing Archers from Billmen, with the numbers of harness, &c. and the property and prestmoney of the several Men, made by the said Commissioners to the Star Chamber.

Extract of Return from the Office *of* Exchequer *of* Account.

Public Records, folio 175, 6, 7, 183.

" Inquisition (post mortem) of John Poulet, Marquis of Winchester, 20th June, 19th Elizabeth."

" Ecclesiastical Subsidies paid in the Diocese of Winchester, &c. 15th Charles II."

Rental of part of the Revenue of Catherine, Queen Dowager of Charles II. in the counties of Southampton, &c.

Rental of the Bishopric of Winchester during the vacancy, 1632.

Account of the Temporalities of the Bishopric of Winchester for one year, sede vacante, 1633.

A Roll, containing the Statutes made at Winchester, dated 13th Edward I. In the Receipt of Exchequer. And,

Similar Rolls, dated from 1277 to 1468. In the Tower.

Public Records, folio 645.

JAMES ROBBINS, Printer, College-street, Winchester.